TWENTIETH-CENTURY PACIFISM

TWENTIETH-CENTURY

PACIFISM

PETER BROCK
University of Toronto

NEW PERSPECTIVES
IN
POLITICAL SCIENCE

VAN NOSTRAND REINHOLD COMPANY
NEW YORK   CINCINNATI   TORONTO
LONDON   MELBOURNE

Van Nostrand Reinhold Company Regional Offices:
Cincinnati   New York   Chicago   Millbrae   Dallas

Van Nostrand Reinhold Company Foreign Offices:
London   Toronto   Melbourne

Published by Van Nostrand Reinhold Company
450 West 33rd Street, New York, N. Y. 10001

Published simultaneously in Canada by
D. Van Nostrand Company (Canada), Ltd.

10   9   8   7   6   5   4   3   2   1

Preface

Twentieth-Century Pacifism IS A SURVEY FOR THE COLLEGE STUDENT and adult reader dealing with pacifism in roughly the half century following 1914. The book is centered on an analysis of the movement which has grown up in our century, combining advocacy of personal nonparticipation in war of any kind or in violent revolution with an endeavor to find nonviolent means of resolving conflict.

On the European continent, "pacifism" includes all efforts to achieve international peace and understanding. In Anglo-American usage, the term is normally limited to the definition given above; the adjective "absolute" or "integral" might well be used for the type of pacifism with which I am mainly concerned in this book. Even inside these narrower limits, however, it is sometimes impossible to divide the pacifists from the nonpacifists. Within the twentieth-century pacifist community itself, a wide spectrum of opinion on the subject of war, as well as on other political, religious, and moral problems, has existed. Pacifist ideals range from rigid vegetarianism, which recoils from killing any sentient being, to conscientious objection, which is confined to fighting in national wars and does not include taking human life in self-defense or in defense of an accepted system of international law.

For their unfailing readiness to help in my research, I owe a debt of gratitude to the Curator and staff of the Swarthmore College Peace Collection, surely one of the finest sources of materials on the peace movement in existence. I also wish to thank my wife for typing the greater part of the manuscript of this book.

PETER BROCK

Contents

TWENTIETH-CENTURY PACIFISM

I. Varieties of Pacifism at the Outset of the Twentieth Century

AT THE OUTSET OF THE TWENTIETH CENTURY THE PROSPECTS for a continuing world peace looked promising. Yet there were dark shadows—increasing armaments, hardening alliances, overseas imperialist rivalries, economic unrest in the industrialized countries, and rising nationalist passions in many areas of the world. The scale of destruction by weapons of war had multiplied many times during the previous century. Most public figures in the West, from semi-absolutist tsars to expansionist presidents, paid lip-service to international peace. Their actions, however, were often more expressive of the *Realpolitik,* of which they accused their nations' opponents, than of the pacifistic international morality on which they prided themselves. Not only did statesmen succumb to nationalist ambitions, but large sections of the population in most advanced countries were also carried away by chauvinist slogans and imperialist designs.

Throughout the European continent, still the center of world civilization, universal military service had long been the rule. Great Britain and the United States, on the other hand, retained the voluntary system for military recruitment. Peace organizations and pacifist sentiments flourished, especially among the middle classes, more vigorously in the latter two countries than in lands where long-term conscription faced the male population. However, the socialist and labor movement in Europe was as strongly influenced by antiwar as by anticapitalist ideology.

Despite signs of an approaching clash between the great powers, few persons could have envisaged that within the first half of the twentieth century the world would be rocked by two successive wars of catastrophic dimensions, or that, by the second half of the century, men would be seriously contemplating the eventuality of universal destruction as a result of the new weaponry. Instead, in the early 1900s Norman Angell in England demonstrated that

1

in modern war conquest would never pay economically. Therefore war, he implied, was not likely to take place if men saw where
their real material interests lay. Although he never claimed that
war and conquest could not actually occur in the future, his arguments illustrate the optimistic outlook of many peace workers at
that time.

Pacifism *stricto sensu*[1] emerged as a political factor only after
the outbreak of war in 1914, mainly in Great Britain and the
United States. Post-1914 pacifism had its roots, however, in previous developments. There are four sources of twentieth-century
pacifism which I consider most important for its understanding:
(1) the doctrine of nonresistance as developed by the Anabaptists
and Mennonites of the Reformation era; (2) the peace testimony
dating back to the Commonwealth period in English history of
the Quakers, who were to contribute substantially to the creation
of an organized Anglo-American peace movement in the nineteenth century; (3) the institutional approach to the problem of
war evolved by these peace societies; and (4) the socialist antimilitarism which emerged, along with the organized labor movement, in the half century before 1914.

MENNONITE NONRESISTANCE

In twentieth-century United States the Mennonites have produced the largest percentage of conscientious objectors. The
Mennonite denomination, a rural community whose members
usually take no active part in politics, was founded by Menno
Simons, a Dutchman who died in 1561. He, in turn, had derived
his faith from the Anabaptists, who originated in Zürich in 1525
in opposition to the Protestant reformer Zwingli. They soon spread
from Switzerland to Germany and Holland. Persecuted almost
everywhere by the authorities, Protestant as well as Catholic, for
their institution of adult baptism as a sign of separation from the
established church, Anabaptists also attempted to separate from
the life of the contemporary state. Their object, like that of certain medieval sects before them, was to restore the fellowship of
the early Christians, to practice the kind of discipleship depicted
in the New Testament.

Thus, from the beginning the Anabaptists regarded government
as incompatible with true Christian discipleship. Though ordained

by God to protect the good and punish the wicked, it was, however, a punishment of the more wicked by the less wicked. Politics was not work for the regenerate or baptized believers. Had not Christ told his followers: "Resist not evil"? How then could they, like soldiers, slaughter their fellow human beings in war or, like magistrates, inflict harsh punishment and even death on malefactors? "Believing Christians are as sheep in the midst of wolves," wrote a Swiss Anabaptist. "They use neither the worldly sword nor engage in war, since among them taking human life has ceased entirely." [2] As their first confession of faith stated in 1527: within their own community "only the ban is used for a warning." [3] An Anabaptist must not resist wrong by violence. Instead, he must suffer whatever evil befalls him, for his reward will come in the life after death.

Yet, an apocalyptic, even violent, strain in early Anabaptism broke out in the mid-1530s in the German city of Münster, where Anabaptists undertook by force to achieve the Kingdom of God here on earth. By no means did all Anabaptists participate. After it was over the pacifist elements rallied under the leadership of Menno Simons and returned speedily to their previous pessimistic view of the impossibility of Christian believers achieving anything good by political action. All desire to change the world disappeared rapidly. The "post-revolutionary" [4] phase of Anabaptism had begun.

For the next 400 years Mennonites (as the Anabaptists were then known) developed in two different directions. First in Holland, and later in Germany, they began to integrate slowly with the rest of the community, abandoning their nonresistant principles along with other peculiarities of dress and habit. This was accompanied by decreasing spiritual impetus and a continuing fall in numbers. On the other hand, in Switzerland (where the church always remained very small) as well as in Russia, the United States, and Canada, to which the Mennonites emigrated in large numbers in search of land and religious freedom, they remained withdrawn from the world up into the twentieth century. Virtually a people apart, they carefully nurtured their pacifism and their hostility to the state, along with many old inherited customs like their German speech from the sixteenth century.

A more militant version of Christian nonresistance was propounded at the end of the nineteenth century by the great Russian novelist, Leo Tolstoy, although he was not directly influenced by Mennonite doctrine. The sources of his pacifism were twofold: his literal acceptance of the perfectionist teachings of the New Testament, and his angry rejection of contemporary Western society, of which war and the state appeared to him essential aspects. To speak of the early Anabaptists and the Mennonites as anarchists would be anachronistic; although their religion tended at times to be excessively legalistic, with Christ's law of love taking on the character of a legal code, while lacking earthly sanctions for its enforcement. Tolstoy, on the other hand, was truly a Christian anarchist—a man who took the inward spirit alone as his guide. His idea of nonresistance to evil was designed as a powerful spiritual weapon for undermining the foundations of the modern Moloch erected by the essentially militaristic state. The state, in his view, must be dismantled entirely and replaced by a voluntarist society before nonviolence could be fully effective.

In many countries of Europe, as well as in North America, his disciples founded Tolstoyan groups. They were small and uninfluential, however. The influence exerted by Tolstoy on the thinking of individuals was more important. In the United States, for instance, persons as diverse as the politician William Jennings Bryan, or the labor lawyer Clarence Darrow, or the social reformer Jane Addams, came under the spell of Tolstoyan nonresistance—without, however, ever accepting it in full. Tolstoy had followers in the Anglo-American Quaker community, especially among those concerned with radical politics or social reform. But the most seminal influence of Tolstoyanism, which will emerge later in this book, was exercised on the Indian nationalist leader, M. K. Gandhi.

THE QUAKER PEACE TESTIMONY

Mennonites urged a politics of withdrawal from the world. At the very beginning, Quakers, or the Society of Friends, sought to transform the world, to establish a realm of the "saints." Later, after early millenarian or perfectionist hopes had been abandoned, they strove rather to reform society than to effect a total change. They aimed at Christianizing politics, for they did not favor relegating the political realm to the unregenerate, as did the Mennonites.

Quakerism first arose in Cromwell's England in the early 1650s. Its founder was a simple shoemaker, George Fox. In contrast to the legalistic emphasis of the Anabaptist-Mennonite tradition, Fox and early Friends stressed the Inner Light and inward experience, in addition to scriptural revelation, as the guide for the spiritual life. After some hesitation and uncertainty Quakers concluded that war and violence, even when employed by the "saints," contradicted the Inner Light of Christ within men. Thus in their declaration to King Charles II in 1660–61, which represents the first clear statement of the Quaker peace testimony, they point to "the Spirit of Christ which leads us into all truth" [5] as the basis of their repudiation of war, and not to any biblical text or to traditional church teaching. By the nineteenth century, a change had come about. Due to evangelical influence on large sections of the Society of Friends, their pacifism became more Bible-centered for a time. "War unlawful for Christians" now figured in the titles of Quaker antiwar literature as it did in the works of other pacifist authors. In the twentieth century there was among those Friends who still cleaved to their Society's peace testimony a return to a pacifism based primarily on the Inner Light and on an intuitional view of the wrongness of war.

Quakers in the seventeenth and eighteenth centuries, especially those who migrated to the American continent, were troubled more than Mennonites were as a result of their refusal to do military service. Whereas the Mennonites did not balk at paying a fine in lieu of service where the state was prepared to offer exemption on these terms (for they regarded it simply as rendering unto Caesar what was justly his), Quaker conscientious objectors demanded unconditional exemption when called upon to serve in the militia. The Society considered that the state had no right to demand money in return from a man who was only acting according to his conscience. Therefore, they suffered distraint of goods and occasional imprisonment for refusing to pay commutation. Those Quakers, who did not follow their Society's discipline in such matters, were liable to be disowned. In addition to being conscientious objectors to military service, a few Quaker radicals also refused to pay not only direct war taxes, which Quakers usually withheld, but also those "in the mixture," i.e., where only an undefined part of the tax went toward war. From the end of the eighteenth century, however, in contrast to the Mennonites in Europe who had to contend with the rising claims of universal military service, the Quaker communities of the British Isles and North America were not faced—except briefly in the American Civil War—with a system of national conscription, for in peacetime Great Britain and the United States, as we have noted, maintained the voluntary system for their armed forces.

Although some early Quakers, like the Mennonites, felt uncertain if government could ever be conducted without a recourse to the sword and if, therefore, true Christians could rightly participate, Quakerism eventually came to regard the magistrate's office as compatible with a pacifist stance. When not excluded by legal restrictions on dissenters, they participated actively in political life. From 1682 until 1756 they actually ruled Pennsylvania, dominating both the provincial assembly and the lower magistracy. This "Holy Experiment" was not altogether successful and eventually led Quaker politicians to sacrifice their pacifism for political power. Pennsylvania's dependence on the home government provided a complicating factor, since its Quaker rulers were never free from the restraints of British imperial policy.

The Mennonites, at least until they assimilated into society as in Holland, had lived physically as citizens of their country but spiritually they were denizens of another world. They were mostly humble people, farmers or craftsmen, who in their European homeland entertained no wish to participate in the political life of the ruling class. They brought this apolitical ethos with them to America. Quakers, on the other hand, soon developed an intense interest in politics. Originally recruited chiefly from the lower strata of the community, Quakerism subsequently became to some degree middle-class and affluent. Moreover, at home and as members of the new and more democratic society across the Atlantic, Quakers prided themselves on being free-born Englishmen and were ready to resist (nonviolently) any attempt by authority to encroach on these rights. Even Proprietor William Penn, himself a Whig by conviction, had difficulty sometimes in controlling his ebullient Friends, who were the subjects of his province of Pennsylvania. It is no wonder, therefore, that—disregarding the apolitical and quietistic trend which gained predominance for a time during the eighteenth century—Quaker pacifism, in contrast to the inward-looking Mennonite tradition of nonresistance, became an outreaching creed and sought to find expression in both domestic politics and international relations.

Thus, quite early in the history of the Society of Friends we find English Quakers, like William Penn or John Bellers, propounding schemes for establishing peace between the nations without, at the same time, requiring their statesmen and citizens to become converts to the unconditional pacifism of the Friends. In nineteenth-century Britain, Quakers were among the earliest promoters of the new peace movement (as well as of a number of other contemporary reform endeavors). In the United States, though they were less active at first, the inspiration of their example was an important factor in developing the peace movement there. Indeed so close was the identification, in the popular mind, of Quakerism with pacifism that in both England and America a pacifist from another nonpacifist denomination (almost all pacifism at that time was religious) would often, in explanation of his position, say simply: "I hold Quaker views on war."

THE INSTITUTIONAL APPROACH OF THE PEACE SOCIETIES[6]

The peace societies, the oldest of which date back to the end of the Napoleonic wars, formed part of a vast movement of reform which included in its sweep such causes as temperance, antislavery, penal reform, women's rights, etc., and embraced Great Britain and North America as well as large parts of the European continent. "The promotion of permanent and universal peace" was the avowed object of these societies. Often, their members shared this concern with a number of other interests; in each country the membership lists of the various reform societies overlapped to some extent.

The London Peace Society opposed all war, though it accepted into associate membership those unable to go quite that far. The American Peace Society, after a long and at times acrid controversy between the supporters and opponents of "defensive" war, decided to remain neutral and receive into full membership all who wished to work to eliminate war from the community of

civilized nations. On the European continent, where the peace
movement was for many decades less flourishing than in Great
Britain or the United States, pacifism in the Anglo-American
meaning of the word was virtually nonexistent.

A radical wing developed within the peace movement in the
United States. Its leader was William Lloyd Garrison, the abolitionist who founded the New England Non-Resistance Society in
1838. Its creed was a kind of Tolstoyanism before Tolstoy (as
Tolstoy himself recognized when he first read this Society's
"Declaration of Sentiments"), repudiating not only war but the
whole machinery of government as incompatible with a consistent
Christianity. A few members even experimented with nonviolent
techniques of resistance—an area that remained virtually unex-
plored, indeed almost totally neglected, by the peace movement
into the twentieth century. The Non-Resistance Society, however,
soon showed signs of declining vigor as its most active members
became absorbed in the antislavery struggle. Some finally lost
confidence in a peaceful solution and, even before the firing at Fort
Sumter, were ready to urge a holy war against the slaveholding
South.

The quasi-millenarian hopes of the New England nonresistants
were perhaps closer to those entertained during the first decade of
Anabaptism over three centuries earlier than to the thinking of the
sober clergymen and merchants who made up the backbone of
the more moderate Anglo-American peace societies. Such hopes
were even more remote from peace workers on the European
continent. Moderates of all kinds were repelled by the nonresistants'
attacks on the institution of government. What above all they
strove to achieve by patient effort was the establishment of
machinery for preventing international war and not any radical
transformation in the political system.

"The [peace] schemes of the nineteenth century all centered on
five fundamentals: arbitration, arbitration treaties and clauses in
treaties, an International Authority or Tribunal or Congress, the
codification of International Law, and [simultaneous and propor-
tional] disarmament. These five essentials were regarded as interrelated and interdependent; it was held to be extremely doubtful
whether, for lack of one of them, any of the others (except arbitration) could be secured." [7] At various periods the emphasis in the

societies' propaganda was placed on one or another aspect of this program, but the combined goal was never lost sight of altogether. Especially in England, the peace cause was intimately bound up, too, with the struggle for free trade. The removal of tariff barriers appeared to be an essential step toward world peace. The peace societies in the various countries kept in touch with each other by means of periodic conferences and later by establishing coordinating bodies which transcended the national boundaries. True, disagreement concerning the inclusion of military sanctions in proposals for international organization continued to divide the Anglo-American societies, which opposed them, from many of their European counterparts, which considered such sanctions to be essential for effective world government. Yet amicable relations prevailed on the whole between peace workers.

The impulse behind this organized peace movement was derived in part—at least in Protestant countries—from the powerful evangelical movement, which also underlay many of the other reform movements of the age. (The Mennonites kept entirely aloof from the peace movement, regarding its attempt to create a warless world among the unregenerate as a utopian dream.) A second source, and perhaps a more fundamental one, lay in the thought of the Enlightenment. Christian pacifists had condemned war as sin. The men of the Enlightenment attacked war as both inhumane and irrational, following in the footsteps of Renaissance predecessors like Erasmus. They denounced war, too, as in total contradiction to their ideal of human brotherhood and unity. Here were the roots of a secular case against war; a pacifism that might be absolute or conditional, but in any case drawing its strength primarily from reason and humanitarian considerations instead of from religion. During the Enlightenment some of the major schemes for universal peace were devised. The Abbé de Saint-Pierre and Jean-Jacques Rousseau, Jeremy Bentham and Immanuel Kant were among those who then turned their pens to this purpose.

The institutional approach of the nineteenth-century peace movement had much to its credit both in countering (in its publications and its organized activities) the age-long glorification of war, and in pressing the material and moral case against the continuance of international war in a supposedly civilized community of nations. The movement's proposals for introducing international organization and a measure of world government in place of the international anarchy that hitherto had prevailed was to be commended. Indeed they have served as a model in many ways for twentieth-century efforts in this area. Yet in one important respect the vision of the peace movement before 1914 failed. It did not penetrate properly the relationship between war and the economic order nor did it detect the hidden seeds of war in the exploitation of labor or in imperialist expansion overseas. True, the peace movement vehemently denounced war for the material destruction it caused, but the movement failed to pursue the matter deeply into the structure of contemporary society. Its protagonists were mainly respectable, middle-class folk, often "do-gooders" whose consciences prompted them to be active in social reform. They were rarely connected with the emergent labor movement and they scarcely ever entertained sympathy for any far-reaching schemes of social reconstruction. This was especially true of the movements in Great Britain and the United States; it constituted in fact the main obstacle to renewal in their activities, not to mention expansion.

SOCIALIST ANTIMILITARISM

By the beginning of the twentieth century organized labor with its political expression in the socialist movement formed a force of considerable importance in the life of many European countries as well as the Americas. Wherever industry developed, there labor eventually strove to exert pressure so as to extract from its rulers better working conditions and a greater say in the affairs of the state. The cause of labor also attracted the support of a small number of persons from the middle and upper classes, who often acquired a position of political and intellectual leadership in the movement.

No socialist or labor party adopted a completely pacifist stand. Marxist parties rejected pacifism categorically. Whereas the left wing regarded it as a bourgeois deviation, the revisionists reserved the right of national defense. In a country like France where the majority of the socialist movement did not claim to be Marxist, the party leader, Jean Jaurès, looking back to the French Revolution with its *levée-en-masse,* urged the creation of a citizen army as the sole viable alternative to a professional service dominated by militarists. Only in Britain's Independent Labour Party were avowed pacifists to be found in any numbers, though there were a few isolated pacifists in the socialist parties of the European continent and in the American labor movement.

Many socialists, especially on the left, favored the class war— at least in theory. Even reformist socialists and trade unionists tended to doubt if the capitalist order would disappear without a final struggle and few among them thought that the workers could carry on a struggle of this kind by nonviolent means. Yet in regard to international war the position of the socialist movement sometimes bordered on pacifism. Socialism at its best expressed an ideal of human brotherhood which transcended frontiers and united races. Until the guns of August 1914 shattered this ideal along with so many others, the international socialist movement condemned war between capitalist governments. War, most socialists believed, resulted from the inevitable clash of economic rivalries. Under the capitalist system every war was in some measure an imperialist war. And in wars the workers suffered, but not the capitalists who fomented them. Since, at that time, in advanced countries power rested exclusively in the hands of capitalist politicians and their allies, this condemnation, if its logic were observed in practice, should have sufficed to prevent socialist or labor support in any future war conducted between capitalist governments.

Actually there was no unanimity among socialists concerning the most efficacious means to prevent war if it threatened to break out. The socialist parties were all willing to stage antimilitaristic demonstrations; however, their leaders were less ready to agree on a strategy to combat war. Ardent antimilitarists like the British ILP leader, Keir Hardie, advocated the proclamation of a general strike as did the antiparliamentarian anarchists and anarcho-syndicalists on the European continent. Other prominent socialists opposed the idea as being either impractical or positively harmful since it might benefit the aggressor. In 1914, as it turned out, the major socialist parties in the countries involved in war backed their respective governments; the workers fought against each other in the ranks of their national armies. Only in countries which shared the Anglo-American pacifist tradition did a comparatively small number of socialists (by no means all complete pacifists) take the conscientious objector stand. A few anarcho-syndicalists adopted it, too, in states like Holland where conscription was not as onerous as in the rest of the European continent. On 6 August, shortly before his death, Keir Hardie wrote: "Ten million Socialist and Labour voters in Europe, without a trace or vestige of power to prevent war! . . . Our demonstrations and speeches and resolutions are all alike futile. We have no means of hitting the warmongers. We simply do not count." [8]

Socialist antimilitarism failed to stop war. It failed even to prevent the working classes in the belligerent countries from becoming infected with chauvinistic passions and hatred of the enemy. Yet from 1914 onward the new pacifism that was generated in the course of the struggle came to possess a social concern that had not been present in the peace movement earlier. Neither Mennonite nonresistants nor Quakers nor the members of the various nineteenth-century peace societies saw at all clearly the connection between the evil of war and the ills of the economic system. There were exceptions, of course, like the eighteenth-century American Quaker, John Woolman, or Tolstoy and his disciples. In the postwar world, however, most pacifists, along with large sections of the wider peace movement, were to become acutely aware of the need for social change in effecting the elimination of war and violence from the world. The exploration of this fresh dimension grew into one of the major tasks facing them.

NOTES

1. Cf. Gene Sharp, "The Meanings of Non-Violence: A Typology (Revised)," *The Journal of Conflict Resolution,* 3, no. 1 (1959), p. 44.

2. Quoted in John Christian Wenger, *Glimpses of Mennonite History and Doctrine,* rev. ed. (Scottdale, Pa.: Herald Press, 1959), p. 153.

3. Quoted in *ibid.,* p. 210.

4. This definition is borrowed from David A. Martin, *Pacifism: An Historical and Sociological Study* (London: Routledge & Kegan Paul, 1965), p. 69.

5. Quoted in Howard H. Brinton, *Sources of the Quaker Peace Testimony* (Wallingford, Pa.: Pendle Hill Historical Studies, n.d.), p. 16.

6. Those wishing to investigate this aspect further can consult the massive works of Christian L. Lange and August Schou, *Histoire de l'Internationalisme,* 3 vols. (Oslo: Publications de l'Institut norvégien, 1919–1963) and of Jacob ter Meulen, *Der Gedanke der internationalen Organisation in seiner Entwicklung,* 2 vols. (in 3 pts.) (The Hague:

Martinus Nijhoff, 1917–1940). See also on a more modest scale A. C. F. Beales, *The History of Peace* (London: G. Bell & Sons Ltd., 1931); Sylvester John Hemleben, *Plans for World Peace through Six Centuries* (Chicago: The University of Chicago Press, 1943).

7. Beales, *op. cit.*, pp. 8, 14.

8. Quoted in David Boulton, *Objection Overruled* (London: Macgibbon & Kee, 1967), p. 42.

II. The Pattern of Conscientious Objection: World War I

WITH THE OUTBREAK OF WAR IN EUROPE IN AUGUST 1914 A NEW epoch in world history began. In the history of the peace movement, too, this date marks the symbolic beginning of a new stage in development. Hitherto, historic pacifism, in the sense of a thoroughgoing renunciation of at least international war and a personal refusal to participate in military service, had been almost exclusively religious in motivation. By the outset of the twentieth century, pacifism of this kind was confined—apart from a few small isolated groups—to the English-speaking world. In fact it had secure roots only in England and the United States. For many persons in these two countries, pacifism was equated with Quakerism on account of the Society of Friends' long witness for peace. Tolerated as the peculiarity of a small sect, war renunciation took on a new character in the popular mind and in the eyes of national leaders when it was found—even if thinly spread—in other churches and among the unchurched masses.

In Great Britain and the United States conscription became the harsh midwife of twentieth-century pacifism. The authorities in these countries had resorted in previous centuries to compulsion to fill the ranks of their peacetime militias and wartime armies. But service was usually selective. In addition, the possibility of commutation offered a way of escape, at least for those with means to pay. Commutation, indeed, was practiced not only in Great Britain and America but on the European continent up into the nineteenth century. Whereas in countries like France, Germany, and Russia universal military service was established in the course of the nineteenth century, in Great Britain after 1860 and in the United States soon after the Civil War militia conscription was finally abandoned, and these two countries went over entirely to the voluntary system. Their imposition in World

14

War I of compulsory military service for all adult able-bodied males, the introduction of which earlier on the European continent had acted as a deterrent to the growth of pacifism, now served instead to reactivate pacifism in the differing political environment of these two English-speaking countries.

THE FRAMEWORK OF CONSCRIPTION

Great Britain

Great Britain entered the war under a Liberal government, many of whose members and followers regarded the idea of military conscription with abhorrence. Before 1914 the call for national service had been a Conservative slogan. During the early months of the war the army had some difficulty in absorbing the volunteers who crowded the recruiting stations to enlist, for the British people greeted the outbreak of war in an upsurge of national feeling and an idealistic enthusiasm for the wronged Belgians. Pressure to introduce a measure of conscription came from the Conservative opposition in parliament and from a widespread sentiment in the country that only by compulsion would "slackers" be forced to take their fair share in the defense of their native land. In July 1915 the government, in an attempt to assuage the growing demands for conscription, introduced national registration. But this did not prove enough. In January 1916, therefore, the first Military Service Act became law. It affected only unmarried men between the ages of 18 and 41. A second act was passed in May of the same year introducing the principle of universal conscription of all able-bodied males, and, in fact, by the beginning of 1918 the upper age limit of those liable to conscription had been raised to 56.

In the debates on the first conscription bill, government spokesmen recognized the right of those holding a conscientious objection to military service to have their scruples respected. This was considered a part of the English heritage of religious and civil liberties. Therefore, conscientious objectors (C.O.'s) were to be exempted, along with men employed in work of national importance or those supporting dependents. Local and Appeal Tribunals were to be set up to hear applications for exemption on one or another of these grounds. In regard to conscientious objectors, provision was made for unconditional (or "absolute") exemption, or for exemption on condition that the applicant undertake noncombatant service in the armed services or that he engage in work which the tribunal considered to be "of national importance." The legislation did not specify that the conscientious objection should be based on religious belief. Although efforts were made in April 1918, during the German advance on the Western front, to get parliament to withdraw all previously granted exemptions, including those given to conscientious objectors, the attempt was not successful.

On paper, at any rate, this legislative provision for conscientious objection was indeed remarkably liberal. If liberally interpreted, it would surely provide satisfaction for even the most sensitive conscience—except perhaps for any who might object to the very act of registration as in itself a compromise with the evil of military conscription. The test of the act's liberality, of course, lay in the spirit in which its clauses were interpreted. A country which believed it was fighting for its existence—and, as many thought, for the salvation of civilization as well—might be inclined to give short shrift to a dissident minority, even when its claims were in theory given legislative backing.

Alternative service, where the tribunal decided to grant the applicant conditional exemption, might be, according to the letter of the law, any activity that the tribunal deemed fit to allocate, even including the applicant's present occupation. But in fact the conditions most frequently granted were consignment to the Non-Combatant Corps or to "work of national importance."

The Non-Combatant Corps, which was set up in March 1916, formed part of the regular army, from which its officers were drawn. Conscientious objectors who were allocated to it had the status of army privates. They wore army uniforms and were subject to army discipline. They were not required to carry weapons, however, or to take part in combat. Their duties included "the repair of roads and railways, sanitation, the provision of huts and baths for soldiers coming out of the trenches, and the manufacture and provision of many necessaries of life." [1] Most conscientious objectors considered that service in the NCC, as well as in the Medical Corps to which conscientious objectors were less frequently assigned, signified becoming part of "the military machine," and they chose prison rather than compliance if there were no other alternative. Some compromised and accepted noncombatant service, though unwillingly. But for members of certain religious sects, such as the Plymouth Brethren or the Seventh-Day Adventists, whose objection was based on a simple and literalist repudiation of killing as unchristian, the NCC appeared as an acceptable alternative.

Work of national importance was a somewhat elastic concept. Usually it meant employment in agriculture or forestry, the food processing industries, the merchant navy or shipbuilding, transport, mining, education, hospital or sanitary services or other public utilities. Unlike the NCC, the work was under civilian control; and the conscientious objector was legally bound to undertake such work until the end of the war emergency—unless his tribunal released him from this particular condition. While some objectors argued that acceptance of work of this kind was (though less directly) as much an abetment of the military system as service in the NCC, many felt that refusal would be carrying logic to undesirable lengths. In fact, only the comparatively small band of "absolutists" held out for unconditional exemption.

The United States

America entered the war against the Central Powers in April 1917. The following month Congress passed a Selective Service Act requiring all males between the ages of 21 and 30 to register for military service. The law exempted from combatant service those who were *bona fide* members of existing pacifist sects (the names of the bodies qualifying as such were not specified, however). On paper, at any rate, neither religious objectors unaffiliated to a pacifist denomination nor nonreligious objectors were eligible for exemption. Thus, American legislative provision for conscientious objection proved considerably less liberal than the British, despite the fact that Secretary of War Newton D. Baker had once had the reputation of being a peace man and that conscription in Great Britain had already been functioning for over a year. Even though leading pacifists and liberals, who could refer both to the advantages of the British legislation and the shortcomings in its practical implementation, pointed out to Baker that his proposed legislation failed to provide either for those who

objected to noncombatant as well as combatant service or for
genuine objectors outside the peace sects, the Secretary of War
refused to extend the range of exemption.

On June 5 registration was held. Most conscientious objectors,
as their counterparts in Great Britain had done, complied while
stating their unwillingness to undertake military service. The local
boards which were set up to administer selective service were
empowered to give noncombatant status only within a narrow
frame of reference. In fact they did not always recognize even
those who were entitled to this classification. Many conscientious
objectors, even though classified as such, were unwilling to accept
noncombatant service. As it turned out, in practice almost all
conscientious objectors (apart from nonregistrants) found themselves, whether recognized or rejected by their local boards, in one
or another of the army camps which had been set up throughout
the country. What to do with these recalcitrant conscripts after
their arrival within the army's jurisdiction was soon to prove a
minor headache to the military authorities and to demand the
attention once again of the administration in Washington. But before we describe the confrontation of these objectors with the
American military machine, along with the experiences of their
British confreres in facing the working of conscription in England,
we must discuss the character of the pacifist movement in both
countries and the categories of objectors who made up its most
active following.

PACIFIST ORGANIZATION

Great Britain

In nineteenth-century Britain the peace movement had been
represented by several rather sedate bodies—eminently respectable,
predominantly middle-class and somewhat limited in their range
of interests. Their main concern was to put before statesmen and
the general public the case for international arbitration. No conflict between civilized nations, they said, was incapable of resolution; with goodwill every dispute could be settled by a panel of
impartial arbitrators. They pleaded, therefore, for the establishment
of a world court to which all governments would be pledged to
bring their suits. There was an International Arbitration League

and an International Arbitration and Peace Association. But the oldest of such bodies was the London Peace Society, which had been founded as early as 1816 under Quaker auspices. It was the only one which had written unqualified pacifism into its statutes, though it admitted to membership all who wished to work for the establishment of a warless world.

By 1914 these bodies were all rather moribund. In theory they continued to maintain an antiwar stand; in practice many of their members supported the war. They took little part in the antiwar movement and after the conclusion of hostilities their activities dwindled away. At the outbreak of war the Peace Society had as its president the Right Honorable Joseph Pease, President of the Board of Education in Asquith's Liberal cabinet and a member of the Society of Friends. Pease approved the declaration of war as the only possible reply to German aggression, but did not relinquish his presidency of the Peace Society until May 1915. On the other hand, the Society's general secretary, the Rev. W. Evans Darby, was a convinced religious pacifist who had served the peace movement devotedly for over quarter of a century. He suffered from ill health, however, and resigned his post at the end of 1915. During the war, wrote the historian of the international peace movement, "the Peace Society remained passive. It never once wavered in its principles, but its existence . . . can be traced only in its annual meetings. The *Herald of Peace* [the Society's organ] virtually died." [2]

The old-time peace associations, then, were in a state of decline at the beginning of the twentieth century. On the other hand, the Quaker Society of Friends, which since the third quarter of the seventeenth century represented the nucleus of religious pacifism in England, had begun toward the end of the nineteenth century to undergo a renewal. In particular, some of its younger and more active members were attempting to deepen the Society's long-standing interest in philanthropy by a concern for social and political problems. Although some Quakers supported the war (perhaps almost as many as a third of the Society's members eligible for military service enlisted in the armed forces), the majority continued to adhere to its peace testimony even in wartime and the Society's official utterances were without exception in support of the pacifist stand. In earlier times—on both sides of the Atlantic—Quakers who joined up were disowned by the Society. This no longer happened in the world wars of this century. But at least in Britain in the 1914–18 war, conscientious objection was as much the stance expected by the Society of younger Friends as military service was expected of active members of most other churches. Quakerism had its peace militants among older members, too. In May 1918 three highly respected Quakers were sent to jail for circulating a leaflet entitled *A Challenge to Militarism,* which they had signed as officers of the Friends' Service Committee. Quaker pacifism, however, was often granted grudging recognition; it seemed to many somehow part of the English tradition for which the war was (allegedly) being fought.

In addition, the Quaker stress on positive peacemaking, on the relief of war's victims, provided a meeting point with those who differed on the subject of the justifiability of war. At first, it was the enemy aliens stranded in Britain by the outbreak of war who demanded the Quakers' attention: a work of mercy that showed courage in those years of "Hun-hating." Later, their War Victim's Relief Committee extended their activities to the war-ravaged lands of Europe. The Quaker star, the badge worn by Quaker field workers and imprinted on the consignments they distributed, became known not only in France but in Russia and Serbia and, in the immediate postwar years in Germany, Austria and Poland.[3] As a result of Quaker relief work, a picture was created in the popular mind of kindly and mild men and women dressed in gray, handing out food and clothes to starving and ragged thousands. Like the legendary "good Quaker" in eighteenth-century France who fired the imagination of Voltaire, this picture was a mixture of fact and fancy. In subsequent years it certainly helped Friends in many areas in their work of political conciliation. It also drew a comparatively small number of people to Quakerism and to pacifism in countries where these had been virtually unknown before. In the long run, however, this twentieth-century legend may have proved to some extent a disadvantage in the Quaker quest for a solution to the problem of war, for, if indubitably it has added to Friends' reputation in the contemporary world, it has also served to largely isolate them in the world's opinion from serious consideration in the realm of politics. With quasi-sainthood bestowed on the Quakers it has not proved too difficult to reject their proposals as the fruits of excessive religious idealism. Thus, Quakers have sometimes been known to wish— at least in theory—a return to the days of George Fox, when the world held them in scorn and misused them and they themselves looked forward not to the quiet life of an apolitical sect, which in the next century they did indeed become, but to the reordering of the whole world according to their peaceable principles.

Whereas before 1914 articulate pacifism had been confined (apart, that is, from labor antimilitarism and the pacifistic internationalism of many liberals) to the Quakers and a sprinkling of clergy and laymen in the nonpacifist denominations, World War I saw the emergence of pacifism in a number of Protestant churches. The pacifists, of course, remained a small minority there, but they were to become increasingly vocal. In politics the Christian pacifist was more often than not a socialist: the war had gravely shaken the long association of liberalism with the peace cause. The saintly Dr. Alfred Salter (later a Labour member of parliament) is an example of the Christian pacifist-socialist alliance. Soon after war broke out he published in the Independent Labour Party's organ, *Labour Leader,* an article entitled "The Religion of a C.O.," which was translated into many foreign languages and circulated in as many as half a million copies.[4] The tone was emotional: the appeal, as in the case of much early socialist propaganda in England, was to the heart rather than the head. "Look!" he wrote, "Christ in khaki; out in France thrusting His bayonet into the body of a German workman . . . Hark! The Man of Sorrows in a cavalry charge, cutting, hacking, thrusting, crushing, cheering. No! No! That picture is an impossible one, *and we all know it.* That settles the matter for me." He called on all Christians, all socialists, to refuse war service and to urge their comrades to take a similar stand.

In December 1914 a group of Christian pacifists "profoundly dissatisfied with the confused utterance of the Christian churches concerning the War"[5] gathered in Cambridge—from their deliberations the Fellowship of Reconciliation emerged. The British Fellowship, which sought to unite the efforts not only of Quakers but of all who based their pacifism on Christian grounds, has always remained small in numbers. It did not aspire to exercise

pressure on public opinion or on government. Its members did
not enter into controversy as to the rights and wrongs of the war.
Their goal of "a world order based on love" was to be reached,
they hoped, by a gradual leavening of society. They were, in a
way, revolutionaries—at least their call for "the enthronement of
love in personal, social, commercial and national life" was surely
a summons to revolution—but they were quiet revolutionaries,
as distant from the political scene as were the first Christians
gathered in an upper room.

Political opposition to the war, however, was not lacking. While
some of its opponents might be practicing churchmen, except for
the four Quaker members of parliament it was not from religion
but from economics and recent diplomatic history that the antiwar
forces drew their ammunition to blast the war establishment. Inside
the House of Commons the peace "party" numbered about forty
M.P.s. They formed a somewhat amorphous group with no formal
organization and with no clearly defined membership. There were
the five ILP-ers, led by Ramsay Macdonald and Philip Snowden,
and a sprinkling of Labour Party members, as well as some
twenty-five independent liberals among whom the most vocal and
cogent critics of the war were representatives of the Union of
Democratic Control such as Arthur Ponsonby and Charles P.
Trevelyan.

The UDC, like the ILP, was not a pacifist body. Many pacifists,
however, supported it and themselves drew support from its de-
nunciations of prewar diplomacy, the "secret diplomacy" of the
European powers including Great Britain, which in the UDC's
view had dragged the country unknowingly into war. Its spokesmen, of whom perhaps the ablest and most industrious was the
journalist E. D. Morel, roundly condemned prewar British foreign
policy for its commitments to France and Russia and for involving
the country in war over Belgium. The war, they believed, was an
unnecessary war. They demanded parliamentary control of foreign
policy in the future and the establishment of an international organization after the war was ended. Meanwhile they called for a
negotiated peace and, while condemning Prussian militarism along
with the military establishments of the Allied powers, they argued
against any attempt to penalize the vanquished if the Western allies
succeeded in pursuing the war to a successful conclusion. De-

nounced as "pro-German" by much of the wartime press, the UDC came to exercise a significant influence on British left wing opinion in the decade or so after the armistice.

The conscientious objectors, too, were branded as traitors and spokesmen of Prussian militarism. As one of the doughtiest champions of the pacifist cause wrote from prison:

I do not anticipate that public opinion is likely to show any appreciable acceptance of the conscientious objector's point of view during the panic of war. We must not, therefore, exaggerate the effect of our efforts on the immediate issue of peace and war. But I am convinced that wise action and persistent propaganda now will assist in creating an opinion which will be eagerly embraced as soon as men and women are freed from the terror of war in their midst.[6]

"Persistent propaganda" was certainly the keynote of the chief pacifist organization in World War I Britain, the No-Conscription Fellowship,[7] of which the author of this letter, Clifford Allen, was chairman. The NCF was in many ways a remarkable body. It drew together under one umbrella devout religious pacifists like Dr. Alfred Salter, the Congregationalist minister Leyton Richards, or the Quaker Edward Grubb who became its treasurer; agnostics like Bertrand Russell the philosopher; a wide variety of socialists of varying degrees of militancy from idealistic ILP-ers to fiery Tynesiders and members of small Marxist sects. It also had more than its fair share of individualist antimilitarists as well as a sprinkling of syndicalists and anarchists. It was indeed a lively organization whose members, when they were not in jail, were constantly debating with each other the issues of war and peace, and striving to convince an unreceptive public of the evils of conscription and of an international system that bred wars like the present one.

Moreover—and this is probably its most remarkable feature— the NCF, unlike many radical bodies, functioned with great efficiency. Its Record Department under the able guidance of an ex-suffragette, who as a woman was not liable to military service, kept a reliable record of the status, experiences and whereabouts of almost all conscientious objectors (with a duplicate file hidden away in case of seizure of the original by the police). The information was used not only to help the men concerned directly, but also to supply information for pamphlets and newspaper

articles in defense of the conscientious objectors' stand and for the
use of sympathetic members of parliament in their speeches and
questions in the House concerning the antiwar movement. Once,
even the War Office had occasion to apply to the NCF for information on a conscientious objector whose whereabouts they
could not trace in their own records. After forwarding the desired
data to the military authorities the NCF received in return "a
courteous note of thanks." [8]

The Fellowship's other departments were no less active than
its records section. The Press Department kept newspapers and
periodicals informed concerning the NCF's activities and about
conscientious objectors in general. (It may have regretted sometimes, of course, what the press did with this information.) The
Literature Department produced over a million copies of pamphlets and leaflets: from March 1916 it issued a weekly journal,
The Tribunal, sales of which at one period reached the considerable figure of 10,000 copies. A Campaign Department organized
petitions asking for the release of imprisoned conscientious objectors, with signatures gathered from persons prominent in public
life who were usually unconnected with pacifism. A Political Department acted as a liaison between the NCF and the peace "party"
in parliament, organized delegations to government, and publicized
the NCF's position in regard to existing and proposed legislation
which touched the interests of conscientious objectors. Finally,
two departments were directly concerned with the conscientious
objectors' welfare: Visitation which kept in contact with those
in prison, army camps or guardroom, and Maintenance which
(under the chairmanship of Ramsay Macdonald, though he was
himself neither a pacifist nor an NCF member) raised money to
help their dependents if in need.

This elaborate organization had not sprung up unprepared upon
the introduction of conscription at the beginning of 1916. The idea
originated with a young socialist journalist Fenner Brockway,
editor of the *Labour Leader.* On 12 November 1914 he had
published in its columns an appeal asking for the names and
addresses of persons between the ages of 18 and 38 who would
refuse combatant service if conscription were imposed. The response was good; Brockway and his associates at once went to
work and within a month the NCF had come into being. Its mem-

bers were drawn mainly from men of military age but sympathizers among older men as well as among women were welcome in its ranks, too. Membership figures eventually reached nearly 10,000; around 6,000 members belonged to the ILP with Quakers as the next largest element.

The primary object of the Fellowship was to challenge the right of government to impose military conscription, even in wartime. This was defense of libertarian rather than pacifist principle. The NCF did, in fact, accept as members all who "from conscientious motives" refused to bear arms. But it also wrote into its "Statement of Faith," [9] in an attempt to satisfy the complete pacifist point of view within the Fellowship, a clause implying that absolute pacifism was a basic article of this faith: members, it was there stated, objected to fighting "because they consider human life to be sacred." This confusion of thought, covered over during the period when all efforts were being concentrated on the struggle against the conscription acts, began to cause dissension as the war neared an end and as the effect of the Russian Revolution began to be felt in Great Britain.

Even earlier the NCF had not been free of controversy. In the first place, there was the question whether the Fellowship should stand out against all proffered alternatives to combatant service. Many of its leaders, including Allen, Brockway, and some Quakers, believed it should oppose at least noncombatant service in the army. There was also some support among the rank and file for a rejection of alternative service of any kind, even when it was of a civilian character, and a conference resolution to this effect was eventually passed by a small majority. However, except perhaps among the more rigid "absolutists," there was a strong feeling in the Fellowship that the question should be left open and each individual member should decide according to his conscience. And, in fact, this remained the policy of the NCF.

A second debate revolved around the objectives of the Fellowship. Should it concentrate on a campaign against conscription as an institution inimical to freedom and in conflict with the British tradition of liberty? Or should it continue as a primarily antiwar and pacifist body? The leadership was split on the issue: as a result the emphasis swung somewhat uneasily between an anti-conscriptionist and a pure pacifist line.

The tactics to be adopted by the Fellowship provided a third topic for heated debate. Should it try to recruit conscientious objectors actively in an effort to defeat the working of the conscription system or was its function merely to act as a self-help organization for conscientious objectors who had already reached their position independently? While the Fellowship did its best to publicize the ideas of the movement, it never attempted any kind of mass resistance to wartime conscription—an action which would have undoubtedly led to its suppression by the government.

As it was, the NCF from 1916 on had its hands full in coping with harassment from the government. There were constant clashes with the authorities. The London police frequently raided the Fellowship's offices, and provincial police raided the houses of district officers and broke up, sometimes with the assistance of unruly mobs of outraged "patriots," public meetings organized by local branches of the NCF. There were prosecutions of members under the notorious wartime Defence of the Realm Acts (D.O.R.A.). Bertrand Russell, for instance, was prosecuted for writing a leaflet published by the NCF, which gave an account of the tribunal hearing and eventual imprisonment of a young socialist conscientious objector. "It is not only I that am in the dock," Russell told the court, "it is the whole tradition of British liberty which our forefathers built up with great trouble and with great sacrifice." He spoke out in favor of "the invincible power of that better way of passive resistance, which pacifists believe to be stronger than all the armies and navies in the world." [10] Earlier in the same year, 1916, five members of the NCF's committee, charged with attempting to hinder army recruiting by the publication of a leaflet entitled *Repeal the Act,* had received a 61-day prison sentence. (The *Tribunal* on this occasion inquired ironically if the government would also consider the Sermon on the Mount a hindrance to recruiting and its author liable to prosecution on that count.)

The NCF, as the threat from the authorities mounted, went partly underground. Vital documents were hidden or duplicated; its departments were located separately and the most important of these, Records, was made into an independent organization; nominal officers substituted for those really responsible in order to prevent the latter's arrest. By early 1918 almost all the leaders of military age had been jailed as conscientious objectors. Leadership was then taken over by the women and older men or by men like Bertrand Russell, who for one reason or another were not liable for call-up. The climax came in the spring of 1918 when the Home Office, worried by signs in the country of increasing radicalism and war weariness, attempted to stop publication of the *Tribunal*. But the police failed to discover who really was the responsible editor. They did succeed in destroying the press on which the paper was being printed. But to their surprise it appeared the following week as usual, though in a smaller format and with a much reduced circulation: the paper continued to be produced on a small hand-press located in a private house.

Thus the NCF weathered the storm of war. It wound up its activities in late November 1919, for with the coming of peace and the ending of conscription it lost its *raison d'être*. A new organizational framework had to be constructed to meet the needs of the pacifist movement in the years ahead. The NCF drew its strength and some of its weaknesses (for instance, a sectarian smugness, that could occasionally approach arrogance, and a readiness to understand the enemy's point of view that sometimes fell over into its justification) from the British tradition of radical dissent. It expressed, too, the English dissenting conscience, which once more, as often in the past, stood in close relationship to political radicalism. The treatment meted out to it by the authorities was frequently deplorable. Yet, it must still be said, the No-Conscription Fellowship could only have functioned in wartime in a country where, at least to some extent, the claim of conscience was still understood, nonconformity tolerated, and radicalism given a respected place in the national tradition.

The United States

"In America," wrote Norman Thomas, "the defense of the conscientious objector was left almost wholly to religious sects such as Quakers and Mennonites, and to political radicals and pacifists." [11] This was in contrast to Great Britain where prominent nonpacifists (including some of unimpeachable Conservative principles)—Lord Hugh Cecil, Lord Parmoor, Professor Gilbert Murray, Bernard Shaw, Arnold Bennett, to cite only a few names— were prepared to speak and write on behalf of the conscientious objectors, even of those who took the absolutist position. In the United States, not only was unconditional exemption unrecognized in law but the "absolutist" found little understanding among non-pacifist liberals and churchmen. Here the popular feeling ran even stronger against the conscientious objector and all who opposed the war than in Britain. An ex-Tolstoyan nonresistant like the lawyer, Clarence Darrow, could write: "The pacifist speaks with the German accent. Even if his words are not against America, the import of all he says is to aid Germany against America and its allies in the war." [12] If a pro-war radical could talk like this, little wonder if the ordinary patriotic citizen should equate pacifism with treason and feel sometimes that the proper place for opponents of the war was swinging from a lamp-post. In addition, the rising Bolshevik scare from the end of 1917 onward served to increase the unpopularity of the antiwar movement. Were not the Bolsheviks against the war and were there not many "Reds" among the con-scientious objectors and the antimilitarists?

The weakness of the pacifist movement in the United States in comparison with its counterpart in Great Britain (where its posi-tion in the country would scarcely be described as strong) derived from several factors. In the first place it lacked the support in the legislature that British pacifists enjoyed. Politicians who were sympathetic to pacifists, like Senator Robert M. La Follette of Wisconsin, were a mere handful. Secondly, the labor movement, which in Great Britain at least contained a powerful antimilitarist wing, though as a whole far from pacifist or antiwar, was in the United States a much less influential element in the life of the nation. The frequent and ruthless suppression of trade unions and labor organization in America at this period is a well known story. The labor movement here could not serve to cushion the blows directed by the authorities against pacifists and antimilitarists, as was the case in Great Britain to some extent. In the third place, it would seem that American society, as it had crystallized in the course of the nineteenth century, while it was certainly far more egalitarian than British society, was at the same time less inclined to tolerate social dissenters. True, a Boston "brahmin" decades earlier might defy with impunity the mores of his social caste and fling himself without suffering too severe a social ostracism into such radical causes as nonresistance, abolitionism or communitarianism. But now in wartime America the drive to conformity swept dissent angrily aside.

No body with the vigor and dimension of the No-Conscription Fellowship emerged on the American wartime scene. Before the United States entered the war there was considerable opposition to the struggle raging across the Atlantic. The millionaire industrialist, Henry Ford, financed a "peace ship," which set sail for Europe in December 1915. Some pacifists participated; yet it was not, properly speaking, a pacifist venture. In addition, a number of ephemeral groups had been formed to canvas for conscientious objection in case war came, but these "mushroom leagues or fellowships" mostly dissolved after America became directly involved in hostilities. "To one who heard the vehemence of their professions," wrote Norman Thomas, "it still remains somewhat surprising, not that they disappeared, but that they vanished so easily, completely, and finally, before the government had time to take really aggressive action against them." [13]

The Socialist Jessie W. Hughan, for instance, had collected from recruits to the Anti-Enlistment League, which she had started up in the spring of 1915, some 3,500 declarations of membership stating: "I, being over 18 years of age, hereby pledge myself against enlistment as a volunteer for any military or naval service in international war, offensive or defensive, and against giving my approval to such enlistment on the part of others." And on the very eve of war we find the veteran worker for peace, Mrs. J. Sergeant Cram, and her "World Patriots" gathering signatures to the following pledge: "I will not kill, nor help kill my fellow-men." [14] In November 1915, as a result of the visit to America of the founder of the British FOR, the Quaker Henry Hodgkin, an American Fellowship of Reconciliation was established. It provided a focal point for the thinking and activities of Christian pacifists; but, like the British branch, in wartime it did not agitate politically, but placed its emphasis on the personal conscience. Some of its members, like the YMCA leader John R. Mott, left the organization after the United States became involved in war. Only in the interwar years did the FOR emerge as the major element in the pacifist movement and a factor not without importance in the development of American political thought.

The old-time peace organizations switched over to support of the war immediately after their country's entry. The American Peace Society, which already had experience of this type of operation at the time of the Civil War, after proclaiming in 1916 "that Jesus Christ was a pacifist," declared in May 1917 its belief that war was unavoidable and its backing of the administration.[15] Even among the Quakers, "many distinguished Friends" publicly proclaimed their "loyalty to the Cause of Civilization, and to the President of the United States" in pursuit of military victory.[16] Officially the Quakers, along with the Mennonites, the Church of the Brethren, and a number of smaller denominations, continued— albeit sometimes somewhat cautiously—to support their historical peace testimonies and to regard the conscientious objector as acting in conformity with his church's traditional stand. Outside these bodies, the clergy (Protestant, Catholic and Jewish) were usually hostile both to pacifism and to the conscientious objectors. A careful student of the subject has calculated that the total number of pacifist ministers was in the whole country scarcely above seventy (including three Jewish rabbis). Some of these men lost their pulpits (even among the Unitarians whose principles were founded on free religion!) and the only Bishop in the company, the Episcopalian Paul Jones of Utah, was forced to resign his see.[17] Whereas the Mennonites, because of their German speech and ancestry were sometimes threatened with mob violence or neighborly boycotts, and the leaders of the Church of the Brethren were at one point threatened with prosecution for impeding the draft if they did not order the immediate withdrawal from circulation of a pamphlet advising members against acceptance of noncombatant service, Quaker pacifism was usually tolerated as an inherited peculiarity of a group that had nevertheless contributed much in the past to creating the American way of life.

No account of American pacifism in World War I would be complete without at least brief mention of the stand of the Socialist Party. As we have seen, socialism in the United States had not succeeded in gaining as secure a foothold in political life as the labor movement had achieved in Great Britain. The American party's wartime stand, however, was as decidedly antiwar as was the British ILP's. On 7 April 1917 the party leaders issued the famous St. Louis resolutions, which affirmed continued opposition to American participation in the war and "allegiance to the principle of internationalism and working-class solidarity the world over." They branded the conflict as a capitalist war between the exploiting classes, in which the workers could have no interest. Whereas a small pro-war section of the party (in addition to a proto-Communist group) split off and founded its own independent organization, the majority of members opposed the war. As in the case of the British ILP, American socialists were free to reach their own decision whether to obey the call-up or to take their stand as conscientious objectors.

The party, of course, was strongly opposed to conscription and agitated, in so far as it was free to do so, against it. In June 1917 Congress passed an Espionage Act, which was used to curb the antiwar press and to imprison individual opponents of the war. In May 1918 an even more obnoxious Sedition Act became law. It increased the penalties for the expression of antiwar opinion, which it construed as a hindrance to enlistment and harmful to the war effort. Colporteurs of anticonscriptionist writings were arrested and stocks of their literature seized by the police. Semi-official organizations, like the American Protective League with a quarter of a million members in 1918, were entrusted with the task of "investigating" possible centers of sedition and espionage. The administration's powers, interpreted very broadly against antiwar radicals, gave rise to snooping, informing, and outbursts of hysteria as well as to the paying off by employers of old scores against persons regarded as dangerous labor agitators. For writing and speaking out against the war, left wing activitists were sent for long terms to the penitentiary. Not merely anarchists like Alexander Berkman or Emma Goldman or syndicalist "Wobblie" (IWW) sympathizers, but veteran socialist party leaders like Victor L. Berger or Eugene V. Debs, a man who professed the profoundest revulsion at the thought of killing a fellow human for whatever cause, found themselves behind bars with sentences often ranging between ten and twenty years. In some cases, terms of imprisonment went even higher. "One who remembers our war-time sentences," to quote Norman Thomas again, "must conclude that life imprisonment would have been the mildest punishment the resourceful leaders of the [British] No-Conscription Fellowship could have expected in the United States." [18]

H. C. Peterson and Gilbert C. Fite have meticulously documented in their study of the *Opponents of War 1917–1918* (1957) the whole dismal story: not only the imprisonment of antiwar leaders and rank and file left-wingers but the tarring and feathering of antiwar agitators by infuriated mobs, the breaking up of meetings by the police, the lashings and beatings perpetrated by vigilante groups and the less virulent but even more frequent minor harrying to which the antiwar minority was subject during these years. "Conservative people who displayed an intemperance that would do credit to the wildest of radicals" and "an extensive picture of intolerance and the demand for conformity" were the phrases used by Peterson and Fite in the foreword to their book in describing the atmosphere of that time. The wartime anti-Red scare merged into the postwar Red panic, and the last of the political opponents of the war were not released from prison until December 1923.

It was not merely popular opinion that was swept by war fever. The intellectual leaders with few exceptions supported the war effort enthusiastically. "To those of us who still retail an irreconcilable animus against war," wrote Randolph Bourne in his now famous essay on "The War and the Intellectuals" first published in June 1917, "it has been a bitter experience to see the unanimity with which the American intellectuals have thrown their support to the use of war-technique in the crisis in which America found herself." In this essay he expresses his amazement at the gullibility with which the educated sections of the American community had followed in the footsteps of their European colleagues and swallowed whole the idea of their country's being engaged in a holy war for democracy and a new international order. "The American intellectuals," he laments, "seem to have forgotten that the real enemy is War rather than imperial Germany." There appeared to be no alternative but to conform. "Dissenters are already excommunicated." Nonetheless, it was, in Bourne's opinion, still worth proclaiming that nothing can justify the evil of international conflict. And, he cries out in frustrated fury, "There must be some irreconcilables left who will not accept the war with walrus tears." [19]

TYPES OF OBJECTORS

In the United States and Great Britain, at least, Bourne's irreconcilable remnant was represented in most tangible form among the objectors to military service. We must turn now to consider the main types of conscientious objection to be found in these two countries.

The two most convenient categories into which objectors may be divided are the religious and the political. This division, however, can be made only with the proviso that it represents an over-simplification. Many religious objectors, especially in Great Britain, regarded the existing social system as evil and war as merely the most flagrant example of a way of life opposed to Christian social justice. On the other hand, many nonreligious objectors looked on human life as something sacred and war in all its forms as the negation of the socialist or libertarian order they sought to create. They, no less than their colleagues who based their convictions on the Christian gospel, drew their strength to resist from the tradition of moral protest fostered in the course of religious dissent in their countries. Even those who did not reject war in all circumstances but foresaw the possibility of a justifiable war, either in defense of a socialist commonwealth or to enforce the decisions of a world government, took their stand as conscientious objectors, instead of entering the war as their comrades on the continent did and attempting to act as antimilitarists in uniform. They acted not merely in this way because this alternative was open to them whereas it was closed to socialists and libertarians elsewhere, but also because, if often only obscurely, they felt that the individual protest was meaningful and that assertion of moral principle had value in itself. As a Quaker wrote of this kind of "selective" objective: "He stands . . . for freedom of conscience in matters of life and death. This . . . is a position entitled to all respect." [20]

No reliable figures are available as to the religious or political affiliations of objectors in World War I. In the United States the religious objectors predominated (they numbered almost 90% of the total), whereas in Great Britain there were considerably more nonreligious objectors of one kind or another than objectors with church ties. In Great Britain it was the Society of Friends that provided the core of religious objection to military service; in America the Mennonites and Brethren provided numerically the largest contingent. In both countries, there were certain sects of a fundamentalist or chiliastic character whose members were forbidden combatant service but recommended to accept noncombatant duties in the army. This was true of the rapidly increasing

Seventh-Day Adventists[21] and the small body of inward-looking Plymouth Brethren. On the other hand, the Christadelphians disfellowshipped members who entered the army even in a noncombatant capacity. And the International Bible Students (another flourishing group, today known as Jehovah's Witnesses), whose militant opposition to the war brought twenty-year sentences for Judge Joseph T. Rutherford and six other leading American Witnesses on the pretext that they were hindering the draft, in most cases claimed a right to unconditional exemption, very frequently without success. Major Kellogg, chairman of the President's Board of Inquiry, has described the Witnesses who appeared before him as follows: "These objectors were of all nationalities. Italians, whose testimony had to be taken through an interpreter, had read "Pastor" Russell [the sect's founder] in the Italian just as Greeks, who knew no English, had read him in the Greek. His pacifism permeates a dozen languages: the immigrant may absorb it in his native tongue before ever he comes to our shores." [22] The Witnesses, in fact, along with the socialists and the adherents of some of the smaller religious sects, represented a proletarian element within the community of concientious objectors, which in Britain was predominantly middle-class and in America had a strong rural, farming admixture. It may also be noted that in World War I Christian pacifism was confined almost exclusively to the Protestant denominations. There were not more than a handful of Roman Catholic conscientious objectors in either Britain or the United States and these were entirely without support among their clergy.[23]

Kellogg, despite strong disagreement with his political views, pays grudging tribute to the socialist objector. "He commonly made," writes the Major, "an unequivocal statement of his case with no apparent concern whether his asserted scruples fell within or without the provisions of the Executive Order . . . The frankness of the Socialists was impressive." [24] For many socialist objectors their stand was not the result of political calculation or a tactical move in the class war but an ethical imperative, an act of obedience to a secular version of the Sermon on the Mount. We find, for instance, the Englishman Herbert Morrison, a future Labour cabinet minister, telling his Tribunal: "I belong to the I.L.P. and Socialism is my religion." [25] This creed was intensely individualistic. Its proponents were socialists because in their view the capitalist system stultified the free development of the individual man; they were pacifists and conscientious objectors because they saw war and conscription as the destroyers of both personal liberty and the spiritual and material welfare of the citizen. "In its appeal to the individual," wrote an English left-winger of the pacifist position, "it is strong by calling upon each to act and decide for himself in matters in which all his ideas are at stake." [26] Though they professed to be agnostics or atheists, these men spoke of "the sacredness of human life" with as much conviction as any birthright Quaker. They preached nonresistance to evil as fervently as any Mennonite. And even if they did not think in terms of the Fatherhood of God, they had made a religion of the Brotherhood of Man.

In the course of 1917, events were to occur on the far side of Europe that were to bring to the surface the hitherto partly concealed distinction among Britain and America's conscientious objectors—between those who opposed war in all circumstances and those who rejected bloodshed only when carried out on behalf of a capitalist government. In the United States, where the objectors had no independent organization of their own, the clash of opinions did not take place within an institutional framework. But in Britain both viewpoints had been represented within the No-Conscription Fellowship: their adherents were united for the time being in the fight against the military service acts and in opposition to the war then in progress. The Bolshevik Revolution in Russia of October 1917, which followed hard in the footsteps of the liberal revolution of the previous February, brought to the fore the question whether continued alliance was possible between those who actively supported violent revolution and those who believed in nonviolent means, even if they might in many instances share the same enthusiasm for the ultimate goal of a classless society.

In April 1917, Bertrand Russell acting in the name of the NCF's National Committee sent a message of fraternal greetings to the new Provisional Government in Russia on the overthrow of the centuries-long tyranny, in the course of which he expressed the Fellowship's refusal to participate in war. It was, however, not the Provisional Government but the Bolsheviks who took Russia out of the war. Sympathy for the transformation of society taking place in Russia was felt in varying degrees of intensity by many members of the NCF. A controversy now ensued within the Fellowship as to the limits of nonviolence. Could a revolution ever be achieved without violence? Should pacifists and antimilitarists support revolution, if social change seemed imperative, even though the revolutionaries resorted to arms to gain their ends? Debate began towards the end of the war and continued into the months after the armistice when the conscientious objectors were being released from prison or alternative service, and men everywhere were turning their thoughts earnestly toward the shaping of the postwar world.

In the middle of 1919 Dr. Alfred Salter wrote: "I have been staggered at the number of discharged prisoners who have told me that they are prepared to take up arms on behalf of the social revolution." He doubted "if one-third of our people are pacifist in the sense that they believe *all* war to be wrong and that *all* methods involving the use of violence to attain a desired end are futile in the long run." He felt sure that the extreme left within the NCF would not oppose conscription if it was imposed by a revolutionary proletarian government.[27] Indeed, even among the complete pacifists there were probably few who went as far as the NCF's first organizing secretary, Aylmer Rose. Expressing "a conscientious objection to the works and methods of Bolshevists, Spartacists, . . . and all others engaged in driving out the old devils of militarism and capitalism by the strangely new devils of civil war, proscription and confiscation," Rose considered that "Bolshevism and Militarism are one and the same thing, only differing in the ends for which violence is proposed. . . . Killing is killing even when you kill a capitalist." "Anti-Bolshevist propaganda seems to me to be an essential part of our work," he forthrightly stated.[28]

From the ranks of the conscientious objectors were to come some of the founding members and early apostles of the British Communist Party. Most leftist objectors, however, remained in the ILP or became affiliated with the rising Labour Party. Whatever their ultimate affiliation, they were now increasingly troubled by the question whether perhaps capitalism and militarism could only be defeated by their own weapons. As one of them wrote soon after release from prison: "To some people, fighting is so evil in itself that no cause could justify it. There are others, and I must confess I am one, who feel bound to investigate whether or not society can be renovated—failing other methods—by those of the soldier, much as I dislike them." [29]

Growing disillusionment on the left with the increasingly authoritarian trend of the Soviet experiment affected pacifists, too. Nevertheless, a clear-cut line between pacifism and the Communist-sponsored peace movement was not to be finally drawn until the 1930s, and even thereafter it was occasionally to become blurred again. "The [war] resister desires a new internationalism," the doyen of British wartime objectors had written, "by which States are concerned less as embodiments of power and more as instruments of social administration." [30] Democratic decentralization, and not centralized democracy, has been the most usual political expression of twentieth-century pacifism. It is not surprising, therefore, that the Soviet behemoth, with its inflated bureaucracy, its suppression of all libertarian tendencies and its ruthless pursuit of power politics, soon lost its attraction for believers in nonviolence, even if they strove to dissociate themselves from the virulent forms of anti-Bolshevism fostered by supporters of the old order in Russia and only too often promoted in the interests of the Soviet Union's rivals on the international scene. Bertrand Russell, who took a prominent part in the work of the NCF and continued active in the pacifist movement after the war was over, well illustrates this point. From the beginning he took up a critical stand towards the Soviet Union while remaining an exacting critic of the policies of the noncommunist world.

Russell, although a socialist, had opposed the war on rationalist and humanitarian grounds rather than because, like some of his NCF colleagues, he wished to stand aside from a struggle which was of concern only to capitalists. It should be stressed at this point that among the nonreligious objectors in Britain and America there was a sizeable minority who refused to perform military service, not on account of any political or economic theory, but primarily because war contravened their ethic, because the bloodshed then going on over the waters seemed neither reasonable nor worthy of an enlightened human being. In this category there were men who forswore all violence as firmly as the religious pacifists; there were others who rejected violence under the present conditions of "international anarchy" but approved its harnessing behind an international authority, the creation of which in the future they saw as the major task before men of goodwill; there were still others who, disapproving of the present conflict as a matter simply of "prestige," considered—balancing the good produced against the evil—that certain wars were justified in the past, whether to settle the empty spaces of the earth or in defense against an inferior level of civilization or for some grand principle.

Of the latter group, Russell was the most cogent spokesman. And it was Russell, too, who provided the most eloquent exposition of the efficacy of nonviolence in the contemporary world in his essay on "War and Non-Resistance," which he published in the American *Atlantic Monthly* in August 1915.[31] He argues his case on strictly utilitarian grounds: his premise for the successful application of nonviolent resistance remains the same. This premise was, basically, that the conflict should be one between civilized nations observing the rule of law in their own communities, yet at the same time lacking any impartial authority to whom to appeal for action "in the general interest and not primarily in the interest of one of the parties to the quarrel." In such circumstances (they were those of contemporary Europe), unilateral disarmament, followed by "passive non-obedience" in case of subsequent invasion by a hostile power, appeared to Russell the most expedient policy for England or any other civilized country. Disarmament would remove any "pretext for invasion"—and with the growing power of public opinion this, Russell believed, was now an important factor. But should any power be tempted, nevertheless, to embark on aggression against a disarmed state, with "fortitude and discipline" on the part of the invaded people a policy of noncooperation would win in the end. As in war, there would be some casualties: some high officials might even be shot by the occupiers—Russell is speaking specifically of the Germans and the English—but all functionaries could scarcely be killed or imprisoned, for this would make the administration of the occupied country impossible. In England's case the Germans might take away the colonies, but their loss, in the view of Russell, the anti-imperialist, would be no tragedy. They might possibly exact tribute by threatening to deprive the country of its food supplies. But would not the consequent lowering of living standards still be preferable to the material and moral destruction of modern war? German militarism could only be permanently undermined by tangible proof that its opponents were themselves ready to do without war.

Russell's essay, though not quite the earliest attempt to envisage the consequences of civil disobedience directed against a foreign occupation, foreshadows the later interest in this problem in the West that was to arise from the Gandhian experiments in nonviolence. It represents an extension of pacifist thinking from a perhaps excessive concern for problems of moral conscience into the realm of international relations. Undoubtedly Russell's discussion has an air of unreality; it is merely a sketch with the details to be filled in later. Moreover, the author vacillates uncertainly between the view that nonviolence is a morally superior method of resistance with the implication, therefore, that it possesses permanent political validity (Gandhi's standpoint), and the opinion that it is merely an expedient technique in the existing state of civilization poised hesitantly between the jungle world of pre-civilization and a coming world order where violence would be employed solely to enforce the rule of law between the nations.

In his advocacy of world government, Russell, the pacifist, shared an enthusiasm felt by many prewar liberals and progressives on both continents. Likewise, among the fighting men there were a number who felt a growing disenchantment with war. The postwar pacifist movement drew many of its most devoted adherents from veterans of 1914–18, like Lieutenant Mark Plowman whom we find in February 1918 writing to his brother: "Bless my soul one need not be a Quaker to think the present war a bit of a failure or object to sticking steel in human flesh." [32] But "Max" Plowman was an exceptional man—at that moment he was awaiting courtmartial for refusing continued service in the army. A more restrained antimilitarism is displayed, for instance, in the letters of another subaltern, Wilfred Owen, the most outstanding of England's war poets, who was killed in action shortly before the armistice. In May 1917 he wrote home from a military hospital in France:

I am more and more Christian as I walk the unchristian ways of Christendom. Already I have comprehended a light which never will filter into the dogma of any national church: namely that one of Christ's essential commands was: Passivity at any price! Suffer dishonour and disgrace; but never resort to arms. Be bullied, be outraged, be killed; but do not kill. It may be a chimerical and an ignominious principle, but there it is. It can only be ignored; and I think pulpit professionals are ignoring it very skilfully and successfully indeed. . . . Thus you see how pure Christianity will not fit in with pure patriotism.

"And am I not myself a conscientious objector with a very seared conscience," he finally bursts out.[33]

With Lieutenant Wilfred Owen, the "conscientious objector with a very seared conscience," we conclude our survey of the types of objectors in the Britain and America of World War I.

THE EXPERIENCES OF THE OBJECTORS

In Great Britain (that is, excluding Ireland where the British did not risk the introduction of conscription on account of the country's rising nationalism) there were some 16,000 conscientious objectors; in the United States, according to the War Department, the figure did not quite reach 4,000. Numerically, this represented a very small percentage of the total number of men drafted for military service: in the United States, for instance, nearly three million men were inducted into the armed forces.

The objectors were divided in their views as to the proper stand to adopt in face of conscription between those who were ready to accept some form of alternative service (most, though, rejected noncombatant duties in the armed services) and those who held out for unconditional exemption. The "absolutists" were stronger in Great Britain than in the United States. They drew their inspiration from the long English libertarian tradition, which had earlier found expression in some measure in political liberalism and radicalism and in religious dissent. Their way of thinking appealed strongly to ethical socialists of the ILP variety as well as to the more socially minded among the younger generation of British Quakers. Indeed, in past centuries the Society of Friends on both sides of the Atlantic had forbidden its members to purchase exemption from service in the militia by paying the small fine which the authorities demanded for this privilege. The state had no right, said Friends, to require anything in exchange for doing what conscience told a man was right. The twentieth-century absolutists were as opposed to military conscription as to war and regarded their noncooperation with the military service acts as a struggle waged for liberty in the tradition of their forefathers.

If Clifford Allen incarnated the position of the British unconditionalists, Roger N. Baldwin, who then served as director of the
National Civil Liberties Bureau, may be taken as a typical representative of American absolutism. In a declaration made in 1918
explaining why he was refusing to register for the draft (a logical
conclusion to which, however, most absolutists were unwilling to
carry their argument), Baldwin stated:

The compelling motive for refusing to comply with the draft act is
my uncompromising opposition to the principle of conscription of
life by the state for any purpose whatever, in time of war or peace.
I not only refuse to obey the present conscription law, but I would
in future refuse to obey any similar statute which attempts to direct
my choice of service and ideals. I regard the principle of conscription
of life as a flat contradiction of all our cherished ideals of individual
freedom, democratic liberty and Christian teaching.[34]

The absolutists felt that to accept any alternative to military
service was to become an accomplice in the working of conscription
for war. And military conscription demanded, too, that a man
sacrifice his life even in a cause in which he did not believe. Like
the old-time Quakers they denied that a government had the right
to ask from one of its citizens any service in exchange for doing
what he thought was right. Thus the state was not entitled to require
alternative service from the conscientious objector to the evil of
war: the demand was inimical to civil liberty as well as a denial of
the rights of the individual. Though mostly socialists by conviction
—many of them were active in the labor and trade union movements of their respective countries—they contested the arguments
put forward by socialists on the European continent in favor of a
citizen militia. The Anglo-American absolutists rejected impa-
tiently the view that compulsory service, at least when it was for
a democratically organized army, not only constituted the most
egalitarian system but would act as a school for the inculcation
of civil virtue in the young male citizenry. In the first place, of
course, if they were also complete pacifists (as most of them were),
the absolutists disapproved of arms even to defend a people's
state. They also considered the spirit of militarism, against the
Prussian form of which the Western allies claimed to be waging
war, as an inevitable concomitant of compulsory military service
in any form. Thus conscription, instead of promoting freedom,

would shackle the development of any country that adopted it. The best service they could render their native land, argued the absolutists, was to make no compromise with conscription. In addition, in wartime the acceptance of alternative service would release someone else for the fighting line, who might otherwise be spared from the clutches of the military: perhaps some unfortunate youth who scarcely had had time or opportunity to make up his own mind on the question of war.

The alternativists, while they were no less opposed than the absolutists to the principle of military conscription, felt nevertheless that in times of national emergency, like a war, the state had the right to demand some kind of service from its citizens. By making provision in law for conscientious objection, the government had shown respect for their scruples, for which they were grateful. They might contrast their privileged position with the fate of the handful of objectors on the European continent where noncombatant service was the only alternative—and one that was only rarely offered—to prison or the firing squad. Unlike their absolutist brethren, the alternativists regarded the carrying on of work under civilian control, even if it were at the behest of a tribunal, as a means whereby they could witness to their pacifist convictions rather than as a tribute extracted from them unwillingly by Moloch. To exist at all in a modern state at war was to contribute indirectly to the military effort, according to the alternativists. They pointed out that even with an unconditional exemption a man could not find release from this dilemma. They doubted if the possibility that acceptance of alternative service might lead in some cases to the call-up of men who were not conscientiously opposed to the war, should deter them from undertaking such work. They were not out primarily, as the absolutists were, to smash the conscription system—they wanted rather to prove that antimilitarism was consistent with good citizenship and that pacifists were prepared to help their country in any way that they conscientiously could.

Thus ran the debate on theory. In practice the alternativists, among whom were represented many fine distinctions of outlook, not infrequently had their cases dismissed and found themselves in army camps or prison along with the more refractory absolutists. Even the most conciliatory group—the noncombatants—on occasion clashed with the military authorities. We must now turn, therefore, to the experiences of the objectors as they took shape separately in Great Britain and the United States.

Great Britain

In Great Britain the main stumbling block to the equitable treatment of conscientious objectors lay not in inadequate legislation but in inadequate staffing of the tribunals set up to administer the legislation relating to exemption from military service, whether on conscientious or other grounds. True, the deportment of some objectors was aggressive and rude; others, especially the young and less well educated, were tongue-tied and had difficulty in articulating their objections to military service; a few would have nothing to do with the tribunals and could not easily have been accommodated under any system of conscription.[35] Even so, while in a few cases the tribunals attempted to be scrupulously fair, the majority only too often displayed complete misunderstanding of the applicants' viewpoint, petty bullying and even crass stupidity. The chief concern of most tribunal members was not to assess sincerity and to satisfy conscience but to provide recruits, especially as the manpower shortage grew, for the armed forces. Therefore, when they were not rejecting applications outright, the tribunals were frequently attempting to press noncombatant service in the army on the objector—even against his better judgment.

Quakers usually fared better than the other religious objectors. Nonreligious objectors, especially if they held radical or socialist (not to speak of anarchist) views, were less likely to gain the type of exemption they sought than those who took their stand on Christian grounds, especially if they were church members in good standing. Some tribunals found it hard to believe that boys in their teens or early twenties could have reached independently a decision to stand as a conscientious objector (although they saw nothing abnormal in the state making up their minds for them and sending them willy-nilly into military service). Many tribunal members displayed by their utterances their conviction that conscientious objectors were cowards or shirkers or even sympathizers with the German cause. Objectors might be told: "Yours is a case of an unhealthy mind in an unwholesome body," or even "You are nothing but a shivering mass of unwholesome fat."[36] The regional

tribunals had been filled with local civic dignitaries, many of them
active in the two established parties. "A pro-war Labour man was
considered a good catch, and a pro-war Quaker—by no means beyond procurement—even better." [37] Doubtless, ordinarily exem-
plars of the middle-class virtues, they had come briefly to hold
authority over the destiny of other men; their sense of fair play
had become clouded by the wartime jingoism that swept the
country. In the gutter press, a campaign was soon under way to
stir up public opinion (including tribunal members) against the
objectors. Moreover, few tribunal members had had previous
experience in the workings of a court. The presence of a "military
representative" at each tribunal sometimes exercised, too, undue
influence on its decisions.

The Local Government Board, when setting up the tribunals
in February 1916, had issued instructions in vain concerning the
conscientious objectors who would appear before them:

While care must be taken that the man who shirks his duty to his
country does not find unworthy shelter behind this provision, every
consideration should be given to the man whose objection generally
rests on religious or moral convictions. Whatever may be the views
of members of the Tribunal, they must interpret the Act in an impartial and tolerant spirit. Difference of convictions must not bias judgment. . . . Men who apply on this ground should be able to feel
that they are being judged by a Tribunal that will deal fairly with
their cases. The exemption should be the minimum required to meet
the conscientious scruples of the applicant.[38]

Even though the Board pointed out clearly that whenever a
tribunal had reason to believe that only unconditional exemption
would satisfy the conscience of the applicant this should in fact be
given, some tribunals continued to assert that they were not
entitled to grant complete exemption to any objector—even in cases
where they frankly admitted the sincerity of the applicant. Still
more tribunals frequently interpreted the "minimum" exemption
which the objector deserved as an exemption from merely combatant duties, regardless of the fact that this would mean the consignment to prison not only of the absolutists but also of men
eager to undertake some form of civilian alternative service.

In April 1919, after the war was over, the War Office—perhaps in an effort to deflect criticism from deficiencies in army policy toward the objectors who had come under military command— issued a revealing statement concerning the effects of so many tribunals' failure to carry out the legislators' intentions. A London liberal newspaper summarized the War Office's findings thus:

As a matter of fact the Army authorities themselves recognize that the lot of the conscientious objector is a hard one. They recognize that he has been the victim of ineptitude. Their view is that many hundreds of men have been thrust into the Army whom the House of Commons never intended should become soldiers. The Tribunals, they consider, rejected the applications of hundreds of these men whose consciences were sincere, and to protect whom the conscience clause was expressly framed by the House of Commons.[39]

To judge another man's conscience is admittedly an almost impossible task. The difficulties of the tribunals were confounded by the fact that many of them were genuinely confused as to exactly which categories of objectors were entitled to exemption. The antiwar movement—at least its more radical section—was for the most part inclined to regard as a *conscientious* objector any man who sincerely objected to taking part in the present war. This distinction would include, for instance, a radical Irish nationalist Sinn Feiner, whose residence in England had made him liable to the call-up—he could scarcely be described as an adherent of nonviolence.[40] One may also sympathize with a harassed tribunal chairman when faced with a member of the International Bible Students Association, whose witness for Jehovah included, it is true, abstention now from the wars of this world but did not exclude participation in fiery apocalyptic conflicts to come. The Central Tribunal, whose decisions were circulated by the Local Government Board for the guidance of the Local and Appeal Tribunals, recommended finally that members of the Association be exempted only from combatant duties (whether with the knowledge that almost all the Witnesses would refuse to accept this classification and end up in jail is not clear). And what should be done with socialists who, while unwilling to commit themselves to a wholesale condemnation of violence in all circumstances, based their antiwar stand not on any accepted religious creed but upon a quasi-religious belief in the brotherhood of man or in the international solidarity of the working class? In actual practice no consistent policy in regard to such cases was ever laid down from above: each tribunal proceeded as it thought fit.

It was the absolutists who received the most attention at the time—in parliament, in the press and with the general public. On the whole they were condemned, or at best regarded as stubborn and misguided fanatics. In July 1916 Lloyd George, then Secretary of State for War (in the Boer War he had been a political opponent of war), expressed to the House of Commons his complete lack of sympathy for the absolutist objectors who, in his view, deserved no consideration, and he promised the House that he would make their path as hard a one as he could.[41] Nevertheless, a few applicants—mostly birthright Quakers, whose cases could more easily be judged by rule of thumb—did receive unconditional exemption either at the local or appellate level. As neither rough handling (even brutal treatment), first in army camps and then in detention barracks, nor subsequent repeated sentencing to civil prisons for essentially the same offense—the notorious "cat-and-mouse" treatment which derived its name from its application to English suffragettes prior to the war—succeeded in breaking the will of the absolutists,[42] voices began to be raised fairly soon in their defense, not only within the pacifist community but among enlightened sections of pro-war opinion.

Attempts by the army authorities in May and June 1916 to covertly ship a number of absolutists to France, where they would be subject to the extremest penalties of military law for continued refusal to fight (34 were actually condemned to death, though the sentences were not carried out) were foiled by the intervention of a group of Liberals led by Professor Gilbert Murray. The Prime Minister, Asquith, who had not previously known of the army's intentions, was genuinely shocked by Murray's revelations, and eventually the army authorities gave up their endeavors to impose this kind of radical solution to the absolutist problem. As accounts of the army's actions were published in the liberal sections of the press and as information concerning the harsh treatment of objectors in barracks and civilian jails percolated through to the public, the government, along with the military, stood accused, by no means without cause, of attempting to browbeat the absolutists into submission, a design, moreover, which was not proving successful on the whole.

In the interwar years the tide of opinion began to turn still more in favor of the absolutists. Their stand acquired a posthumous reputation (by no means undeserved) among the growing number of persons who were becoming disillusioned with the outcome of the war. The absolutist objectors had stood firm against the all-mighty modern state: their challenge had a completeness, a consistency that was less apparent in the position of the more conciliatory alternativists. This shift in opinion had been foreshadowed by some pacifists earlier. In the spring of 1919 in an article summing up "What the conscientious objector had achieved," Bertrand Russell wrote: "The absolutists have won in the contest of endurance: they have shown that the will to resistance is stronger than the community's will to persecution." [43] The absolutists indeed represent the liberal tradition carried to its extremity: their successful defiance of conscription, however, could only have been achieved in a community which, even in wartime, had not entirely abandoned its respect for this tradition.

To move, as we shall now do, from the roughly 1,700 absolutist objectors to the 3,400 men who accepted noncombatant service in the armed forces is to swing the discussion from one end of the pacifist spectrum to the other. The difference between the two stands was by no means necessarily a question of varying firmness in pacifist conviction or contrasting temperament. "It took a considerable degree of moral courage to appear in public with the brass letters 'N.C.C.' (Noncombatant Corps) on the uniform." [44] And when members of the NCC were ordered to do work they considered an infringement of their noncombatant status, or when Seventh-Day Adventists were required to perform duties on their Saturday Sabbath, they endured—if more briefly—similar treatment to that being meted out to the absolutist objector. It was chiefly by their ideological background that the men who served in the NCC (or in the Royal Army Medical Corps with noncombatant status) were distinguished from their colleagues who would accept only civilian work or no condition for exemption at all. For the sects which strove, with a fine disregard of anything but a literalist interpretation of the Ten Commandments, to fulfil

the Biblical injunction, "Thou shalt not kill," noncombatancy of
this sort provided a quite acceptable minimum which their adherents could conscientiously accept.

A curious anomaly in a twentieth-century Europe at war has
been the Friends' Ambulance Unit, which was set up in the early
months of the war by a group of young Quakers.[45] The FAU
had no official connection with the Society of Friends. Some
Quakers disapproved of its close connection with the army. Although its 1,200 members remained civilians and subject only to
their own internal discipline, the Unit worked in uniform alongside the regular forces. Its commander overseas held an honorary
captaincy and there was an unwritten agreement that its members
would not engage in peace activities while in the FAU. As a former
member expressed it, the FAU in fact was "a strange hybrid of
pacifism and militarism." "Its personnel consisted mostly of Quakers, but not entirely. . . . Some were ardent Christian pacifists.
. . . Some based their pacifism on broader grounds. Some were
in the 'Unit' out of deference to their Quaker upbringing. Some
[at first] were simply men in a hurry to take part in the war without the tedium of military training." Permitted to act as pacifists
at war by the British military authorities, members of the FAU
were regarded by the French Army, to which some of them were
attached for ambulance duties, "as amiable and efficient cranks."
"Our pacifism was put down to some eccentricity of religion. We
discussed it freely, and were treated with respect, sympathy and
almost complete incomprehension." [46]

For those objectors in whom the impulse to render humanitarian
service prevailed over the desire to protest the war (and who
were fortunate enough to get accepted by the Unit) the FAU
appeared to provide an excellent outlet for their energies. However, after the introduction of conscription early in 1916, a crisis
occurred. Apprehension grew that the FAU was becoming simply
part of the military machine. The Unit's adjutant, himself now
convinced "that the Unit is no longer a place for the strong peace
man" and about to move over to an absolutist stand, reported:
"A good many of my boys are getting restless, being afraid that
C.O.'s will be forced either into the N.C.C. or into prison, and
that if so they must resign [from] the F.A.U. and take their share
of the hardships." [47] Opinions differ as to the contribution made

by the Unit's work in World War I. Did it prove that, in a liberal democracy, pacifists even in wartime could still find a place inside the military framework and yet preserve their peculiar witness intact? Or did it, instead, show that modern war demanded a more radical protest from its opponents than the patching up of the wounds inflicted by the opposed military machines? The argument, as we shall see, was reopened again with the coming of World War II.

Apart from men assigned to the FAU or confirmed by a tribunal in their membership in the Unit, over 5,000 objectors were given exemption from combatant service on condition that they undertook civilian work of national importance. Job allocation was mostly carried out under the auspices of the Pelham Committee (so called from the name of its first chairman). In addition, in the early summer of 1916, under pressure of liberal opinion in the country which was becoming increasingly scandalized by official treatment of the conscientious objector, the Home Office set up a scheme for reviewing cases of imprisoned objectors and releasing those considered genuine "on their undertaking to perform work of national importance under civil control." It became apparent thereafter that among the over 6,250 men who refused to abide by their tribunal's decision, only a minority were thoroughgoing absolutists. Roughly 3,750 accepted work under the auspices of the Home Office Scheme. To some pacifists this was a disappointment. Bertrand Russell, for instance, wrote around this time: "Odd things give me a sense of failure—for instance, the way the C.O.s all take alternative service, except a handful." [48] Fervent, occasionally bitter, debate took place within the NCF concerning the merits and disadvantages of the Scheme. Although Clifford Allen and many other influential NCF members, including the whole National Committee, opposed it as an unjustifiable compromise with militarism and an attempt to split the united front of those engaged in fighting conscription, the feeling among imprisoned objectors and in the organization at large continued to run in favor of accepting the Scheme (though, of course, with the proviso that full support should still be given to the men who wished to resist conscription à l'outrance). Moderates, like the Quaker M.P. T. Edmund Harvey, even felt that the Scheme had positive value. Not merely did it demonstrate the government's goodwill and desire to avoid the persecution of genuine conscience, it would also serve to show, in his view, that the imprisoned objectors were prepared to shoulder the burdens of citizenship by hard and, at the same time, useful work.

English prisons of the early twentieth century still retained in their regimen much of the harshness of the nineteenth-century system—in particular, the silence rule and a sense of complete isolation oppressed the wartime prisoners of conscience. The system's "silent inhumanity . . . scarcely dreamt of in proper society" [49] made outstanding exponents of penal reform in the postwar years out of some absolutist objectors, like the socialist Fenner Brockway and the Quaker Stephen Hobhouse. At the time these rigorous conditions, the after-effects of which in a few cases are known to have resulted in death, undoubtedly led objectors not infrequently to a reconsideration of their absolutist stand and to a readiness to exchange prison for civilian work, especially if they felt their health and sanity threatened by prolonged incarceration. However, most of the "schemers," as they were called, were men who had landed in jail not because they refused to accept any alternative to military service, but as a result of their tribunal's failure to recognize the sincerity of their objection to army service. They, therefore, welcomed the Home Office Scheme as an attempt by the government to rectify the tribunal's mistaken judgment.

Yet many of them were soon to lose their enthusiasm. In the first place, labor was of a semi-penal character and carried out in conditions not vastly different from those the men had left behind in jail. Nevertheless, the gutter press repeatedly reported that the Scheme was pampering and coddling its "conchies" (as objectors were derisively called in Great Britain). Sometimes work centers were actually located in prisons; asylums and workhouses were also used for this purpose. Men who accepted the Scheme were required to undertake whatever work was allotted them by the committee which administered the Scheme. This Committee framed the regulations which governed daily activities, including a ban on all peace activities. Remuneration and conditions of labor were not subject to collective bargaining in any form, which particularly riled the many socialist objectors among the schemers. Discipline in cases of disobedience was enforced by the threat of return to prison for completion of sentence and subsequent army call-up. In fact, some schemers preferred to go back voluntarily to jail rather than to continue to work under conditions they considered intolerable.

A recent writer on World War I conscientious objection in Britain has given the following severe, but by no means unwarranted, judgment on the Home Office Scheme:

Despite the liberal intentions of those who planned the H.O. scheme, it proved to be a discreditable shambles. It never came within measuring distance of giving conscientious objectors the "work of national importance" they were promised. It insisted on punishing men officially declared to be genuine in their conscientious objection. Above all, it went a long way towards justifying its rejection by the absolutists as a diversionary fraud—and towards increasing their numbers.[50]

Revolutionary events in Russia and the approaching end of the war led to unrest among imprisoned objectors as well as among those in Home Office camps. The signing of the armistice increased these feelings of dissatisfaction still further. In jail, political activists like Clifford Allen as early as mid-1917 had refused to work as a form of protest against prolonged imprisonment—contrary to the advice, however, of Dr. Alfred Salter and other religious pacifists, who felt that the men were endangering their health and sanity in an empty gesture of defiance. Early in 1919 militants resorted to even more radical forms of protest including the hunger strike (a weapon of resistance used also by militant suffragettes and by Sinn Feiners) in an effort to gain release. The prison authorities answered this at first by forcible feeding, bringing on death in one instance on account of the roughness with which the operation was conducted. The NCF did not officially approve these prison strikes. Instead, it concentrated on mobilizing liberal public opinion behind the demand for freeing objectors who remained in prison: in November 1918 there were still some 1,500 of them. The NCF had been unable to prevent parliament in the Representation of the People Act of June 1918, which gave the vote to women over the age of 30, from disqualifying all conscientious objectors from exercising the franchise for a period of five years, and there was continued postwar discrimination against conscientious objectors in municipal and government employment. But with the war over, feeling against the objectors began to gradually subside.

The release of imprisoned objectors, however, commenced in earnest only in April 1919: it was completed by the following August. In November of the same year, after some discussion, the NCF, believing that its work was done and that a new organizational framework was needed for the tasks of the pacifist movement that lay ahead, decided to dissolve. The wartime objectors in Great Britain had represented a small and outcast minority. While the fighting raged their fellow citizens had given scant attention to their views; insofar as they noticed them at all, they, for the most part, regarded them with a mixture of apprehension and contempt. "The question seemed trivial at the time; it had great effect later." [51]

The United States

The administrative pattern of conscientious objection in the United States differed considerably from that which prevailed in Great Britain. For one thing there was nothing equivalent to the British system of tribunals, which required every applicant for exemption to present a statement of his belief. Neither the American local selective service boards nor other bodies dealing with conscientious objectors, whether army court-martials or the War Department's Board of Inquiry, permitted this procedure. Organizations like the leftist American Union against Militarism or the Emergency Peace Federation or the National Civil Liberties Bureau, which fought against conscription and for the rights of the conscientious objector, did not provide the latter with a forum for airing his views in the same way as the NCF was doing for his British counterpart. Newspapers rarely gave space to letters from opponents of the war. Little wonder, then, that Norman Thomas in his book on American conscientious objectors in World War I complains that "their dialectic skill was confined to controversies with officers, judges and jailers, and left little record." [52]

A second major distinction between the two patterns lies in the fact that in the United States, as we have seen, the law granted exemption only from combatant service (and that solely for religious objectors). Therefore, the experiences of the American conscientious objectors are set, at least at first, almost entirely within the framework of the army camps to which they were required to report along with their fellow draftees.

Of the 64,693 men who had registered a claim to noncombatant classification, the local boards recognized 56,830 as sincere. Since the authorities were not anxious to touch those who could be deferred on nonconscientious grounds, only 20,873 were actually inducted into the army in the period before the Armistice. But of that number—and this is a surprising fact—considerably less than 4,000, which is less than a fifth of the total, made use after induction of their "Certificate of Exemption from Combatant Service" issued to them by their local selective service board; for it must be remembered that in the War Department's total figure for conscientious objectors of 3,989 were included some whose applications for objector status had been rejected by their local boards. We can only guess at the reasons for the small number which stuck by its original determination not to fight. A genuine change of heart—as, for instance, in the case of the later war hero, Sergeant Alvin C. York—or the growing pressures of war feeling in the country or uncertainty and isolation probably all contributed to this rapid shrinking of the community of objectors.

Once in camp the conscientious objectors presented the military authorities with an awkward problem—except for those religious objectors who were willing to accept noncombatant service in the armed forces. The latter were assigned to the Medical Corps, the Quartermaster Corps and the Engineer Service, even though this last assignment included construction of fortifications and defenses as well as work on camouflage. The Seventh-Day Adventists, as in Britain, were occasionally in trouble over their refusal to work on Saturdays. They and other noncombatants were sometimes put in detention, too, for refusing orders to carry rifles (still others were ready to accept rifles when issued but would not produce them for drill). Eventually noncombatant soldiers were provided with certificates guaranteeing their immunity from transfer to combatant units without their consent—which had occasionally been attempted earlier—and were expressly exempted from carrying sidearms. It later became the administration's policy to exert pressure on all objectors in camp—whether acknowledged sincere by local boards or not—to accept noncombatant service. Altogether around 1,300 men accepted this status.

At first the army authorities were at a loss to know exactly what to do with the remaining objectors: doubtless, they had many more urgent tasks requiring their attention. As a result, treatment of objectors varied greatly from camp to camp. In some places religious objectors belonging to churches generally known to be pacifist were shown more consideration than other objectors. Isolated objectors were more likely to meet rough and sometimes cruel treatment than those held in large cantonments; as were those, like the Russian-speaking Molokans or the German-speaking Hutterites, who combined imperfect mastery of the English language with what was regarded as eccentricity in dress or personal appearance. The War Department, indeed, deplored any man-handling of objectors, and instances where this did occur were usually the result of overzealous junior officers acting on their own initiative. Though the army did not cease its endeavors to persuade objectors to accept some sort of service, in the large camps, at any rate, it soon stopped any attempt to impose drill or military duties. In the end the only work usually required of them was performance of camp chores such as cooking and tidying up. This regimen, which was finally confirmed by the War Department, but not until June 1918, was indeed monotonous but gave plenty of opportunity for reading and study—and for endless discussions among a motley community, which included *inter alia* college educated urban Quakers, militant and agnostic socialists and anarchists, pious ploughboys from fundamentalist Mennonite communities of the rural mid-West, as well as illiterate Negro sectaries from the deep South and long-haired devotees of the esoteric House of David.

If the army was puzzled to know how to proceed with the objectors, many of the objectors, young men in their twenties often away from home for the first time, were equally uncertain as to the right behavior in the circumstances. "You apparently, when you reached camp, did not know what you could and could not conscientiously do and have been floundering ever since," an official of the American Friends Service Committee told a young Quaker. The AFSC advised Quaker objectors to think out the implications of their position carefully beforehand. Without forethought it was very easy to slide unthinkingly into acceptance against one's true inclinations of at least noncombatant duties. The AFSC gave objectors, who were unwilling to become noncombatant soldiers, three pieces of advice: first, refuse to wear a uniform as this may be misunderstood as readiness to accept service in the army; secondly, do not take army pay since to do so is really inconsistent with your stand; thirdly, do not obey military orders, even when seemingly unconnected with war. "Planting flowers around the hospital grounds," wrote another AFSC worker," sounds like an innocent kind of work but you have seen the principle involved: as this work is under the military and therefore as you cannot, in accordance with the principles of the Society of Friends, conscientiously perform work under military [command], you cannot conscientiously do this work." [53]

As early as September 1917 the Secretary of War had directed the army, in regard to Mennonite objectors, not on any account to employ force to make them wear uniforms "as the question of raiment is one of the tenets of the faith." Eventually, this ruling was also extended to most other objectors. In the following month the Secretary of War issued instructions that objectors be segregated within the camps from other draftees and placed under specially selected officers, who would treat them "with tact and consideration." [54] He expressed a hope that in this way what browbeating and coercion had failed to achieve milder methods would accomplish—namely, the renunciation by many of their objector status. At once a problem arose in relation to men who claimed to be conscientious objectors but had not been recognized as such by their local boards. (In practice camp commanders hitherto had usually solved the problem by treating as legitimate objectors all who continued obdurate in refusing army service after varying degrees of harassment.) In December the Secretary of War issued a further directive: until further notice all claimants to that status should be segregated as conscientious objectors. The War Department still appeared to be hesitant concerning the best policy to be adopted. Therefore, it continued to drift along uncertainly.

The position, however, was becoming increasingly unsatisfactory. Since the army regarded an objector as a soldier subject to military discipline, minor infractions of regulations caused either by the objector's defiance of authority or by his conscientious scruples—or by a mixture of both—could lead to his trial by court-martial and sentencing to a stiff term of detention in a

military prison. The inflamed state of public opinion made it difficult for Congress to extend the existing terms of exemption for
conscientious objectors. Many persons then agreed with ex-President Theodore Roosevelt in considering objectors as either slackers
(at best) or plain traitors. But in March 1918 a law was passed
allowing the furloughing of draftees in general to civilian work
if deemed in the national interest. The way was now open for the
War Department to rid the army of its remaining refractory objectors, including those who had been rejected earlier by the local
boards. The process of sifting the "sincere" objectors from the
"insincere" began in earnest at the beginning of June with the
setting up of a Board of Inquiry consisting of two judges and the
dean of Columbia University's Law School. Objectors deemed
"sincere" after appearing before the Board and unwilling to accept noncombatant service were usually directed to undertake agricultural work or in a few cases employment in industry. Prior to
the Armistice about 1,200 men had been furloughed in this way.
In addition 99 men were permitted to join the Friends Reconstruction Unit in France[55]—naturally they were mostly members of the
Society of Friends but a few non-Quakers were included in this
group. A court-martial was the fate of men considered "insincere"
by the Board (under this designation were included most of the
political objectors who held a selective objection to the current
war) and of those who refused the proffered furloughing or
"whose attitude in camp [in the words of an order of the Secretary
of War, dated 27 April 1918] is sullen and defiant" or who engaged in political propaganda. Altogether some 450 objectors were
sent to military prisons. Finally, at the time of the Armistice 940
objectors (of whom 225 sought noncombatant status only) still
remained in camp awaiting assignment by the Board of Inquiry.

The three members of the Board seem to have made every
effort to be scrupulously fair to the men who appeared before
them. But it was often difficult for highly trained lawyers to comprehend, in particular, the motives and values of rural religious
sects, from which many of the objectors came. It was hard, too,
for these respectable members of bourgeois society to appreciate
the antiwar militancy of working class agitators, whose passion for
building a new social order, after they had destroyed the old,
sometimes reached an almost religious fervor. The Board's chair

man, Major Kellogg, for instance, found the Quaker objectors from middle-class homes nice boys (his Board usually exempted them without more ado) and he admired at least the dialectical skill of the socialists who argued the case against capitalist wars. But for the Mennonites,[56] mostly farming folk with little formal education and sometimes an imperfect mastery of the English tongue, he had little but a contemptuous pity. "Civilization," he writes, "apparently has passed them by. . . . They remain a curious and alien survival of an old-world people, an anachronism amid the life of today." [57] What is perhaps more curious is the fact that the major for all his learning appears to have been utterly unaware of the sociological transformation and the currents of intellectual and spiritual renewal that were already at work in the American Mennonite community.

The men who were furloughed on the Board of Inquiry's recommendation to work in agriculture were technically still regarded by the army as soldiers. But this was largely a formality. They were given work on private farms and the farmers paid them current wage rates—with the proviso that anything above $30 per month, i.e., the pay of a private soldier, should be forwarded to the Red Cross. The men were not permitted to leave their employment without permission, and they were not allowed to take a job in the area of their home (a ruling that was designed to prevent ill feeling on the part of those whose sons had had to leave home for the army). In fact, most furloughed objectors were assigned employment in the vicinity of the camp in which they had previously been held. In some cases local "patriots" attempted to whip up resentment in their local community against the assignees. When this happened, however, the army intervened at once: these men were soldiers, it explained, and were engaged on work of national importance and any attempt to harass them would not be tolerated. After the war was over, objectors on furlough from the army were demobilized along with the regiments to which they had been nominally assigned. On leaving service each man received a certificate stating: "This is a conscientious objector who has done no military duty whatsoever and who refused to wear a uniform." [58]

Thus we find that the American military authorities' policy for dealing with objectors who were prepared to undertake alternative civilian service but would not accept noncombatant status in the army compares not unfavorably with that devised by the British government. It was indeed long delayed owing to political hindrances which held up the application of a satisfactory solution to the problem. The War Department was circumscribed, too, by the legal framework of exemption which, on paper at any rate, permitted conscientious objector status only on religious grounds. Though the furlough system allowed the objector rather less freedom of choice and movement than the conditional exemption which tribunals in Great Britain were entitled to grant applicants, it was considerably more generous than the British Home Office Scheme. However, the American system of dealing with conscientious objection had, apart from the fact that it was much more closely controlled by the military than its British counterpart, a further major shortcoming: Congress omitted from the legislation any provision for the absolutists who would be satisfied only with unconditional exemption. True, unconditionalists were much less numerous in America than in Great Britain, but for those who did take that stand there was no alternative but jail.

The best that may be said of American military prisons of World War I (known officially as disciplinary barracks) is that they were perhaps no worse than those in Britain. Concerning the fate of the American prisoners of conscience, whether absolutists or political objectors, who were incarcerated in them, Norman Thomas has written: "Most of [their] experiences . . . can be paralleled by cases of the maltreatment of ordinary military prisoners, though it was less frequently that the latter were so persecuted." [59] Overcrowding and subjection to a savage discipline framed to break the will of recalcitrant soldiers were the common lot of all inmates, conscientious and otherwise. The objectors, however, since many of them refused to work under a military regime, received more than their share of solitary confinement and punishment diet. Some were shackled for hours on end to the bars of their cells. However, following the public protest which stemmed from publicity in the press, the War Department in December 1919 forbade altogether the manacling of military prisoners. Two Hutterites, the Hofer brothers, died in jail from the results of ill treatment experienced in Alcatraz and Fort Leavenworth (Kansas).

At their court-martials objectors usually received inordinately lengthy sentences, though not longer, it must be said, than were normally meted out to military offenders. Seventeen objectors got commuted death sentences (one objector who was somehow sent overseas indeed narrowly escaped execution, his reprieve being due only to his volunteering to fetch the wounded from No Man's Land); 142 were given life sentences. Sentences of 20 to 25 years can be regarded as average; they were not cut down on review. However, no objector was kept in jail for much more than three years, since the release of the last group took place towards the end of November 1920. As in Great Britain, after the conclusion of the Armistice, work strikes were organized by the political radicals in protest both against their continued incarceration and the inhuman conditions prevailing in the jails. In several instances the objectors succeeded in extending the strike as to include the other military prisoners; many of these were not really criminals so much as offenders against military discipline, who felt indignant at the thought of being held captive for long years after the war was ended.

In World War I the prison community of conscientious objectors in America was indeed small, especially if one remembers that, according to the War Department's figures, there were as many as 171,000 draft dodgers who escaped service. Those objectors sentenced by court-martial amounted to less than one eighth of the total number of objectors. Several hundred nonregistrants and objectors to undergoing the army medical examination were tried in the ordinary courts where they received relatively short terms in civil prisons. On release, however, they were automatically registered for military service and thereby became liable for forcible induction into the army if they failed to present themselves voluntarily in camp. As thoroughgoing absolutists, most of them eventually found their way to the court-martial chamber. American pacifism of this period certainly had its radical wing. But whereas in Great Britain the typical objector (at least in the public image) was the absolutist, who shunned so far as he was able all association with the military machine, most American objectors sought a viable compromise with the state at war, which would leave them free to serve their country according to the dictates of their conscience.

CONSCIENTIOUS OBJECTION OUTSIDE GREAT BRITAIN
AND THE UNITED STATES

In the countries of the British Empire where conscription was introduced, the pattern followed in dealing with conscientious objectors was roughly the same as in the mother land. The percentage of draftees who applied for conscientious objector status was, however, lower than in Great Britain and the objectors were drawn almost exclusively from pacifist sects. In Canada, for instance, Quakers, Mennonites, and Brethren in Christ possessed a hereditary claim in law to exemption from military service. The turbulent Dukhobors of British Columbia, a sect of Russian origin whom Tolstoy had aided at the beginning of the century in their emigration to Canada, were rarely touched after conscription had been introduced in 1917 (over the opposition, it may be noted, of the French Canadians). The scruples of religious objectors prepared to accept noncombatant service or farm work were given consideration by the government. But for the nonreligious there was even less organizational support for their stand than in the neighboring United States. Some of them endured imprisonment and maltreatment. In general pacifists in Canada suffered from a more extreme sense of isolation than their fellows did in Great Britain or the States.

On the other side of the globe both Australia and New Zealand had introduced compulsory military service for teenage boys in 1909. When youngsters began to be jailed for refusing to drill—among them a handful of Quakers and children of pacifist parents —there was a public outcry which was unsuccessful, however, in putting an end to the scandal for the time being.[60] Wartime conscription, however, was not imposed in Australia. In New Zealand it came into operation in June 1916 despite lively opposition, inside parliament and out, from the small Labour Party, whose activists continued thereafter to agitate against conscription and to carry on antiwar propaganda. Some of them were arrested and imprisoned for sedition. The New Zealand government interpreted conscientious objection very narrowly. Only members of prewar pacifist denominations (this meant mainly Quakers and Christadelphians, both very small groups) were granted exemption and this exemption was only from combatant duties. Since both Quakers and Christadelphians were conscientiously opposed to service within the armed forces, the act's exemption clause was virtually of no effect. Eventually the government did set up a farm camp scheme for those willing to accept alternative service of a civilian character—but not before the imprisonment of some 400 objectors, a small party of whom were even shipped by the military overseas to the Western front in France.[61]

Respect for conscientious scruples in regard to military service was not confined to countries where English was spoken. Yet outside the British Empire and the United States recognition of the right to exemption on this account was minimal. Where it did exist it almost invariably applied solely to birthright members of certain small nonresistant sects who were usually excused only from combatant duties. In Tsarist Russia, however, Mennonites could apply for assignment to the civilian forestry service or army hospital work. Their brethren in Germany, on the other hand, where Mennonitism steadily dwindled throughout the nineteenth century and nonresistance was largely abandoned by those remaining in the church, could obtain only noncombatant duties in the army; most young Mennonites accepted full military service.

Under the Tsar, wartime objectors from non-Mennonite Russian sects and Tolstoyans were usually jailed for periods of four to six years: the February Revolution of 1917 brought them release. And the Bolshevik government, after it came to power in October, was eventually persuaded (but not until January 1919) to confirm the assignment of *bona fide* religious objectors to useful civilian work, an arrangement which was already in practice informally, and even to grant unconditional exemption in certain exceptional cases. In 1918, however, while the grip of the central government on the country was not yet firm, cases occurred not only of the imprisonment but also of the shooting of conscientious objectors. Treatment at that time was mainly a question of the disposition of the local authorities.

Before the war the Nazarenes in Hungary, where the sect had adherents especially among the South Slav peasantry, were allowed to serve in the Medical Corps. After the outbreak of hostilities, however, many members of the sect were imprisoned—and some even were executed—for their pacifist stand. A long term of imprisonment, too, was the best the occasional Tolstoyan anarchist

objector could hope for from the military authorities of the Central
Powers, who also resorted to putting objectors—including the
handful who opposed the war on socialist grounds—into the lunatic asylum. In Germany, Seventh-Day Adventists, despite their
readiness to do noncombatant service in the army, usually ended
up in jail, for they were a sect comparatively new in that country.[62] In France and Belgium, no provision at all existed for any
kind of exemption on grounds of conscientious objection. In
France, though, where a lonely intellectual like Romain Rolland
might attempt to stand "above the battle" (the title he gave to his
book: *Au-dessus de la mêlée* [1915]), a vigorous antiwar campaign did eventually emerge. This movement, however, understandably enough, did not advocate conscientious objection. The outlook for the conscientious objector was scarcely less bleak in the
neutral countries of the European continent. Before the war only
Norway exempted religious objectors from military service of any
kind. In no country could nonreligious objectors gain official recognition until in 1917 Denmark instituted an alternative service
system for which no religious test beyond sincerity was required.
In Holland, where during World War I there were many hundreds
of anarchist objectors, the most the government would concede
them unofficially was noncombatant army service.

Pacifism of the type that postulated a personal stand against war
possessed two powerful institutional bases in the English-speaking
world that were absent on the European continent: the nonconformist conscience, incarnated in its most sensitive form in the
Quaker Society of Friends, and the radical political individualism
which found expression within the labor movement in such bodies
as the British ILP. European socialists of the left abhorred war as
fervently as their British or American equivalents, but they did
not become conscientious objectors. There were almost no Quakers
on the continent at this date; the Protestant churches represented
the establishment and were anything but nonconformist in relation
to the demands of the state. Only in Russia was there a powerful
indigenous sectarian movement but there the sects' often wild and
apocalyptic messianism failed to move a religious Orthodoxy that
remained the strongest bulwark of the Tsarist regime.

In Great Britain a lingering tradition of aristocratic liberalism
and in the United States a retreating, but not quite vanished,

frontier democracy still retained sufficient strength in the community at large to cushion the shock of a failure to conform in wartime to the mores of society. Over large areas of the European continent, on the other hand, men either succumbed to the spell of *la gloire* or abandoned international solidarity in favor of the defense of the Fatherland. Those who continued to oppose war either remained secluded intellectuals isolated in their studies from any form of action or pursued international peace by entering the ranks of their national armies and working there, if they could, for the social revolution, which would destroy the roots of war along with capitalism. Conscientious objection was the path chosen only by a few obscure and harmless religious sectaries and a handful of eccentric radicals.

In Great Britain and the United States, the conscientious objectors of World War I belonged in the tradition that stretches back at least to the seventeenth century, to the English Revolution and its Puritan antecedents. Of this ancestry were not only the Quakers and other religious objectors of Protestant background but the agnostic socialists and *enragé* libertarians, who opposed conscription not necessarily from a repugnance to all violence but always in the belief that a personal witness of this kind held value. By their stance they proved their right to this genealogy. A young Englishman of the post-1918 generation, who fell in the Spanish Civil War fighting on the side of the Loyalists, wrote not long before his death of the conscientious objectors of the 1914–18 war: "We look [back] with respect and gratitude" to them for their "personal integrity and intellectual courage." [63]

NOTES

1. Quoted in David Boulton, *Objection Overruled* (London: Macgibbon & Kee Ltd., 1967), p. 131.

2. A. C. F. Beales, *The History of Peace* (London: G. Bell & Sons Ltd., 1931), p. 283. Evans Darby was succeeded as secretary by the Rev. Herbert Dunnico, subsequently a Labour member of parliament. In World War II, ironically, Dunnico—still secretary of the now almost defunct Peace Society—was a supporter of the extreme anti-Germanism of Sir Robert (later Lord) Vansittart.

3. See A. Ruth Fry, *A Quaker Adventure: The Story of Nine Years' Relief and Reconstruction* (London: Nisbet & Co. Ltd., 1926).

4. Reprinted in John W. Graham, *Conscription and Conscience* (London: George Allen & Unwin, Ltd., 1922), pp. 46–50. Italics in the original.

5. From a leaflet entitled *The Order of Reconciliation: Draft* [ca. 1915], in Archives, Swarthmore College Peace Collection: Great Britain, FOR. Henry Hodgkin, first chairman of the British FOR, wrote to an American Quaker (letter to William I. Hull, dated 28 April 1915, in *ibid.*): "Our experience of peace organizations in existence before the war has been a very distinct shock to us. Some of the strongest peace men in the country . . . are now supporting the war. They say that they are doing so as pacifists, because they believe that it is a war which will end war, that it is one against the spirit of militarism, and so forth. Now, it seems to us that this shows that they have never really grasped the full Christian position in regard to war."

6. Letter dated 14 December 1916 in Arthur Marwick, *Clifford Allen: The Open Conspirator* (Edinburgh and London: Oliver & Boyd, 1964), p. 37. For Allen, see also Martin Gilbert, ed., *Plough My Own Furrow* (London: Longmans, 1965).

7. The NCF has recently been the subject of a detailed monograph: Thomas C. Kennedy, "The Hound of Conscience" (Ph.D. diss., University of South Carolina, 1968).

8. Boulton, *op. cit.*, p. 177.

9. Printed in Graham, *op. cit.*, p. 174.

10. Quoted in Boulton, *op. cit.*, pp. 183, 184.

11. Norman Thomas, *Is Conscience a Crime?* (New York: Vanguard Press, 1927), p. 261. This volume was originally published as *The Conscientious Objector in America* (New York: B.W. Huetsch, Inc., 1923).

12. Clarence Darrow, *The War* (New York: National Security League, 1917), pp. 13, 14.

13. Thomas, *op. cit.*, p. 69.

14. Jessie Wallace Hughan, *Three Decades of War Resistance* (New York: The War Resisters League, 1942 ed.), pp. 8, 9.

15. *Advocate of Peace* (Washington, D.C.), 78 (November, 1916), p. 288; 79 (May, 1917), pp. 134, 135. See also Ray H. Abrams, *Preachers Present Arms* (New York: Round Table Press, Inc., 1933), pp. 161–164.

16. See, for instance, the leaflet *Some Particular Advices for Friends & A Statement of Loyalty for Others* (Philadelphia and Baltimore, 1918), signed by 120 prominent Quakers from these two Yearly Meetings. It is reprinted in the *Advocate of Peace*, 80 (May, 1918), pp. 146, 147.

17. Abrams, *op. cit.*, chap. XI. For clerical opposition to wartime pacifism, see pp. 131–142.

18. Thomas, *op. cit.*, p. 70. Cf. Milton Cantor, "The Radical Confrontation with Foreign Policy: War and Revolution, 1914–1920," in Alfred F. Young, ed., *Dissent: Explorations in the History of American Radicalism* (DeKalb: Northern Illinois University Press, 1968), pp. 215–249.

19. Randolph S. Bourne, *War and the Intellectuals: Collected Essays, 1915–1918* (New York: Harper Torchbooks, 1964), pp. 3, 13, 14. In his posthumously published essay on "The State" (pp. 65–104), Bourne develops his quasi-anarchist critique of the modern state as an instrument of power inseparable from the waging of war. "War is the health of the state" (p. 71). However, Bourne—despite some of his wartime utterances—was not an absolute pacifist: he approved of certain spontaneous manifestations of armed resistance exemplified in his view, for example, in the French people's resistance to invasion in 1792.

20. Edward Grubb in *The Tribunal* (London), no. 171 (21 August 1919), p. 1.

21. See Francis McLellan Wilcox, *Seventh-day Adventists in Time of War* (Takoma Park, Md.: Review and Herald Publishing Association, 1936).

22. Walter Guest Kellogg, *The Conscientious Objector* (New York: Boni and Liversight, 1919), p. 52. In fact, the Witnesses' "pacifism" does not preclude participation on God's side in a future Armageddon.

23. See H. Gordon Moore, "Catholic CO.'s in the Last War," *Pax Bulletin* (High Wycombe), No. 35 (September, 1943), pp. 7, 8.

24. Kellogg, *op. cit.*, pp. 173, 174.

25. Quoted in Fenner Brockway, *Bermondsey Story* (London: George Allen & Unwin Ltd., 1949), p. 65.

26. H. P. Adams, *The Failure of War* (London: No Conscription Fellowship, n.d.), p. 8. See also Brockway's pamphlet *Socialism for Pacifists* (Manchester: The National Labour Press Ltd., n.d.).

27. *The Tribunal*, No. 167 (14 July 1919), p. 1. Italics in the original.

28. *Ibid.*, No. 156 (8 May 1919), p. 4; No. 166 (17 July 1919), p. 1. Earlier the NCF had greeted with enthusiasm the German Spartacist Karl Liebknecht's antiwar stand; while before the Russian Revolution the future Soviet Commissar for Foreign Affairs, Georgii Tchitcherin, then a Menshevik refugee in England, had been one of the organizers of an NCF branch recruited from opponents of the war among the exiled Russian revolutionaries.

29. H. P. Adams, "Problems of Revolution," *ibid.*, No. 160 (5 June 1919), p. 1.

30. Clifford Allen his Preface to Graham, *op. cit.*, p. 23.

31. Republished in *Justice in War Time* (London: George Allen & Unwin Ltd., 1924 ed.), pp. 38–57. See also pp. 19, 27, for discussion of justified and unjustified wars in the past.

32. Dorothy L. Plowman, ed., *Bridge into the Future: Letters of Max Plowman* (London: Andrew Dakers Limited, 1944), p. 99. See *The Faith Called Pacifism* (London: J. M. Dent and Sons Ltd., 1936), for his fully matured standpoint.

33. Harold Owen and John Bell, eds., *Wilfred Owen: Collected Letters* (London: Oxford University Press, 1967), p. 461.

34. Quoted in Thomas, *op. cit.*, p. 27.

35. See James Scott Duckers, *"Handed Over"* (London: C. W. Daniels, Ltd., 1916), for the wartime experiences of a London solicitor, a liberal by political persuasion and a libertarian by inward conviction, who refused to recognize the right of any Tribunal to judge conscientious objection.

36. Graham, *op. cit.*, p. 71.

37. Boulton, *op. cit.*, p. 124.

38. Quoted in Graham, *op. cit.*, p. 67.

39. Quoted in *ibid.*, pp. 326, 327, from the *Daily News,* 7 April 1919.

40. To my knowledge only one radical Irish nationalist of any prominence was also a complete pacifist: Francis Sheehy Skeffington. During Easter Week 1916, the English repaid him for this irregularity in conduct by shooting him.

41. Cf. A. J. P. Taylor, *English History 1914–1945* (Oxford: The Clarendon Press, 1965), p. 73, n. 4: "Lloyd George lacked physical courage.

The air raids of the first war, and still more those of the second, terrified him, and he rarely spent a night in London."

42. Mrs. Henry Hobhouse, *'I appeal unto Caesar': The Case of the Conscientious Objector* (London: George Allen & Unwin, Ltd., n.d.) is an importance source for the treatment of the absolutists.

43. *The Tribunal,* No. 154 (24 April 1919), p. 2.

44. Wilcox, *op. cit.,* p. 260.

45. See Meaburn Tatham and James E. Miles, ed., *The Friends' Ambulance Unit 1914–1919: A Record* (London: The Swarthmore Press, 1919).

46. Olaf Stapledon, "Experiences in the Friends' Ambulance Unit," in Julian Bell, ed., *We did not Fight* (London: Cobden-Senderson), pp. 363, 364, 367.

47. T. Corder Catchpool, *On Two Fronts* (London: Headley Bros., 1918), pp. 105, 107–110.

48. Letter to Lady Ottoline Morrell, September, 1916, in *The Autobiography of Bertrand Russell,* Vol. II (London: George Allen and Unwin Ltd., 1968), p. 74.

49. Kennedy, *op. cit.,* p. 436.

50. Boulton, *op. cit.,* p. 219.

51. Taylor, *op. cit.,* p. 54.

52. Thomas, *op. cit.,* p. 23. See Ernest L. Meyer, *"Hey! Yellowbacks!":* *The War Diary of a Conscientious Objector* (New York: The John Day Company, 1930) and Harold Studley Gray, *Character "Bad": The Story of a Conscientious Objector* (New York and London: Harper & Brothers, 1934), for informative accounts from the points of view, respectively, of a political and a religious objector.

53. Arle Brooks and Robert J. Leach, eds., *Help Wanted: The Experiences of Some Quaker Conscientious Objectors* (Philadelphia and Wallingford, Pa.: AFSC and Pendle Hill, 1940), pp. 13, 27–29, 31.

54. Quoted in Thomas, *op. cit.,* pp. 89, 90.

55. For the relief activities of American Quakers during and after World War I, see Rufus M. Jones, *A Service of Love in War Time: American Friends Relief Work in Europe, 1917–1918* (New York: The Macmillan Company, 1920); Mary Hoxie Jones, *Swords into Ploughshares: An Account of the American Friends Service Committee 1917–1937* (New York: The Macmillan Company, 1937). John Forbes, *The Quaker Star under Seven Flags 1917–1927* (Philadelphia: University of Pennsylvania Press, 1962) provides a detailed and well documented account of Friends' negotiations for undertaking relief work with the governments of France, Serbia, Austria, Bulgaria, Germany, Poland and Russia. The author stresses the close connection between the Quakers' pacifism and their impulse to carry on foreign relief.

56. See the artless account given by J. S. Hartzler, *Mennonites in the World War, or Nonresistance under Test* (Scottdale, Pa.: Mennonite Publishing House, 1922 ed.).

57. Kellogg, *op. cit.,* pp. 37–42, 66–69.

58. Quoted in Thomas, *op. cit.,* p. 119.

59. *Ibid.,* pp. 146, 147.

60. See John Percy Fletcher and John Francis Hill, *Conscription under Camouflage* (Adelaide: Co-operative Printing and Publishing Company of South Australia, Limited, 1919); Leslie C. Jauncey, *The Story of Con-*

scription in Australia (London: George Allen & Unwin Ltd., 1935), chaps. I–III.

61. See H. E. Holland, *Armageddon or Calgary* (Wellington, N.Z.: The Maoriland Worker Printing and Publishing Co. Ltd., 1919); as well as Archibald Baxter, *We will not Cease* (London: Victor Gollancz Ltd., 1939) for an account of his experiences en route to, and at, the Western front.

62. The most detailed account of conscientious objection in the German and Austrian empires during World War I is given in a pamphlet by Martha Steinitz, Olga Misar and Helene Stöcker, *Kriegsdienstverweigerer in Deutschland und Österreich* (Berlin: "Die neue Generation," 1923). See Markus Mattmüller, *Leonhard Ragaz und der religiöse Sozialismus,* Vol. II (Zürich: EVZ—Verlag, 1968), chap. VI (B) and (F), for wartime conscientious objection in neutral Switzerland and the stand of one of its foremost defenders.

63. Bell, *op. cit.,* Introduction, p. xv.

III.   The Gandhian Philosophy of Nonviolence

IN THE AUTUMN OF 1914 AN INDIAN LAWYER IN HIS MIDDLE forties, who had recently stopped off in England on his way back to his native land after a prolonged residence in South Africa, began to recruit volunteers among Indian students for an ambulance corps, which he hoped would serve with the British armed forces. This was roughly at the same time that English pacifists were taking the first steps to launch their campaign against the threat of conscription. It is unlikely that the Indian lawyer, whose name was Mohandas Karamchand Gandhi (1869–1948),[1] then met any of the men who were to lead the conscientious objector movement in Great Britain. Their purposes scarcely coincided. The Indian wished to prove his compatriots' devotion to the British Crown, the British pacifists hoped successfully to defy their government's efforts to make them fight for King and country. Gandhi, however, was soon to become the greatest exponent of the philosophy of nonviolence that the world had hitherto known.

During his 21-year stay in South Africa, Gandhi had led a moderately successful campaign of passive resistance by members of the country's Indian colony against the legal discrimination to which they, along with all other non-white groups, were subjected by the ruling minority.[2] What was at that date unique about Gandhi's leadership was that he not only deliberately rejected violence to gain the just rights of his countrymen, he had also begun to evolve a technique of extra-legal action to achieve this goal. It was neither the way of parliamentary government, for Indians in South Africa were deprived of most democratic rights, nor, of course, was it rebellion or civil war, for at its very center stood the principle of nonviolence.

After his return to India in 1915 Gandhi was to apply this technique in order to gain his country's freedom, with results that shook the British Empire to its foundations and sent ripples round the globe. A new method of winning political independence and social justice, even of defending a country against outside aggression, without the degradation and destruction of violence and war made its appearance. Before we examine the principles behind, and the practice of, Gandhian nonviolence, we must enquire briefly whence Gandhi derived the intellectual inspiration to launch nonviolence on a surprised world. Were its origins basically in the Hindu religious tradition in which Gandhi himself was reared? Or should we rather seek its roots in the thought of the West to which, by his education, Gandhi became affiliated?

THE ROOTS OF GANDHIAN NONVIOLENCE

Gandhi himself admitted that neither his beloved *Bhagavad-Gita*, nor the other Hindu religious classics, nor contemporary Hindu practice condemned war or preached the need for nonviolence in group relations. But all living religions are in a state of evolution. "What . . . I have done," said Gandhi, "is to put a new but natural and logical interpretation upon the whole teaching of the *Gita* and the spirit of Hinduism." [3] What he in fact achieved was the transformation of traditional Hindu ideas into something new. In many cases the terminology remained the same, and thereby acceptable even to conservative Indian minds, while the meaning given bore a revolutionary significance. He poured the wine of Western political thought into the old bottles of Hindu tradition; out of the resulting explosion he created a new ethic and a dynamic political technique.

The idea of *ahimsa,* for instance, of non-injury to any living creature, which went back deep into the Indian past and is found in Buddhism and among the Jains as well as in the Hindu religion, Gandhi completely remolded. He made a politico-social obligation from what had been primarily a personal duty. The same thing occurred with his treatment of the search for truth (*satya*), which Hinduism posited as the paramount goal of religion. Gandhi here created a gospel of social action where before there had been only an individual quest. Or take *tapasya,* the ascetic ideal of self-restraint and self-sacrifice which the holy men of India expressed in its most austere form—Gandhi strove to harness such self-discipline to social ends. To him the true end of *tapasya* was not withdrawal to the caves but return to the market place. A similar

socialization, as it were, occurred in Gandhi's use of traditional
Hindu concepts such as *Karma*, which for him became not an
impersonal destiny but an exemplification of the theorem that
immoral actions lead relentlessly to bad ends; or such as non-
attachment to earthly objects, which Gandhi forged into an instrument for changing this world.

Historic India possessed certain techniques of passive resistance
which sought to exercise pressure in order to achieve a given goal.
There was *dharna*, for instance, a kind of sit-down strike pursued
even unto death. A creditor might use it in an endeavor to extract
repayment from a debtor; if he died, his spirit would haunt the
latter. A similar element of coercion and absence of outgoing love
were present in the fast, in the *hartal* (a token shut-down by workshops and businesses to express dissatisfaction at some official
enactment), and in *hijrat*, a voluntary exile in protest against
government action for which there was no legal remedy. When
Gandhi employed *dharna*, the fast, or the *hartal*, however, he
sought to eliminate so far as possible the coercive element and to
replace it by the requirement always to respect the opponent's
personality.

Thus his Indian background supplied Gandhi with the vocab-
ulary and the symbols of his nonviolent philosophy.[4] The set of
values he affixed to them he derived from a quite different source.[5]
As a young student in London he had come upon the New Testament. In the Sermon on the Mount he read the injunctions to love
enemies and not to resist evil by violent means. From two other
favorite authors, Ruskin and Emerson, he took over the idea
of utilizing military heroism and discipline for peaceful goals
and of directing man's warlike instincts into creative, instead of
destructive, channels. There should be a new chivalry of peace
which would incorporate all the moral virtues formerly contained
in war. Thoreau's famous essay on civil disobedience to unjust
acts of government he first read in 1907 when he had already been
conducting his own campaign of civil disobedience against racial
discrimination for nearly fourteen years, almost from his first arrival in Natal in 1893. But the essay provided him with confirmation, and an eloquent apologia, for the line of action he had been
pursuing, as well as an impulse to further extend its range to meet
new injustices.[6]

The most seminal Western influence on Gandhi may have been that of Tolstoy. He read the latter's *Kingdom of God Is Within You* in 1894, soon after its first publication, and was immensely impressed by it. Tolstoy's bold denunciation of modern civilization, with its latent violence and essential falsity, and his call to a simple life struck an answering chord in the Hindu, whose religion taught him non-injury, asceticism and the illusoriness of the visible world. Tolstoy's search for the truth in all the world's religions matched Gandhi's syncretic approach to spiritual problems, which he inherited from his Indian background. Yet in Gandhi the sharp edges of Tolstoy's philosophy are softened: with the former, existing society must be transformed by the spirit of love rather than rejected in a passion of hatred. To Gandhi the political arena and not the self-contained community was the directest way to reach a nonviolent society. "Gandhi is a Tolstoi in a more gentle, appeased, and . . . in a more Christian sense," writes Romain Rolland, "for Tolstoi is not so much a Christian by nature as by force of will." [7] Tolstoy, when shortly before his death he heard of Gandhi's campaign in South Africa, at once recognized their basic spiritual affinity. In a moment of vision the Russian foresaw the tremendous impact that Gandhi's actions (and thus indirectly his own ideas) would make on the world. "Your work in Transvaal," he told him, "which seems to be far away from the centre of our world, is yet . . . most important to us supplying . . . weighty practical proof in which the world can now share and in which not only the Christians must participate but all the peoples of the world." [8]

Scholars have argued concerning the primacy in Gandhi's development of Western or Eastern influences. Did he merely seek confirmation in Christianity and in the writings of Western thinkers of concepts that already lay buried deep in his own mind? Or did he go back to the Indian scriptures and traditions only to seek confirmation there of truths he had learned elsewhere? Certainly the final result of Gandhi's exploration of truth was a synthesis of two traditions. Without his Indian background the shape of his political and social philosophy, including his views on nonviolence, would have been very different. If he had remained without contact with Western ideas, on the other hand, it is extremely doubtful if he could have evolved a revolutionary technique of political action on the basis alone of the Hindu tradition combined with his native talent for social action.

THE PRINCIPLES BEHIND "SATYAGRAHA"

Truth

For Gandhi, as for early British Quakers, life itself was conceived as an experiment in reaching truth. Man, then, must continually strive for the truth; yet, and this was equally important, man could never perfectly know truth. His vision was always defective, fragmented, and one-sided, despite all his efforts to discover truth. For truth, Gandhi came to eventually believe, was God. So long as man was on this earth, chained to the wheel of being, he could not become one with God; even though all his efforts must be directed through single-minded pursuit of truth toward approaching nearer to God.

Since man's perception of truth was by the very fact of his humanity overcast by error, no theology, no philosophical system, no political creed enjoyed a monopoly on the truth. Out of man's frailty, however, there could be generated an element of strength. For, once admitting their proclivity to err and their partial vision of reality, men could work together in the search for truth. They would become, for all their differences, *satyagrahis,* who would harness the force of truth (*satyagraha:* truth-force) behind all their earthly endeavors. The atheist, for instance, who genuinely sought the truth possessed unknowingly that faith in God which Gandhi postulated as an essential prerequisite in the *satyagrahi.*

Satyagraha excluded the employment of violent means. Since man was incapable of reaching absolute truth, he should not take it upon himself to punish error. Patience and sympathy, so long as these virtues were not made excuses for palliating what was believed wrong, were the weapons of *satyagrahis* or nonviolent soldiers, as it were, in the cause of truth. Unlike weapons of violence they were consistent with respect for the opponent's personality, for his vision of the truth (however seemingly mistaken in the issues at stake) and for the common quest for truth on which all mankind was engaged. And a *satyagrahi,* moreover, was obliged constantly to examine his own position to see if his opponent were not in some way nearer to the truth than himself.

Non-injury

In pursuing truth, use of the right means was indeed essential. Practice of *ahimsa,* or non-injury to all sentient beings, who were essentially one in the unity of all being, was inextricably tied to this search. "If there is a dogma in the Gandhian philosophy, it centers here: that the only test of truth is action based on the refusal to do harm." [9] On this point alone did Gandhi require complete agreement from those who followed his leadership. To Gandhi, *ahimsa* signified very much more than non-killing. It included that, of course, but it demanded, too, a positive outreach towards even the evildoer, a love of the sinner along with abhorrence of the wrong done by him. Love, however, should not remain an abstract virtue. As in other spheres Gandhi wished to "socialize" it, to see it materialize in some form of humanitarian service or in a demonstration of resistance to injustice, which in turn would creatively transform the political scene.

Ahimsa, Gandhi insisted vehemently, was never the path of "the timid or the cowardly." "It is the way of the brave ready to face death. He who perished sword in hand is no doubt brave, but he who faces death without raising his little finger and without flinching is braver." On the other hand, a man who should yield his possessions "for fear of being beaten" was devoid of *ahimsa* and a true coward. Gandhi always counseled men to choose violence rather than yield through cowardice. "But . . . nonviolence is infinitely superior to violence, forgiveness is more manly than punishment." [10]

"My *ahimsa* is my own" was a typical remark of Gandhi's. Not everyone could succeed in expunging from his thoughts as well as from his actions every trace of hatred for an opponent. And in regard to animals and insects Gandhi, unlike the Jains whom he knew and admired, never saw his way to observing complete nonviolence (although the problem obviously bothered him from time to time). He, himself, as a good Hindu practiced vegetarianism—but he did not demand it of all *satyagrahis.* Monkeys, he believed, might be killed if they threatened to become

a pest and reptiles if they became a nuisance. He did not believe
in kindness to animals if it were at the expense of human beings.
At the same time, he felt that this restriction of nonviolence was
due to his own shortcomings, to his failure somehow to come
upon the right attitude, rather than to a failure in the absolute
quality of *ahimsa*. Snakes and scorpions would respond to the
force of truth, if only man knew how. The sacredness of all
sentient life was the ideal; yet each man could only go so far
in recognizing this truth as his limited vision allowed.[11]

Self-sacrifice

A third element in Gandhian nonviolence, perhaps the hardest
for Westerners to comprehend, was *tapasya,* suffering voluntarily
undergone not for its own sake, as with the ascetic Yogis (or certain Christian orders), but as a demonstration to an opponent
of one's seriousness of purpose and as a guarantee of sincerity.
In striving for the right a *satyagrahi* should be prepared to endure
unto death. He must be ready to detach himself from material
things. Self-suffering, then, acted as a purifying process by which
the dross of life was purged away. In this fashion, even after
persuasion has failed, the opponent's heart may ultimately be
melted; he may be impelled to relinquish a wrong position and
join in common pursuit of the truth. By a kind of shock treatment
dramatizing the position of the *satyagrahi,* writes Bondurant, "suffering operates . . . as a tactic for cutting through the rational
defences which the opponent may have built . . . This process
may be referred to as catharsis." [12] There was, of course, an
element of expediency in all this. Further, there was clearly a
danger, which even Gandhi was not always able to avoid, of
coercion in disregard of the opponent's true convictions. In order
to escape the guilt of causing the death of a fasting *satyagrahi,* for
instance, or to avoid the consequent opprobrium in the eyes of
public opinion, the opponent might come to terms. But this, in
Gandhi's view, would not signify a real reconciliation unless the
opponent's heart was also won.

Tapasya, in addition to purifying the nonviolent combatant
(as prayer helped to purify and strengthen the medieval knight
of chivalry), acted also as a means of mastering the animal passions (fear, anger, hunger, greed, sexual desire), thus enabling

the *satyagrahi* more easily to direct his energies into nonviolent channels. As Gandhi wrote:

Non-resistance [*satyagraha*] is restraint voluntarily undertaken for the good of society. It is, therefore, an intensely active, purifying, inward force. It is often antagonistic to the material good of the non-resister. It may even mean his utter material ruin. It is rooted in internal strength, never weakness. It must be consciously exercised. . . . The acquisition of the spirit of non-resistance is a matter of long training in self-denial and appreciation of the hidden forces within ourselves. It changes one's outlook upon life. It puts different values upon things and upsets previous calculations.

Gandhi believed that *satyagraha* could generate sufficient spiritual force to transform the world. Indeed it would be enough for the release of this tremendous energy if only "one person" were possessed fully by the force of truth (*satyagraha*), "even as one general is enough to regulate and dispose of the energy of millions of soldiers who enlist under his banner even though they know not the why and wherefore of his dispositions." [13]

The Common Welfare

Gandhi, as has often been pointed out, was no systematic philosopher or cloistered theologian. He was above all a social actionist, one who aimed "to revolutionize politics by ethics." [14] The revolutionary nature of his politics lay in technique but, despite the assertions of some writers, he did not by any means neglect social theory. Indeed he regarded the structure of a nonviolent society as a matter of basic importance.

"Truth and *ahimsa*," he wrote, "must incarnate in socialism." [15] By socialism he meant not a centralized, industrialized state socialism but a decentralized, peasantist society with the overwhelming majority of the population living in largely self-sufficient, democratically run village communities and gaining their livelihood in agriculture or by handicrafts. Poor, yet self-supporting, these villages would constitute the surest bulwark of a nonviolent order. Due to their poverty they would not tempt aggressors, and by supplying their essential needs on the spot, they could more easily defy a conqueror in case of necessity than a complex technological civilization. Even Hitler, Gandhi once said, would be incapable of crushing the 700,000-odd villages of India, if they adopted

nonviolence.[16] In a village society coercion in government would
be reduced to a minimum: this provided an additional argument
in its favor.

Gandhi's socialism was essentially a populist socialism. It did
not go much beyond the principle of labor ownership in the
village lands and of trusteeship in respect to other forms of
property. A *satyagrahi,* a follower of nonviolence, must be ready
to relinquish his wealth if this were necessary for the common
welfare. *Sarvodaya,* the welfare of all (the title Gandhi used for
his translation of Ruskin's *Unto This Last* into Gujerati), expresses
in compact form the essence of Gandhi's social philosophy.

Was Gandhi, as his Marxist critics have maintained, merely a
reactionary pleading for the preservation of an archaic social order?
True, he believed that the traditional structure of society should
be altered only where good reason existed for change—and then,
of course, only by nonviolent means.[17] But the populist democracy
that he urged on his fellow countrymen approached more nearly
the mutualist anarchism of the Proudhonist variety than the
social conservatism of Western political thought (though Gandhi
himself, unlike the anarchists, never advocated the abolition of
the state, despite elements of coercion seemingly built into its
very structure, or of the redemptive aspects of the punishment of
wrongdoing). Decentralization of power seemed to Gandhi the
best way not only to guarantee the maximum good of all but
also to reduce the exercise of this power to a minimum, to provide
a firm foundation from which to extend the practice of *satyagraha,*
and to gradually permeate society with the ethic of nonviolence.

THE PRACTICE OF "SATYAGRAHA"

Pursuit of truth, non-injury, readiness to suffer and the common
good of all members of society: these were the principles which
must guide the follower of nonviolence. In bridging the gap,
however imperfectly, between ethic and practice lay the heart
of Gandhi's genius and the essence of his contribution to the
twentieth-century world.

Nonviolence, Gandhi emphasized constantly, must never be
employed frivolously, without just cause. A *satyagraha* campaign
should crystallize around some truth—or rather, it must embody
some aspect, admittedly partial, of universal truth. In South Africa

(where Gandhi had originally coined the word *satyagraha* to replace the more negative term "passive resistance") the struggle had been against legal discrimination of the Indian minority on grounds of race. The campaign, it should be pointed out, did not include the oppressed African majority in its scope. After Gandhi's return to India, he embarked on a series of struggles, either led by himself or by one of his deputies, which were directed not solely against the British authorities but sometimes against Indian wielders of religious or economic power, too.

In the Vykom Temple Road *Satyagraha* (1924–25), for instance, the object was to vindicate "the right of every human individual to pass along a public road without discrimination on the basis of caste," for here the untouchables had been forbidden to use the highways around the temple. In the Bardoli campaign of 1928, "the granting of an impartial enquiry into the enhanced assessment of land" was the demand for which the *satyagrahis* undertook action: the provincial government had arbitrarily raised the taxation imposed on the local peasantry, who now sought relief from this injustice. Sometimes a labor dispute, such as occurred in 1918 at Ahmedabad between laborers and textile-mill owners, provided the occasion for the exercise of *satyagraha*. It was "the social justice underlying the demand for increased allowance"—a 35% increase for the workers to cover a steep rise in cost of living over recent years—that embodied the truth for those who engaged in this campaign. Those campaigns that were directed against the foreign occupying power aroused the most controversy, since 'truth' was matched here not against a group, however powerful, of private citizens but employed against the British in order to bring about a change in the law of the land or even a totally new regime. Near the beginning of his political career in India, Gandhi had launched a struggle of this nature: the unsuccessful nationwide *satyagraha* in 1919 against the obnoxious Rowlatt Act, which *inter alia* allowed preventive detention for political offenses. The famous Salt *Satyagraha* of 1930–31, the largest-scale effort ever mounted by Gandhi, was directed overtly towards political goals: at first "the removal of laws [creating a government monopoly of salt manufacture] which worked a hardship upon the poor" and broadening later to resistance against "the subjugation of India by a foreign power," whose continued presence in the country appeared contrary to the interests of its inhabitants.[18]

The 'truth' embodied in a campaign of *satyagraha* was not open in Gandhi's view to negotiation. Only a conviction as to their inconsistency with what was really true should lead *satyagrahis* to alter or abandon their avowed objectives. Gandhi has been accused of undue rigidity on this point: surrender and confession of error on the part of the opponent was his goal, it was claimed, instead of a compromise formula such as was aimed at in labor conciliation—an outcome that may not perhaps be completely just by absolute standards but remains a reasonable approximation of what each side wants. Gandhi, it was said (not without some justification), aimed at victory: a nonviolent victory, it is true, but victory nevertheless. Yet essentially what Gandhi strove for was agreement and conciliation between the conflicting parties—provided this did not involve a compromise concerning what was right. The victory, at least in theory, should not mean the triumph of either contestant; it should signify the victory of truth itself.

Techniques

Satyagraha is not merely a philosophy of nonviolence; it is also a technique for the creative resolution of conflict. It does not aim at the elimination of conflict from human relationships. Conflict is admitted as a built-in element of the human situation. But conflict, Gandhi claimed, may be directed into creative, nonviolent channels with a proper understanding of the means necessary for this purpose. Thus *satyagraha* is not a perfectionist ethic or a counsel of withdrawal, but a tool for the collective achievement of practical objectives.

There are two major types of *satyagraha* in action, both of which were employed on different occasions by Gandhi: noncooperation and civil disobedience. Noncooperation does not normally involve the breaking of any human law (though of course in certain circumstances it may do so). It can be directed either against the state or against some private group in the community. A *satyagraha* movement of noncooperation, if concerned with fighting against an economic wrong, might take the form of a strike, walk-out or sit-in or of a boycott of goods; one aimed at political injustice could involve, for instance, the protest resignation of civil servants from their posts or the renunciation of official titles and honors or the boycott of some educational or cultural institution. The second type of *satyagraha,* the best known and the more widely practiced—civil disobedience—involves by its very nature the breaking of man-made laws in the name of a higher law expressing truth. Nonpayment of taxes, refusal of compulsory military service, or the manufacture of some prohibited article (here the breaking of the state monopoly by making salt practiced by Gandhi and his followers in 1930 is the best known instance) are examples of such principled disobedience. For successful *satyagraha* nonviolent suffering of the penalties of disobedience— manhandling, imprisonment or even death—is absolutely essential.

A *satyagraha* movement is essentially a group movement; sometimes, as in British India in 1930–31, a mass movement. Indeed, Gandhi's model of a nonviolent society envisaged the participation of the whole community to some degree in its nonviolent defense. He did, however, conceive of an individual form that might be used on occasion: token or, better said, "representative" *satyagraha.* Whereas, for instance, the undertaking of a fast by one or more carefully selected individuals might be an efficacious, as well as nonviolent, means of exposing the public to the truth which a *satyagraha* movement was expressing and of directing the opponent's mind toward a recognition of that truth, widespread fasting on the part of *satyagrahis,* however dedicated, was likely to lead to disaster. Not only was it uncertain if the necessary discipline and powers of endurance existed among large numbers, but there was a serious danger of the coercive element latent in the fast becoming uppermost and obscuring the nonviolent basis of the campaign.

A supplementary form of *satyagraha* is the positive program of constructive work, which should always accompany the more negative forms of nonviolent struggle, whether noncooperation or civil disobedience. Only with such a program in existence would it normally be possible, Gandhi thought, to find a creative solution to a conflict situation, for a program of this kind points the way to the achievement of a just society. Gandhi centered his constructive program in the village and its needs, but this, of course, was conditioned by the Indian situation and was by no means an essential characteristic. In fact the idea is an old one: "Ye shall know them by their fruits" [Matt. 7:16]. Under Gandhi's leadership *satyagrahis* engaged in such activities as communal reconciliation, the fight against untouchability, the promotion of village industries and handicrafts, basic education, the improvement of sanitation and health services, and the cultural development of the country's backward tribes. The social reconstruction and relief work of Quakers in the West, alongside their more negatively framed objection to war, have independently expressed the same concept in a different environment.

In choosing the target of the *satyagraha* campaign, the symbolic element is extremely important. In handing back their decorations and honors to the British government, Indian *satyagrahis* were not protesting against the honors system as such. When Gandhi embarked on his famous Salt March to the sea at Dandi, his efforts were not directed primarily against the salt monopoly. It was the oppression of the poor deprived in this way of cheap salt, one of the basic constituents in their daily fare, against which nonviolent struggle was to be waged. And from social injustice the campaign eventually turned to direct its efforts toward the winning of national independence, *swaraj*. Gandhi always insisted on the need for extreme care in choosing the right symbol on which to focus a *satyagraha* movement. The inner meaning of the symbol must be clear to all; the truth which it sought to express should shine forth so that even the simplest soul might understand what was at stake. Just as a party leader fighting an election in a democratic state must possess an almost instinctive sense of the popular mind in order to choose the right slogan on which to win the election, so Gandhi in his way knew how to convey both to his followers and to the wider public whom he hoped to win over, and even to the opponent with whom reconciliation on the basis of truth must eventually be achieved, the essentials of his nonviolent struggle in a single symbolic act. This might be the illegal panning of salt or insistence on the right of all to use a public way or the withdrawal by workmen of their labor: what was important was the truth symbolized. To gain this truth men followed Gandhi. In winning men for the truth there was need for a kind of divine expediency.

In Gandhian strategy, however, resorting to civil disobedience or noncooperation should come only after every effort has been made

to reach an acceptable solution—as well as preparing for a successful employment of nonviolent resistance should it eventually become necessary. Thus, as it were, negotiation and preparedness are
developed alongside each other. In addition, the various stages
in mounting a resistance movement must be carefully modulated
so as to provide flexibility in negotiation and also to allow for a
gradual stepping up in intensity. First, persuasion must be used to
deflect the opponent from his wrong course and an agreement
sought with him that would be honorable to each party without,
however, betraying the principle at issue. At the same time the
satyagrahis must develop their constructive program and, above
all, put over to the public as clearly as possible (and insofar as
they have access to means of communication) the reasons for
their stand. In case direct conflict is not averted, a sympathetic
public can be of immense value in upholding the morale of the
nonviolent campaigners. If negotiation of the issue reaches a dead-
lock, then the second stage begins. This consists of an attempt to
dramatize the issue by voluntary suffering on the part of the
satyagrahis or selected members of their movement. If their earn-
estness at the negotiating table or their eloquence in stating their
case to the public fails to move the opponent, then perhaps their
willingness to suffer for the cause—whether vicariously by their
leaders undergoing a fast or in some other way—may convince
him of their sincerity and the rightness of their cause. Only when
this approach has failed to produce any effect should the movement
embark on the third and most decisive stage: either civil disobedience or noncooperation.

Even after the lines are drawn and some form of nonviolent
coercion (for attempts by some Gandhians to deny the presence
of a coercive element appear disingenuous) is employed, the door
should always be left open for renewed talks and negotiations
and an agreed settlement. "If . . . the nonviolent struggle itself
[brings] to light relevant facts which the *satyagrahis* failed to take
into account when drawing up their proposals for a settlement,
these proposals will be amended." [19] So long as there is no agreement—despite genuine efforts to reach one on the part of the
satyagrahis—the strength of their movement and its effectiveness,
Gandhi believed, lay above all in their moral quality. Intellectual
attainments or intuitive gifts have their value, of course, and

physical courage is essential, too, but they can only supplement, not replace, moral worth. Even moral worth is valueless in a *satyagraha* campaign unless accompanied by moral discipline. The campaigners' behavior should always be in consonance with their nonviolent principles: they must refrain from reacting violently to any injury suffered, submitting peacefully to arrest or confiscation of property while at the same time refusing to obey unjust orders whatever the consequences. They should never utter angry words whatever the provocation. Willingness to abide by the decisions of the campaign leaders was likewise basic to *satyagraha*'s success: if a campaigner experiences a fundamental disagreement with their direction, he should withdraw altogether. The *satyagrahi* was a soldier, but a volunteer not a conscript. Gandhi stressed four essential qualities in a perfect *satyagrahi:* courage, patience, self-reliance, freedom from covetousness.

Is *satyagraha,* then, a technique only for those near to attaining perfection? Are only saints, a small band of elect spirits, ripe for engaging in such nonviolent confrontation with evil? Should its use be confined to specially selected groups, a kind of nonviolent order of chivalry? Gandhi stoutly denied that nonviolence was a prerogative of a spiritual elite. It was a weapon that could be wielded by the ordinary man, one that would serve to elevate as well as defend him. "The religion of non-violence," he said, "is not merely for the *rishis* [i.e., holy men] and the saints. It is meant for the common man as well. Nonviolence is the law of our species as violence is the law of the brute." [20] It is the latent capacity for nonviolence that distinguishes man from the beast.

Satyagraha was capable of becoming a mass movement. But Gandhi fairly soon came to realize that some training for nonviolence was essential if it was to be conducted on a wide scale. Where, as in the Vykom Temple Road *Satyagraha,* specially selected volunteers of high moral caliber were alone involved, the maintenance of a nonviolent stance was comparatively simple even over a long period of time. In campaigns where large numbers were utilized, the danger of a lapse into violence, of destructive outbreaks against the opposing forces, was a serious one. Gandhi learned his lesson in 1919 during his campaigns against the Rowlatt Act. After some of the participants in areas where he was not present in person had turned to violence, Gandhi at once called off the campaign. "I had called on the people to launch upon civil disobedience before they had . . . qualified themselves for it," he wrote later, "and this mistake seemed to me of Himalayan magnitude." [21]

Whereas the successful employment of *satyagraha* demanded dedicated leadership committed to the principle of nonviolence and, if possible, some degree of previous instruction in nonviolent ideas and techniques for all participants, the rank and file did not need to share in full the rigorous moral and physical discipline that Gandhi imposed on himself. He took all who volunteered and were willing to abide by the rules. He never demanded that all those who joined him on a campaign cease to eat meat or become celibates or give up their worldly possessions. He did not even ask them to pledge themselves to be nonviolent for the rest of their lives, though he did expect of them unqualified non-violence for as long as they were part of a *satyagraha* movement. And he hoped, of course, that their experiences as *satyagrahis* would eventually make them convinced adherents of that "law of love that rules mankind . . . the supreme and only law of life." [22]

Gandhi pointed to the way unlettered peasants and simple work-men by the thousands had adopted nonviolence during the various campaigns he led in person or through his deputies. In the Salt *Satyagraha* of 1930–31 the movement had reached mass dimen-sions. Was not Gandhi indeed the great awakener of the Indian people, the first to arouse the peasant millions to action after centuries-long apathy? Yet, undeniably, the larger the movement grew the greater became the risk of violent outbreaks and thereby a nullification of all that *satyagraha* stood for.

Apart from preliminary instruction of those taking part in a *satyagraha* movement, including the training of specially chosen volunteers to deal with large crowds, Gandhi devised certain methods for averting violence or containing it once it had erupted. Most important were his efforts to decentralize leadership by strengthening what Bondurant has called "secondary leadership" and to see that those responsible for organizing a campaign were well known in their own district and aware of its needs and prob-lems, and able, thereby, both to enjoy the confidence of the people and to control the local *satyagraha* movement. The creation of a chain of leadership stretching downwards would also help to remove some of the disadvantages resulting from large-scale arrests at the top. Even after the campaign commanders had disappeared into jail, the movement might continue to function—and to function nonviolently, which was even more vital to its success—if it was firmly rooted in the community. Secondly, Gandhi occasionally used *satyagraha* itself against those who had resorted to violence: to shame them into a return once more to nonviolence. This technique, however, presupposes that the violence has not gone too far. It also presumes a certain basic unity of thought between the nonviolent and the now violent campaigners. It would be much less effective, for instance, with those who wished purposely to provoke violence for their own ends. And its successful employment would be considerably more difficult for those not possessing the charisma of a Gandhi, whose threat to fast unto death could serve to bring even the violent part of India to heel. Of potentially wider application was a third Gandhian method for dealing with outbreaks of violence. This consisted in either continuing the campaign at a lower pitch of intensity, a kind of tactical withdrawal in order to gather strength for further nonviolent conflict, or in carrying on only in areas uncontaminated by violence, a deployment of forces that could be executed more easily, of course, if the movement were decentralized. Lastly, if violence spread despite every effort to restrain it, Gandhi advised calling off the *satyagraha* altogether. On more than one occasion he terminated a campaign on this account. Just as a battle lost will not convince a general of the futility of war, so Gandhi's confidence not merely in the moral superiority but in the ultimate success of nonviolence was not shaken by a defeat.

A problem faced by Gandhi in many of his campaigns was that of maintaining the morale of his followers after the first enthusiasm had worn off. He stressed the need for retaining the initiative on the side of the *satyagrahis*. Thus in the Salt *Satyagraha* as the excitement generated by his march to the sea began to wane and there was a danger of the campaign petering out in anticlimax, he inaugurated a series of nonviolent raids on the government salt depot. Successive parties of volunteers advanced against the cordon of police, who kicked and beat them mercilessly without evoking a violent response. Meanwhile, throughout the length and breadth of India the illegal manufacture of salt, sometimes only in symbolic quantity, proceeded. The jails filled, but the participation of the masses in the movement was kept up for twelve months until negotiations, which finally led to Indian nationalist participation in the Round Table Conference in London, were initiated between the Indian National Congress, on whose behalf Gandhi was directing the campaign, and the British authorities.

It has frequently been asserted that *satyagraha* is something peculiarly Indian without appeal to persons from other religions and cultural environments. Although, undoubtedly, some of its techniques need adaptation if they are to become easily acceptable outside India, there was evidence early in Gandhi's career that his nonviolence was not so narrowly circumscribed.

It soon succeeded, for example, in reaching out to, and rooting itself among, the Muslim Pathans of the Northwest Frontier Province (now part of Pakistan). Under the leadership of Khan Abdul Ghaffar Khan,[23] who founded in 1929 an organization on the Gandhian model known as Khudai Khidmatgar (Servants of God) to work for social reform and national development, the Pathans in large numbers—in the thirties over 100,000 of them gave their allegiance to the Khudai Khidmatgar—supported the method of *satyagraha;* though it is not clear if, despite a strict pledge exacted by their leader, they all adopted nonviolence as a total principle of action. Around 1920, Gandhi, who wished to enlist for his movement the support of India's Muslim community, had persuaded the Muslim *Ulema,* the highest religious authority in the land, to agree that, despite the warlike tradition of Islam, the faithful might still practice nonviolence "as a policy." [24] Ghaffar Khan himself (like the Bahais) sought confirmation in the Quran and in Islamic history for his quest for peace. To his fellow Pathans, warlike mountain tribesmen who had been feuding and raiding for centuries, he praised nonviolence, willingness to suffer rather than to kill, as an act of bravery demanding greater courage than death in battle (while Gandhi, during his tour of the Province in the autumn of 1938,[25] typically, told them it would nevertheless be better for them to kill as of old if they were unable to accept nonviolence as the superior method of overcoming evil). Acting independently but in loose alliance with the Indian nationalists, the red-shirted Servants of God undertook civil disobedience against the British with even more fervor and readiness to sacrifice than their Indian allies. Shootings, hangings and firing at demonstrators did not lead these frontier disciples of Gandhi to relinquish their nonviolent stance; on one occasion troops belonging to the British-run Indian Army refused to shoot at the Pathan *satyagrahis*. The point to be stressed here is that the Pathans were a people to whom such traditional Hindu concepts as *ahimsa, tapasya, satya,* etc., were unfamiliar. They were not peace-loving sedentary peasants or effete urban dwellers, but hardy and pugnacious hillsmen.

The Nonviolence of the Weak

Writers who have argued that *satyagraha* is simply a technique and that Gandhi "possessed no ideology" [26] appear to me to have missed the essence of his teaching. Without a desire to achieve truth, without the endeavor, at least, to preserve a loving attitude toward the opponent, *satyagraha* becomes a dead thing; it is nonviolence only in name, not necessarily in itself wrong but morally neutral. True nonviolence, then, is not merely a method of waging war by other means, it is an attempt at raising group conflict onto a new level, at "ethicizing" politics. This is the core of Gandhi's teaching.

In speaking of "the nonviolence of the weak," Gandhi, as Howard Horsburgh has pointed out,[27] meant two different things. He might be referring to the practice of nonviolence by those who had adopted it simply because they were too cowardly to resist by arms, although they had no objections to armed conflict. This attitude Gandhi condemned utterly (though he seems to have felt voluntary exile [*hijrat*] might be an allowable form of action for those who lacked either sufficient courage to undertake violent resistance or sufficient conviction to initiate nonviolent action). "I would rather have India resort to arms in order to defend her honour," he told his countrymen, "than that she would, in a cowardly manner, become or remain a helpless witness to her own dishonour." [28] But he might also mean by the phrase a more honorable and a not necessarily ineffective stance. He could be referring to those who adopted nonviolent techniques of resisting wrong not from cowardice, or from a principled objection to all violence, but from expediency—from a belief that use of violence in the given circumstances would be self-defeating and ineffectual. Many of Gandhi's most respected colleagues in the Indian nationalist movement—Jawaharlal Nehru, to cite just one name—belonged to this class. They accepted Gandhi's leadership (until his temporary retirement from active politics in 1934), and were prepared to accept, too, the discipline of *satyagraha,* because arms were not available to the Indian people and military superiority was overwhelmingly on the side of the British *raj.* But they did not disavow resorting to arms if conditions changed.

Gandhi believed, as they did, that nonviolent resistance to injustice was possible for a nation forcibly deprived of weapons. He also believed, as they did not, that it remained morally the preferable, and ultimately the more effective method of resistance even where military success was attainable.

But this did not mean that *satyagraha* was not open to debasement either through abuse as to the occasion of its use or through the lack of a truly nonviolent spirit behind the campaign. For nonviolent action of this latter kind Gandhi used the term *duragraha* (stubborn persistence). "Forms of passive resistance are usually forms of *duragraha,*" writes Bondurant.[29] Most strikes, boycotts and demonstrations, come within this category; though obviously preferable to armed clashes over the issues in dispute, they usually fall short of those qualities—produced only as a result of conscious will to reconciliation—which provide the creative dynamic of Gandhian nonviolence.

In addition, certain activities, though formally nonviolent, are of such a nature as really to involve violence. Gandhi, for instance, forbade acts of sabotage such as the destruction of railways or bridges, even where no danger of loss of life existed. Unlike some Western exponents of nonviolence, he regarded them as totally incompatible with a nonviolent ethic; he took the same stand, too, toward a policy of scorched earth to obstruct the advance of an aggressor. He did, however, recommend—and his followers carried out—the burning of British-manufactured cloth, so long as it was the property of those taking part, as a protest against the economic oppression of his country. Willingness to sacrifice one's possessions outweighed in his mind the element of violence latent in this act. Gandhi usually disapproved of nonviolent obstruction (*dhurna*): this might be practiced, for instance, as an adjunct to picketing. In order to reach a building being picketed, the *satyagrahis'* opponents would have to walk over their prostrate bodies: in Gandhi's view this signified an unwarranted degree of coercion. He did, however, advocate the employment of *dhurna* against a foreign invader: a subject which will be touched on a little later in this chapter. Concerning social ostracism applied to those opposing a *satyagraha* campaign (something akin to the shunning or avoidance of sinning members— *meidung*—practiced by Mennonites), Gandhi exhibited considerable uneasiness. Somewhat reluctantly he gave it his approval, provided every care were taken that ostracized persons were not deprived of the means of life. Yet in practice it may often prove difficult to draw a workable distinction here between regard for the human needs of an opponent, including a readiness to carry on continuous dialog with him, and disapproval of his actions expressed in a ban on social intercourse.

Civil Disobedience and Democracy

Gandhi conducted his *satyagraha* campaigns within the context of alien rule. If he sometimes directed noncooperation toward Indian groups or institutions, civil disobedience was practiced in respect to a state dominated by the British. Gandhi scarcely outlived the coming of independence.

For all his passion for local democracy he did not expect, or even desire, the disappearance of the state. But is not a nonviolent state perhaps a contradiction in terms? Gandhi believed that it was not. He wrote in 1940, when the outlook for a free India looked more promising than at the outset of his *swaraj* campaign twenty years earlier: "A state can be administered on a non-violent basis, if the vast majority of the people are nonviolent. So far as I know, India is the only country which has a possibility of becoming such a state." [30] This possibility had arisen from the fact of a considerable body of men there pledged to nonviolent policies, a nonviolent elite built up through Gandhi's efforts over the previous decades. But Gandhi was also clear that a believer in nonviolence could not, consistently, enter a government that was not based on nonviolence—even if he felt that his presence could help to mitigate the extent of violence employed in ruling the country.[31] In this he obviously differed from some of his disciples in nonviolence, like Rajendra Prasad, for instance, who became independent India's first president, or from some pacifist politicians in the West who, while preserving their personal objection to war and violence, have become members of nonpacifist administrations.

Might a nonviolent government do away with all forms of coercion? In this case Gandhi answered no. At least for a long time to come, and for as long as man possessed only an imperfect understanding of the strength of nonviolence, some degree of coercion (nonviolent coercion) would be needed to stave off anarchy. Gandhi was willing to concede that

even in a non-violent state a police force may be necessary. This, I admit, is a sign of my imperfect *ahimsa*. I have not the courage to declare that we can carry on without a police force as I have in respect of an army. Of course I can and do envisage a State where the police will not be necessary; but whether we shall succeed in realizing it, the future alone will show.

The police of my conception will, however, be of a wholly different pattern from the present-day force. Its ranks will be composed of believers in non-violence. The people will instinctively render them every help, and through mutual co-operation they will easily deal with the ever decreasing disturbances. The police force will have some kind of arms, but they will be rarely used, if at all. In fact the policemen will be reformers. Their police work will be confined primarily to robbers and dacoits [i.e., murderers]. Quarrels between labour and capital and strikes will be few and far between in a non-violent State, because the influence of the non-violent majority will be so great as to command the principal elements in society. Similarly there will be no room for communal disturbances.[32]

This of course is more a model, a golden age projected into the future, than an analysis of current trends. Several comments may be in order at this point. In the first place, Gandhi clearly envisaged the gradual withering away of the police apparatus in a nonviolent state. At the beginning the guardians of the law may even carry some light arms for use in dire emergency but, as the nonviolent ethic permeates ever more thoroughly the communal life, the need for coercion will lessen until physical force of any kind becomes an anachronism. Secondly, just as—let us say—strikes (according to Soviet theory) are unnecessary and even harmful in the workers' state, so in a nonviolent state civil disobedience would seem to be out of place, unless we can conceive of two sets of opposing *satyagrahis* locked in nonviolent combat.

Thirdly, the role of the police in a nonviolent society is in Gandhi's model to be filled by a nonviolent corps specially trained to carry out its functions with a minimum of physical force. One may ask in parenthesis if Gandhi really meant, as his words taken literally imply, to approve the use of lethal weapons by disciples pledged to observe non-injury under all circumstances. (We have probably a further example here of the inconsistencies in which his writings abound: "one result of his persistent habit of thinking in public." [33] Or it may be that, at first, at any rate, the nonviolent police would have to be recruited from persons whose adherence to nonviolent methods was as yet incomplete.) In the thirties Gandhi became interested in the idea of a "peace brigade," which would substitute for the ordinary police where there was danger of violence breaking out, e.g., in communal disturbances. Members of the brigade, all believers in *ahimsa,* would receive specialized training in such things as riot control or the remedial treatment of hooligans, robbers and dacoits; they would be given a distinctive uniform and would thereafter serve either full- or part-time.

Finally—and this point is basic to a proper understanding of Gandhi's idea of a nonviolent state and its apparatus for maintaining domestic order—he postulated not merely full adult democracy but the creation of a society with some measure of economic equality and close communal ties, where the individual would not easily become alienated from the community and on this account driven to violence by destructive urges. For Gandhi this society, so far as India was concerned, could only become incarnate in the village.

Between Gandhi's ideal nonviolent India and the British-dominated India of his own day lay a third alternative: a free India which did not accept Gandhi's belief in *ahimsa,* at least in group relations. As the father of the reborn nation and revered leader of its independence movement, Gandhi had hoped to steer his people along the path of nonviolence. But the majority of the leaders of the Indian National Congress, as its historian has remarked sarcastically, did not intend it to remain merely a "humanitarian association or World Peace Society;" [34] they aimed at creating ultimately a modern nation-state. They were unwilling to forgo the usual insignia of this institution including a national army and an armed police apparatus. For them, *satyagraha* had been a convenient means for attaining independence; to Gandhi, on the other hand, *ahimsa* was a principle of life. But he had approved the idea of taking over the functions of government—by nonviolent means of course—as the final stage in the strategy of *satyagraha.* The creation of a parallel governmental structure, and a boycott of state institutions controlled by the alien ruler, were to be the immediate prelude to the achievement of *swaraj.*

In an independent and democratic India, or indeed in any country whose citizens shared in choosing their government and in making the laws, Gandhi saw no place normally for civil disobedience; indeed it might even prove harmful to the community, undermining respect for legality and leading either to anarchy or to the setting up of a dictatorship in reaction. In these circumstances he would probably have agreed *mutatis mutandis* with his old opponent Lord Irwin (later Halifax), who was Viceroy of India at the time of his Salt *Satyagraha,* when the latter claimed that if a movement, however nonviolent, aimed at making government impossible, the administration had no alternative between resisting its demands or abdication. For Gandhi, of course, the decisive factor in justifying civil disobedience or not was the dependence of the regime on the popular will. Even in a democracy, however, he did envisage the possibility of applying civil disobedience creatively where a popular majority consistently ignored the rights of some minority.[35]

All this did not mean that Gandhi considered that, once national independence was won, nonviolence was only relevant in marginal instances. Quite the contrary. But its role, he believed, had shifted; its aim was not a direct confrontation with the established order but its transformation by constructive effort and personal example into a nonviolent community. The violence, which swept the country in 1942 after the arrest of Gandhi and other Congress leaders at the outset of their "Quit India" campaign against British wartime rule and which soon degenerated in some areas into guerrilla warfare, proved a shock to him, exposing as illusory his earlier optimism concerning the degree to which his people had accepted nonviolence. His experiences *vis-à-vis* the fierce and bloody communal disturbances in 1946 and 1947, on the eve of independence, were even more traumatic. Yet to Gandhi they indicated the need for a more intensive application of nonviolence to the problems of the community. During a walking tour of Noakhali, a remote and densely populated rural area where Hindus and Moslems lived side by side and where the bloodshed had been among the worst, Gandhi wrote prophetically: "The work I am engaged in here may be my last act. If I return from here alive and unscathed, it will be like a new birth to me. My *ahimsa* is being tried here through and through as it was never before." [36]

Gandhi was dead within fifteen months of writing these words, a victim of the communal hatred he had sought to remove from society. We shall see in a later chapter how his successors in the nonviolent movement in India, as well as his disciples in the West, were likewise to be faced with the problem of the proper role of nonviolence in a modern democratic society.

Satyagraha v. the Totalitarian State

For Gandhi's critics and admirers alike, it has not been the free society but the totalitarian state that has seemed to present the most serious challenge to the universal validity he claimed for the nonviolent method of conflict resolution. Could a *satyagraha* movement, could a Gandhi, emerge in a totalitarian environment similar to that which existed, for example, in Hitler's Germany or Stalin's Russia? And even if nonviolent resistance to tyranny had begun, could it possibly have made any headway in such circumstances?

Gandhi's civil disobedience, it has been argued,[37] was conducted in countries such as South Africa and British India where, however circumscribed, certain constitutional freedoms did exist and where the rule of law prevailed within a restricted area. Moreover, at home in England where the ultimate policy decisions were taken, public opinion had considerable weight in directing government action and this opinion was to some extent colored by liberal and humanitarian thought. Many of Gandhi's opponents, too, were men of high personal rectitude (General Smuts, for instance, or Lord Irwin)—persons with whom meaningful and creative dialog could be carried on. Would this be possible with the ruthless thugs who often initiate and execute the policies of totalitarian regimes? Moreover, would the moral appeal of nonviolent resistance operate in regard to men who consider their opponents as racially inferior?

To these questions no certain answer can be given for, as Bondurant has remarked, "we do not have any direct empirical evidence." Certain stages in *satyagraha* would obviously be impossible against a totalitarian opponent: for example, the publicity and propaganda on behalf of the campaign, which Gandhi regarded as specially important on account of their effectiveness in winning the sympathies of the populace at large for the *satyagrahis'* cause. But even totalitarian regimes depend on the cooperation of their citizens and are sometimes amenable to the influence of world opinion; civil disobedience, *if* it could be organized on a wide enough scale, might topple them or at least bring sweeping concessions. "The problem centers upon the extent to which this noncooperation can be obtained." [38] Noncooperation would almost certainly require some amount of prior knowledge of nonviolence among the population, though it is just possible that the situation would generate spontaneously, as it were, sufficient momentum to carry the movement along until experience of *satyagraha* technique was acquired empirically.

Two further points may be added here. First, violent resistance employed internally against a totalitarian state, insofar as it has been tried, has not proved particularly effective. Nonviolence appears to possess at least as good a chance of success against a modern police state as do violent methods of opposing it. The consequences of a nonviolent failure, moreover, might possibly be less disastrous than those following the failure of violence against such a regime. In the second place, despite all precautions taken to preserve secrecy (which, incidentally, Gandhi with his insistence on openness of action might not have approved), the danger of a *potential* Gandhian movement being nipped in the bud would certainly be great. Yet the situation appears not dissimilar to that in which a country finds itself when it begins to rearm against an outside threat. There is likewise here a danger period when, if attacked, the country would certainly suffer defeat. The risk involved by its action, however, is not usually held to invalidate its rearmament.

Gandhi expressed confidence in the ability of nonviolence to

overcome, even within a totalitarian setting. He pleaded with the
Jews in Germany to adopt nonviolence (as well as with the Czechs
in 1938 and with the British in 1939–40 *vis-à-vis* external aggression). He never claimed that nonviolent resistance under such
circumstances did not involve risk or would not almost inevitably
lead to considerable loss of life. He contemplated stoically (some
might say with an Oriental calm) the possibility of thousands
dying in the course of a *satyagraha* movement. This attitude, as he
explained, did not stem from his holding life cheap or regarding
it as a kind of nonviolent cannon fodder; it flowed from his belief
that nonviolence would prove ultimately the method of resistance
least wasteful of human life and resources, and one, too, that was
more ennobling and morally sound than insurrection or war. To the
famous Jewish philosopher Martin Buber, *satyagraha* such as
Gandhi envisaged against the Nazis appeared to augur no more
than "a martyrdom cast to the winds." [39] For Gandhi, nonviolence
could not fail in the long run for it represented the law of the
universe.

"SATYAGRAHA" AND WAR

The Gandhian philosophy of conflict and the techniques of
satyagraha emerging from it were applied in practice by the
Mahatma exclusively to group relations within the state. International relations were a branch of politics on which Indians under
British rule could make little impact. Foreign policy decisions
affecting India were made in London and not in Delhi. Gandhi,
therefore, "had no occasion to show how this non-violent strategy
could work in the face of an invading army." [40] Nevertheless, he
stressed that violence within the state and violence between states
formed an organically interrelated problem. He insisted, too, on the
relevance of nonviolence as an instrument for obtaining and maintaining justice in the relations between states. It is this last aspect
of nonviolence that has been of primary concern to the pacifist
movement in the West.

Before discussing Gandhian ideas concerning nonviolent resistance to aggression, we must deal briefly with the problem of
Gandhi's attitude to the wars in which Indians during his lifetime
became involved, albeit as a passive factor, as well as to the

possibility of military preparation on the part of a future independent India.

Gandhi and Pacifism

In 1939, on the occasion of Gandhi's seventieth birthday, a Western admirer greeted him as "the greatest living exponent of successful pacifism." [41] Yet, as the reader has already seen from the opening paragraph of this chapter, his career reveals a certain ambiguity on the issue of war. This ambivalence has led some writers, both pacifist and nonpacifist, to the conclusion (in my view quite erroneous) that Gandhi cannot be regarded as an unconditional opponent of war.

Of course it is true, as has been shown, that he preferred violent resistance in the face of injustice and tyranny to a cowardly, if formally nonviolent, submission. He appreciated martial valor. "If," he once wrote, "war had no redeeming feature, no courage and heroism behind it, it would be a despicable thing, and would not need speeches to destroy it." [42] But he never failed to point out that, in his opinion, nonviolent resistance was the best way. Again, he did not object to military conscription in a free country (such as he hoped India would become) for those who had not accepted the principle of nonviolence: an attitude, of course, that was repugnant to many libertarian pacifists in Europe and America. As an Indian nationalist, he resented their British rulers' depriving his countrymen of the right to carry arms: he saw in it a mark of inferiority and enforced cowardice rather than a sign of nonviolence. But he wholeheartedly supported *conscientious* objectors in their refusal of military service and contemplated sympathetically the proposal that pacifists refrain from paying taxes for war purposes. However, "military service is only a symptom of the disease which is deeper," he adds significantly. Conscientious objection, like patriotism, is not enough: state and society must be remolded in the spirit of nonviolence.[43]

More controversial, and more difficult for Westerners to comprehend, was Gandhi's seeming support of the British war effort on several occasions. In South Africa, during the Boer War and in the Zulu rebellion in Natal in 1906, and then again in World War I, he rallied to the cause, helping to recruit Indians for ambulance duties at the front and himself participating actively in such work. Indeed, he went further and urged his countrymen to enlist for combatant service. "How could you do that, Gandhi, you who stand for fraternity and moral resistance?" a Dutch pacifist once asked him indignantly.[44]

The explanation Gandhi gave of his wartime actions testifies to his honesty and to the sincerity of his basic devotion to nonviolence, if not always to the strength of his logic. "There is no defence for my conduct weighed only in the scales of *ahimsa*," he admitted. At the time, however, he had believed that only if Indians showed their willingness to back Britain's war effort to the hilt would the mother country be ready to acknowledge their right to self-government and equality within the Empire. Since only a handful of Indians at that period accepted Gandhi's teaching on nonviolence, and since in these circumstances creative action against war did not appear possible, loyalty to the British Empire was the only attitude he could honestly recommend to his countrymen. "My repugnance to war was as strong then as it is today," Gandhi wrote later, "and I could not then have, and would not have, shouldered a rifle"; even though objectively he had to acknowledge there was little difference between combatant service and the type of Red Cross work in which he participated. Yet, "so long as I lived under a system of government based on force and voluntarily partook of the many facilities and privileges it created for me, I was bound to help that Government to the extent of my ability when it was engaged in a war, unless I non-cooperated with that Government and renounced to the utmost of my capacity the privileges it offered me."

Gandhi developed a more militant stand against war only after Indian loyalty had failed to evoke the expected reward from Great Britain and he had begun to reassess his earlier stance. "If another war were declared tomorrow," he stated in 1928, "I could not, with my personal views about the present Government, assist it in any shape or form; on the contrary I should exert myself to the utmost to induce others to withhold their assistance and to do everything possible and consistent with *ahimsa* to bring about its defeat." [45]

Should "the present Government" be replaced by an independent Indian administration, Gandhi obviously reserved the right to give it qualified support, even though it did not share his confidence in nonviolence. Had a free India become involved in war during his lifetime we might have witnessed again ambulance-corpsman Gandhi, and even Gandhi "the self-appointed recruiting sergeant" (as he once called himself), urging that those who could not renounce violence should fight rather than bow down to wrong. But under the *swaraj* of his dreams, as he once said, there would indeed be no need for arms. A nonviolent nation could defend justice and its own integrity without their aid.

Nonviolent Resistance to Aggression

Gandhi's approach to international relations assumed the existence of the sovereign state. Like Mazzini and the liberal nationalists of nineteenth-century Europe, Gandhi, however, conceived of a natural, God-willed harmony between the political entities into which the world was divided. He shared with Mazzini, too, the idea of national mission.[46] For Gandhi the mission of his India, however apostate, was to show the world, under his tutelage, the way to nonviolence, to a new universalism subsuming but not eliminating the separate national states. "My patriotism," he wrote, "includes the good of mankind in general. Therefore my service [to] India includes the service of humanity." [47] He did not appear interested in the finer problems of nationalist theory or in the dilemmas of self-determination as revealed with special acuteness, for example, in the interwar experience of East Central Europe. But he presumed the state to be normally the expression of a national consensus.

Righteousness, not peace, was for Gandhi the goal of society, not only in its internal relations but as reflected in the international community of nation-states. Nonviolence was a means toward achieving this goal, a method of adjusting human relations on a higher ethical plane than civil violence or war.

With the contemporary peace movement in the West, Gandhi shared many practical proposals for avoiding war. While remaining, it is true, somewhat suspicious of institutional machinery for settling disputes (the League of Nations or the United Nations, for instance) he did give his support at one time or another to such measures as informal third-party arbitration, disarmament, world government and an impartially administered international police force. He viewed them as means to avoid war and achieve justice in a world that had not yet embarked on the higher path of nonviolence. But nonviolence with Gandhi was far from being a doctrine of nonintervention or an instrument for upholding the international (or domestic) *status quo,* for justice might sometimes require alterations in the existing order.

In regard to the employment of nonviolent resistance against aggression, in the practice of which he hoped (though later with decreasing optimism) that an independent India would lead the way, he was already being questioned as early as 1920. What, asked his critics, would India do if the British withdrew and left the country to the mercies of the wild mountain tribesmen, who coveted the riches of the Indian plains? "If India returns to her spirituality," Gandhi answered, "it will react upon the neighbouring tribes; she will interest herself in the welfare of these hardy, but poor people, and even support them, if necessary, not out of fear but as a matter of neighbourly duty." [48] Thus, here in embryo we already see Gandhi applying the techniques of domestic *satyagraha* to an external situation. The power of nonviolence, if combined with a constructive program to remedy grievances, would prevail. He pleaded, in addition, for India to become self-sufficient in respect to the basic necessities of life: food, clothing, etc. In this way, it would form a less tempting prey for an invader.

His success in converting the bellicose Pathans to nonviolence in considerable numbers showed at least that it could touch the hearts of so-called backward races. (Of the Afghans, Gandhi once remarked: "They are a god-fearing people." [49]) The trouble, it became clear, would be with civilized barbarians, whose will to aggression remained unappeased even after steps had been taken to remove any injustice from which they might be suffering. Could *satyagraha* be applied with success in this case? Gandhi believed that it could. He spoke (in 1931) of the need to re-enact the battle of Thermopylae, to present "a living wall of men and women and children" [50] in an effort to block an invading army or an army in transit to invade another country. He advocated this despite the element of coercion involved in this form of passive resistance, which the Indians have called *dhurna.* From what he had seen of the behavior of his *satyagrahis* in the recent civil disobedience campaign—ordinary human beings transformed by a cause—he felt confident that such heroism and such discipline did not require supermen or saints. And although he never expanded the idea, he advocated the creation of a nonviolent army if a country adopted this method of defending itself.

To the victims of Fascist aggression in the 1930s—China, Abyssinia, Spain, Czechoslovakia, and Poland—he recommended (though scarcely with any hope of his advice being followed) the adoption of nonviolent resistance. "I present Dr. Benes with a weapon not of the weak but of the brave," he wrote in the autumn of 1938. "History," he admitted, "has no record of a nation having adopted non-violent resistance." But through the practice of non-violence a people could preserve, if not its life, at least its "honour" intact—for Gandhi the most valued possession of all. Unlike some Western pacifists, he condemned the Munich settlement root and branch. "Europe has sold her soul," he wrote, "for the sake of a seven days' earthly existence. The peace Europe gained at Munich is a triumph of violence." And he accused England and France of cowardice for not backing Czechoslovakia by arms against German threats.

At the same time Gandhi refused to admit that even Hitler and Mussolini were "beyond redemption," since "belief in non-violence is based on the assumption that human nature in its essence is one and therefore unfailingly responds to the advances of love." "The hardest metal yields to sufficient heat." Yet the efficacy of non-violence did not stem from the essential goodwill of the opponent "for a successful non-violent resister depends upon the unfailing assistance of God which sustains him throughout difficulties which would otherwise be insurmountable. His faith makes him indomitable." [51]

We can see from the above that, unlike some contemporary Western pacifists, Gandhi did not consider that in modern war there could be no real aggressor (though he did share many of their reservations concerning the 1918 peace settlement). He believed that it was usually possible to assess relative blame in international disputes. "My sympathies are wholly with the Allies," he told the British in 1939, for instance. And throughout his career he had rarely remained neutral in international conflicts. Moreover, *satyagraha* itself was based on the idea of the justice of one's own side over the opponent's. Gandhi held that the strength of nonviolent resistance lay not merely in the ethical character of the means but in the righteouness of the *satyagrahis'* cause. Should some imperfection be found in their case, then the wrong must at once be righted before the campaign could be permitted to continue. In somewhat similar fashion, in World War II he called upon the British to free India and relinquish their empire; he also urged them to adopt nonviolence in resisting Hitler.

He was prepared to approve a liberated India's support of Britain's war effort if he could not persuade his countrymen (as he knew he almost certainly could not do at that time) to follow him in adopting nonviolence. As a critic of Gandhi has remarked: "Even after he had completely abjured violence he was honest enough to see that in war it is usually necessary to take sides." [52]

The arrival of the atom bomb seemed to Gandhi (as well as to many who had previously felt his doctrine to be too otherworldly) to confirm his belief that the world's future lay in the development of nonviolent resistance. The only alternative to it might now be mankind's eventual suicide. True, the time for nonviolent Thermopylaes might have passed, along with more conventional military techniques, but in the nuclear age, when war threatened universal annihilation in the process of repelling aggression, *satyagraha* appeared to offer, if the nations could be persuaded to adopt it, a viable technique for achieving a measure of justice between states.

Gandhi's last years were clouded not only by the menace of nuclear warfare but by the fratricidal conflict between Hindus and Moslems, which accompanied the birth of an independent India and Pakistan. Gandhi's heroic struggle to reconcile the two communities, undertaken at the risk of his life, was mentioned earlier in this chapter. In his attitude toward India's freshly emergent neighbor, Gandhi unwittingly illustrates some of the difficulties involved in the relationship between nonviolence and international justice. Gandhi had steadfastly opposed the creation of Pakistan, regarding a Pakistani nation as a fiction (at that date perhaps not an altogether unjustified conclusion). It is true that he finally threw the weight of his influence against any *satyagraha* movement aimed to prevent the emergence of that state as a result of partition. However, he conditionally approved India's taking armed action against Pakistan in certain instances, e.g., the occupation of Kashmir by an Indian army. "I could never advise anyone to put up with injustice," Gandhi said. "If all the Hindus were annihilated for a good cause, I would not mind it." [53] But the problem of where injustice lay in the dispute between India and Pakistan appears to be one not so easily resolved by even nonviolent techniques.

On January 30, 1948, Gandhi fell victim to the bullet of a Hindu fanatic. His worldly estate consisted of little more than the scanty garments he was wearing. His legacy to the world was infinitely more substantial. It offered mankind release from its containment within the vicious circle of violence and war.

NOTES

1. The best biographies are Louis Fischer, *The Life of Mahatma Gandhi* (New York: Harper & Brothers, 1950); B. R. Nanda, *Mahatma: A Biography* (Boston: Beacon Press, 1958); Geoffrey Ashe, *Gandhi—A Study in Revolution* (London: Heinemann, 1968). There is material on nonviolence, too, in the eight-volume life of Gandhi by D. G. Tendulkar, *Mahatma* (Bombay: V.K. Jhaveri & D.G. Tendulkar, 1951–1954; 2nd ed., Delhi: Government of India, 1960–1963). The vast extent of the literature on Gandhi, much of which touches on the subject of his nonviolence, may be seen by perusing Jagdish Saran Sharma, *Mahatma Gandhi: A Descriptive Bibliography* (Delhi: S. Chand & Co., 1955). For subsequent years, see the periodic bibliographies published in the English-language edition of the journal *Gandhi Marg* (New Delhi, 1957ff.), which also includes articles on Gandhi and nonviolence. The multivolume *Collected Works of Mahatma Gandhi* (Delhi: Government of India, 1958ff.) will eventually contain almost everything that he wrote and much that he said. For a study of his nonviolence, M. K. Gandhi, *Non-Violence in Peace and War* (Ahmedabad: Navajivan Publishing House, Vol. I, 3rd edition, 1948; Vol. II, 1949) is at present the most useful collection. It is cited below as Gandhi, *Non-Violence*. Penderel Moon, *Gandhi and Modern India* (London: The English Universities Press Ltd., 1968), is a very recent—and readable—addition to Gandhian studies. [A 1968 edition of Sharma's descriptive bibliography, which brings the entries down to January of that year, has reached me as this book goes to press.]
2. Gandhi's own account is given in his *Satyagraha in South Africa*, translated from the Gujarati (Ahemdabad: Navajivan Publishing House, 1928).
3. Gandhi, *Non-Violence*, Vol. I, p. 123.
4. See Indira Rothermund, *The Philosophy of Restraint: Mahatma Gandhi's Strategy and Indian Politics* (Bombay: Popular Prakashan, 1963), Chap. III: "Gandhiji and the Hindu Tradition."
5. I owe this thought—and much else in the chapter—to Joan Bondurant, *Conquest of Violence*, revised ed. (Berkeley and Los Angeles:

University of California Press, 1965), by far the most useful exposition hitherto of "the Gandhian philosophy of conflict."

6. George Hendrick, "The Influence of Thoreau's 'Civil Disobedience' on Gandhi's *Satyagraha*," *The New England Quarterly*, vol. 29, no. 4 (December, 1956), pp. 462–471. See also Harrison Hoblitzelle, "The War against War in the Nineteenth Century: A Study of the Western Background of Gandhian Thought" (Ph.D. diss., Columbia University, 1959).

7. Romain Roland, *Mahatma Gandhi: The Man Who Became One with the Universal Being*, translated from the French (London: George Allen & Unwin, 1926 ed.), p. 36.

8. Letter dated 7 September 1910, reprinted in Kalidas Nag, *Tolstoy and Gandhi* (Patna: Pustak Bhandar, 1950), p. 74. I have slightly corrected the grammar of the last clause quoted.

9. Bondurant, *op. cit.*, p. 25.

10. Gandhi, *Non-Violence*, Vol. I, pp. 76 and 1.

11. *Ibid.*, pp. 67, 69.

12. Bondurant, *op. cit.*, pp. 228, 229.

13. Gandhi, *Non-Violence*, Vol. I, p. 63.

14. Dhirendra Mohan Datta, *The Philosophy of Mahatma Gandhi* (Madison: The University of Wisconsin Press, 1961), p. 127.

15. M. K. Gandhi, *Towards Non-Violent Socialism* (Ahmedabad: Navajivan Publishing House, 1951), p. 12.

16. Gopinath Dhawan, *The Political Philosophy of Mahatma Gandhi* (Ahmedabad: Navajivan Publishing House, 1957), pp. 195, 331, 332.

17. Cf. Nirmal Kumar Bose, *Studies in Gandhism*, 3rd rev. ed. (Calcutta: Merit Publishers, 1962), p. 65.

18. Bondurant, *op. cit.*, pp 50, 61, 71, 83, 100.

19. H. J. N. Horsburgh, *Non-Violence and Aggression: A Study of Gandhi's Moral Equivalent of War* (London: Oxford University Press, 1968), p. 22.

20. Gandhi, *Non-Violence*, Vol. I, p. 2.

21. M. K. Gandhi, *An Autobiography: The Story of My Experiments with Truth*, translated from the Gujerati (London: Phoenix Press, 1949), p. 392.

22. Gandhi, *Non-Violence*, Vol. I, p. 266.

23. See D. G. Tendulkar, *Abdul Ghaffar Khan: Faith Is a Battle* (Bombay: Popular Prakashan, 1967). After the creation of Pakistan, Ghaffar Khan's movement there was suppressed on account of its leader's desire to see a separate "Pakhtunistan" erected in the area inhabited by Pathans. Despite his fervent nationalism, however, the "frontier Gandhi" retained his belief in nonviolence.

24. Gandhi, *An Autobiography*, p. 414.

25. See Pyarelal, *A Pilgrimage for Peace: Gandhi and Frontier Gandhi among N. W. F. Pathans* (Ahmedabad: Navajivan Publishing House, 1950).

26. The phrase is from W. K. Hancock, *Four Studies of War and Peace in This Century* (Cambridge: Cambridge University Press, 1961), p. 59. Chap. III, "Non-Violence," is a fairminded but critical account of *satyagraha*.

27. Horsburgh, *op. cit.*, p. 64.

28. Gandhi, *Non-Violence*, Vol. I, p. 1.

29. Bondurant, *op. cit.*, p. viii.

30. Gandhi, *Non-Violence*, Vol. I, p. 265.

31. *Ibid.*, p. 244.

32. *Ibid.*, p. 333. See also pp. 144–146, 372.

33. Bondurant, *op. cit.*, p. 7.

34. R. C. Majumdar in Martin Deming Lewis, ed., *Gandhi: Maker of Modern India?* (Boston: D. C. Heath and Company, 1965), p. 56.

35. W. H. Morris-Jones, "Mahatma Gandhi—Political Philosopher?" *Political Studies* (Oxford), vol. 3, no. 1 (1960), pp. 30, 31.

36. Letter dated 24 November 1946, quoted in Pyarelal, *Mahatma Gandhi: The Last Phase*, 2 vols. (Ahmedabad: Navajivan Publishing House, 1956–1958), Vol. I, p. 387.

37. For example by Hancock, *op. cit.*, pp. 81–88.

38. Bondurant, *op. cit.*, p. 226.

39. From letter dated 24 February 1939, reprinted in Peter Mayer, ed., *The Pacifist Conscience* (London: Penguin Books, 1966), pp. 270–282.

40. J. P. Kripalani, "Gandhian Thought and Its Effect on Indian Life," *Cahiers d'histoire mondiale* (Neuchâtel), vol. 5, no. 2 (1959), p. 419.

41. Laurence Housman in S. Radhakrishnan, ed., *Mahatma Gandhi: Essays and Reflections on His Life and Work* (London: George Allen & Unwin Ltd., 1949), p. 123.

42. Quoted in Paul F. Power, *Gandhi on World Affairs* (Washington, D.C.: Public Affairs Press, 1960), p. 38.

43. Gandhi, *Non-Violence*, Vol. I, pp. 106–108.

44. B. de Ligt, "Mahatma Gandhi on War: An Open Letter to Gandhi and His Reply," *The World Tomorrow* (New York), vol. 11, no. 11 (November, 1928), p. 446. De Ligt also published a strongly critical study of Gandhi's attitude to contemporary wars: *Een wereldomvattend vraagstuk —Gandhi en de oorlog* (Utrecht: Erven J. Bijleveld, 1930).

45. Gandhi, *Non-Violence*, Vol. I, pp. 49, 69, 71–75. See also pp. 23, 24.

46. See the citations from Gandhi in Dhawan, *op.cit.*, p. 343.

47. Gandhi, *Non-Violence*, Vol. I, p. 31.

48. *Ibid.*, p. 5.

49. *Ibid.*, p. 9.

50. *Ibid.*, p. 109.

51. *Ibid.*, pp. 149–155, 175, 178.

52. George Orwell, "Reflections on Gandhi," in *Shooting an Elephant and Other Essays* (London: Secker and Warburg, 1950), p. 109.

53. Gandhi, *Non-Violence*, Vol. II, p. 191.

IV. Pacifism and War Resistance: The Interwar Years

THE COMMUNITY OF WAR RESISTERS

IN WORLD WAR I THE OCCURRENCE OF CONSCIENTIOUS OBJECTION had been confined almost entirely to the English-speaking world. In the interwar years pacifists attempted to implant their ideas in areas with a different political and cultural tradition. Only in India, as we have seen, was Anglo-American pacifism grafted successfully onto the Hindu doctrine of *ahimsa* to produce the Gandhian philosophy (a process, however, which took place as the result of a reaching out from the Indian side rather than from any direct Western initiative). Otherwise, pacifism in this period still remains largely an episode in the history of Great Britain and the United States.

Yet some progress was made in diffusing pacifist concepts beyond the Anglo-American cultural orbit. Expansion, however, was of very limited dimension. Even though, for instance, Christian pacifism acquired a notable convert in Japan in the saintly Toyohiko Kagawa and a few others in both China and Japan came under the influence of Quaker or other pacifist missionaries from the West, the Far East was scarcely touched. In India the protagonists of nonviolence were at that date so involved in the nationalist movement that no indigenous pacifist organization emerged there either. In the countries of Latin America, the Near East, and among the scarcely emergent peoples of Africa, pacifism aroused scarcely an echo. The same may be said of large parts of southern Europe, where deeply ingrained Roman Catholicism provided an environment unpropitious to the spread of pacifism which drew its inspiration largely from Protestant dissent, as well as of the lands of Orthodox culture in the Balkans.

In Russia, however, the existence of several million sectarians, who were hostile to the power structure of the state and rejected the authority of the Russian Orthodox Church, could have provided a potentially rich mission field for pacifist propaganda. Some of the sects, including the most numerous, the Baptists, already had pacifist leanings; they provided some conscientious objectors during the recent war and the troubled times that followed.

At first, therefore, the pacifist outlook in the Soviet Union looked promising. As a result of representations from the United Council of Religious Groups and Communities for the Defense of Conscientious Objectors, led by Tolstoy's former secretary Vladimir Chertkov, a decree was issued on 4 January 1919 that provided not merely alternative civilian service but unconditional exemption for those whose conscience forbade them to undertake such service. The machinery of exemption was placed almost entirely in the hands of the objectors' own Council. True, exemption was confined to religious applicants and the wording of the decree seemed to imply that membership in an actual pacifist denomination was needed before an absolutist could win his case, nevertheless, apart from the British provisions of 1916, the decree was more liberal than any legislation hitherto dealing with conscientious objection.

By subsequent amendments to the decree, however, the administrative functions of the Council were whittled away and the Council itself dissolved in 1921. The Soviet government may have been alarmed by the fact that by 1920 in the Moscow area alone some 30,000 persons had come forward as conscientious objectors. In 1924 exemption was confined to members of certain specific pacifist sects (among which the Tolstoyans were not included) and in the following year further restriction took place when only birthright members were declared eligible for exemption. After visiting the Soviet Union toward the end of the decade, the American advocate of civil liberties, Roger Baldwin, reported: "The restrictions on private pacifist and anti-militarist propaganda and activity in Russia are on the whole more severe than under any other government, or than under the czar." [1] In April 1929 the last of the pacifist organizations—the Tolstoyan Vegetarian Society in Moscow—was closed down. All open pacifist activity ceased. Although very limited provision for conscientious objectors was included in the Military Service Law of 1930, it was omitted altogether in 1939 on the pretext that it was no longer necessary, since no applications for exemption had been submitted during the previous two years.

Among members of Lenin's entourage there were some who had been sympathetic to the conscientious objector stand and had worked alongside Tolstoyans and nonresistant sectaries in defiance of the Tsarist government. The Marxist Vladimir Bonch-Bruevich, the Dukhobors' friend, was one of these who, after the Bolshevik Revolution, became a prominent figure in Soviet cultural and academic life. From the mid-twenties on, however, Stalin's destruction of the old Bolsheviks, his intensified campaign against all manifestations of religion as a counter-revolutionary element, the purges of the thirties, and the fervent Great Russian nationalism that eventually re-emerged under his leadership created an atmosphere hostile to the spread, even on a limited scale, of pacifist ideas. The Soviet inspired peace movement of the interwar years (like the post-World War II Communist peace movement) was for export; home-grown pacifism was ruthlessly suppressed. That there were objectors to military service in the Stalinist era is certain; some may have succeeded in getting themselves assigned to noncombatant duties, others may have been imprisoned or shot. A veil of silence hung over their fate; only one fact is certain, that they were few in number and utterly isolated.

In Western Europe, France remained largely immune to pacifism in its Anglo-Saxon form. Although antimilitarist ideas were rife on the extreme left, its adherents rarely refused military service. Left wing writers, especially those who were active in the campaign against the peace treaties, sometimes toyed with the theory of conscientious objection. A minority of pacifist clergy and laymen existed within the small but intellectually vigorous Protestant Reformed Church. (However, the hard-won respect of their church did not prevent the sentencing of pastors like Henri Roser or Philippe Vernier to long and repeated terms of imprisonment for their failure to answer the call to the colors.) In Belgium, Flemish nationalists sometimes refused military service. In Holland under the leadership of men like the anarchist Bart de Ligt, the concept of revolutionary nonviolence was developed.[2] It won the allegiance not only of agnostics and atheists but of a handful of clergy in the established Reformed Church, who in 1928 initiated the organization of an International Union of Anti-Militarist Ministers and Clergymen to represent their ideas. Small pacifist groups also sprang up in the Scandinavian countries as well as in Switzerland.

Somewhat ironically, it was on two former enemies (Germany and to a lesser extent Austria) that Anglo-American pacifism made its greatest impact during the decade and a half following 1918, until Hitler's accession to power put a stop to all pacifist activity. The pre-1914 peace movement in Central Europe had possessed notable exponents in the German–Austrian, Alfred H. Fried, and the Bohemian Baroness von Suttner (née Kinská). But this traditional form of pacifism, as everywhere on the European continent, remained rather academic, socially conservative, and opposed to political radicalism of any kind. It upheld the right of national states to wage defensive war and reacted coldly to the idea of individual resistance to military service.[3] In Weimar Germany the radical pacifist societies were frowned on not merely by the political center and right but also by the social democrats who, like most socialists on the European continent, looked askance at individual war resistance. Pacifists like Carl von Ossietsky, editor of *Die Weltbühne,* who in the late thirties became both a prisoner in a Nazi concentration camp and a winner of the Nobel Peace Prize, were foremost in the campaign against German militarism and secret rearmament. They opposed the efforts of the right wing to cast exclusive blame for Germany's misfortunes on the Versailles peace treaty (at this point running counter to most pacifists in the victorious countries, who saw in Germany's treatment at Versailles an act of injustice that stood at the very root of the world's troubles). The energetic Fritz Küster, editor of the militantly pacifist *Das Andere Deutschland,* the circulation of which rose at one period to 15,000 copies collected among his fellow countrymen pledges to refuse war service and to support a belligerent government. Societies arose dedicated to the furtherance of (potential) conscientious objection and to propagating the slogan: "No More War." A lively *Linkspazifismus* (Left Pacifism) advocated refusal of military service in all wars between capitalist states, while reserving the right to defend the workers' fatherland. Even among German Catholics, whose church hitherto had been everywhere hostile to the radical pacifist stand, a peace association of both priests and laymen came into being with a program not unsympathetic to the position of the personal objector to twentieth-century war. But time was to show that neither enthusiastic public meetings and crowded demonstrations on behalf of peace nor mass signatures to antiwar declarations signified much once the public mind and the machinery of state were bent toward war by an unscrupulous demagogue.[4]

It was, of course, the absence of conscription, along with war disillusionment and the postwar experience in Germany and Austria—a result of these countries' defeat in World War I and the treaties imposed on them at its conclusion—that had provided an opportunity there for proselytizing for the cause of conscientious objection. Disenchantment with war and the return of the voluntary system, along with the legacy of endurance bequeathed by their objectors of 1914–18, were the main reasons why, throughout the interwar years, in the United States and Great Britain, pacifism—or war resistance, to use the term increasingly favored by those considering *pacifism* too negative—flourished even more freely.

In the United States the Fellowship of Reconciliation soon showed itself to be the most vigorous and intellectually alive exponent of pacifism. Its political program will be discussed in greater detail later in this chapter. Apart from a very few small societies pledged to war resistance, pacifists who wished to join an organization but could not accept the FOR's religious basis had only the War Resisters League, established in 1924. However, this body, which had less than a thousand members in 1928, grew very slowly, reaching a peak of 12,000 members in 1942 after the outbreak of World War II. Both the FOR and WRL were predominantly middle-class: teachers, students, Protestant clergy, and housewives provided the bulk of their membership. In the thirties and early forties denominational pacifist fellowships were formed within the major Protestant churches: Methodists, Baptists, Episcopalians, Lutherans, Disciples of Christ, Unitarians and Universalists. Once again, however, numbers remained extremely small; it was the ministry rather than the laity which provided the backbone of these groups.

The British FOR, unlike the American section, did not stand in the center of pacifist activities in Great Britain. It continued to see its task as one of leavening society rather than leading the crusade for a new social order. In numbers much smaller than the American FOR, it concentrated primarily on the still by no means easy task of winning adherents within the Protestant churches to a pacifist interpretation of Christianity; in its efforts it was aided, too, by denominational affiliates.

Just as during World War I conscientious objection in America had been in the main religiously motivated and in Britain politically oriented, so in interwar Britain—in contrast to the Christian-based American FOR—the central pacifist organization united the religious and the nonreligious under one umbrella. After the dissolution of the No-Conscription Fellowship in November 1919, a new body had been set up early in 1921 to take its place. But this No More War Movement, the leadership of which was provided by the pacifist radicals of the old NCF, lacked something of the drive of the wartime organization. Membership grew rapidly during the twenties but the NMWM did not succeed in mobilizing under its direction the mounting wave of antiwar feeling in the country, which manifested itself toward the end of the decade. In the 1924 parliament which saw the coming to power of the first Labour government, sixteen M.P.s (of whom three were in the government) had been conscientious objectors in the recent war. Many prominent members of the labor movement joined the NMWM, which had socialism as well as pacifism written into its program. Yet the NMWM was not able to draw into its activities the hundreds of thousands of labor supporters who then voted for war resistance motions at conferences and congresses. It was only in the mid-thirties, after the deteriorating international situation had led organized labor to abandon its pacifist sympathies and thereby deprived the NMWM of most of its impetus, that anything approaching a pacifist mass movement was generated from the inchoate antimilitarism of the time. The Peace Pledge Union which emerged in 1936, and with which the NMWM eventually fused in 1937, had a membership of around 125,000 shortly before the outbreak of war in 1939. We shall have to return to the PPU for further discussion later in this chapter.[5]

A Pacifist International

The pacifist movement found institutional expression not only in national societies but in international organization. The twentieth century indeed has been an age of internationals. Socialist and cooperative internationals, Communist "Red" and peasantist "Green" internationals do not exhaust their number. It was natural, therefore, that after the war the ex-conscientious objectors of Britain and America, along with a handful of sympathizers from the former allied, enemy and neutral lands, should band together in some form of fellowship, which would provide a basis, they hoped, for the expansion of the movement beyond its Anglo-American heartland.

Thus the International FOR dates back to a conference held at Bilthoven (Holland) in October 1919. There the fifty participants had solemnly acknowledged "each his own share in the sins of his own country in connection with the war and the making of so-called peace," and proclaimed their "shame for their part in the failure of their respective churches to maintain a universal spirit during war." [6] Although a few Roman Catholics collaborated in its work, sections affiliated with the International FOR drew supporters chiefly from Protestant clergy and laity. Its strongly emphasized Christ-centeredness remained a potential barrier to its spread to lands with a different religious tradition.

This religious exclusiveness did not feature in the program of the War Resisters' International, which was set up—under the name *Paco,* the Esperanto word for peace—in 1921 with four affiliated sections located in Great Britain, Holland, Germany and Austria. The WRI was prepared to accept into membership any group whose members individually assented to the International's pledge: "War is a crime against humanity. We therefore are determined not to support any kind of war and to strive for the removal of all the causes of war." [7] This meant, however, that, whereas pacifists of any or no religious persuasion were free to join the WRI, organizations that did not require an individual pledge of war resistance were debarred from affiliating. Thus, if the International FOR would have had to refuse membership to Mahatma Gandhi (had he applied), the WRI could not enter into full communion with such staunchly pacifist bodies as the Women's International League for Peace and Freedom,[8] the International Co-operative Women's Guild, the leftist International Anti-Militarist Bureau or even the peace committees of the Society of Friends, because they contained members who could not entirely accept the pacifist position. We must add to this dogmatic rigidity as a factor in slowing down expansion the fact that among the less socially committed pacifists there were many who felt unable to accept the nonviolent social revolution, to which both the International FOR and the WRI were explicitly committed in their programs, and that numerically large groups of potential conscientious objectors—the Seventh-Day Adventists and the Jehovah's Witnesses, for instance, or most American Mennonite communities —remained aloof, if not actually hostile, to any collaboration with pacifists outside their own fold. Though the WRI by 1939 could claim fifty-four sections in twenty-four separate countries, in fact it had failed so far to make much headway outside Great Britain and the United States. Elsewhere its affiliated groups mostly remained tiny conventicles alternatively ignored or suppressed by the powers that be.

By the early thirties civilian service schemes for conscientious objectors had been set up in the four Scandinavian countries as well as in Holland. But apart from Austria and Weimar Germany compulsory military service remained the rule throughout the European continent. Even the Quakers, whose name had become a byword for peaceableness in many countries on account of their postwar relief activities, failed anywhere to root Quakerism deeply, in part because of the difficulties involved in adjusting a pacifist religious ethic in a conscriptionist country.[9] For some war resisters numbers of adherents were a matter of complete disinterest: what was important was the purity of the idea. The French novelist Romain Rolland, one of the most outstanding Western exponents of the Gandhian philosophy, spoke for these in his letter of greeting to a Ukrainian conscientious objector imprisoned in the Soviet Union:

I want to tell you [he wrote] that I am never worrying about the near or future success of ideals which I know to be true, healthy and sacred. The success does not concern us. We are servants of our ideals. We have only to serve them bravely and faithfully. Whether we shall be victors or vanquished this matters little. It is a joy to serve the eternal and to sacrifice oneself for it. I do not love at all those who so ardently expect a sort of human paradise on earth, and I have no confidence in them. These are weak people who in order to act morally feel that they must be promised an earthly reward, either for themselves or for their own people. The reward lies in your own self—it does not come from outside. It lies in our faith, our struggles, our courage.[10]

But probably few pacifists, however dedicated, shared Rolland's seemingly complete indifference to earthly success or his utter contempt for numbers. They would have been happy to see pacifist movements arise on the European continent as broadly based as the American and British ones (they would likewise have been pleased if Anglo-American pacifism had been able to further extend its influence), and they were depressed at their inability to make any really perceptible impact in these politically important lands. "Regarded from the sociological standpoint we are today a sect," complained in 1928 a young pacifist scholar of Jewish background, who had recently emigrated from Prague to Palestine. "We must become a movement," he went on. "It is undoubtedly of great spiritual value that we have begun as a sect, a small group, a community of people united by one idea, who have gone out to seek to discover men who already belong inwardly to this sect." If pacifism was to prove an effective agent for creating a peaceable world, however, it must advance beyond the sectarian stage in its evolution to become a full fledged movement. Kohn pointed to the major obstacle to development: conscription. "If we wish to free the world from the compulsion to kill men," he concluded, "then we must strain every nerve against compulsory military service." [11]

But throughout the European continent, and especially in its central and eastern areas, conscription possessed an almost sacral quality; it formed part of the national myth of the newly arisen successor states. To refuse military service even on religious grounds appeared to most citizens of these countries to challenge not only their hard-won security but the very idea of the nation state. It was with the notion of providing for youth a substitute— something along the lines of William James's "moral equivalent of war"—which would be acceptable to those patriots still clinging to the older martial concepts that Pierre Cérésole, a Swiss convert to Quakerism, initiated in 1920 a *Service Civile Internationale* (IVSP).[12] Its volunteers who were recruited on an international basis with any young person eligible, whether pacifist or not, undertook manual labor of the pick-and-shovel variety.

They worked on land reclamation or afforestation; they helped in the reconstruction of towns and villages which had been devastated in earthquakes or floods; they participated in building projects for the needy. Cérésole always hoped that his IVSP would act as a prototype in conscriptionist lands for government-approved schemes of alternative national civilian service. In his native Switzerland there was no choice for a conscientious objector between noncombatant service in the army or prison, and until middle age he himself went regularly to jail for refusing to participate in the annual periods of military training. However, the British section of the IVSP, soon the largest and most active, with its tradition of fighting conscription on libertarian grounds, opposed this concept of IVSP's functions and wished to dissociate the organization from any compromise with the state. In the United States in World War II, on the other hand, the IVSP was taken as a model for the association of government and pacifists in running civilian public service camps for conscientious objectors. How this worked in practice will be discussed in a later chapter.

After World War I was over the attempt to create an effective international pacifist movement failed. Pacifist societies, even in the two countries where the movement had roots going back before 1918, remained extremely small and weak when compared with the numbers and influence of other contemporary political movements. Yet in both the United States and Great Britain, as well as in most European countries, antiwar sentiment grew even after Hitler's accession to power presaged again the world's descent to war. Abhorrence of war was by no means equivalent to pacifism: the longing for a peaceable world was felt by millions who had no sympathy with war resistance. Even so, during the twenties and thirties, hundreds of thousands of men and women (especially young people) were vaguely attracted to the pacifist idea. In the English-speaking world many of them toyed with the idea of refusing to fight should another war occur. They were not, for the most part, associated with any pacifist organization; if they were, this often did not go beyond signing some pledge of war resistance. We must now consider more closely what pacifists were saying about war and peace during the years between the two wars.

THE PACIFIST CRITIQUE OF WAR

The Moral Approach

The center of the pacifist argument against war, whether clothed in theological terms or urged on purely secular grounds, was moral protest. The liberal publicist Oswald Garrison Villard's description of war as "the sum of all villainies" is one with the Mennonite theologian Donovan E. Smucker's cry: "War is sin! War is hell! War is organized atrocity." [13] Christian antimilitarists called for the recovery of the pacifist vision of the early church, which had been obliterated with Constantine's conversion and the subsequent subservience of church to state. A Dutch professor of theology, G. J. Heering, for instance, wrote an influential book significantly entitled *The Fall of Christianity* (1930), in which he pleaded for a total renunciation of war by the churches. Secular humanist pacifists, on the other hand, linked up with the eighteenth-century Enlightenment's vision of a world with reason enthroned, from which war would be forever banished.

The killing of the innocent in modern war was a favorite theme of pacifist literature: women and children would be the first victims of air attack, poison gas and economic blockade. This surely was a complete negation of both reason and Christian morality. But the waging of war entailed not only material destruction but the mutilation of the human personality in war; soldiers became mere killing machines obliged to obey the orders of their superior officers, even if they considered them wrong, or face death at the hands of a firing squad. In any case, war always penalized those bearing no responsibility for its outbreak; the really guilty ones might escape. Many pacifists believed that another war, whoever won, would bring the destruction of democracy and the imposition of some form of military dictatorship even in countries which till then had enjoyed parliamentary rule. Pacifists deplored the glamor of war, a relic of the barbaric past; its glorification in ceremonies and monuments was particularly harmful in that it helped to cloak the squalid realities of battle. Youth must be shown a better way in which to expend its energies and idealism than armed struggle. Workcamps on the IVSP model seemed a modest contribution to solving this problem.

In particular, pacifists in their writings pointed to the moral deception practiced by each side in the recent world conflict in order to maintain morale among their citizenry. Governments, including those of Great Britain and the United States, had resorted both to lies to cover up the true causes of the war and the real reasons for its prolongation, and to slandering the enemy with the object of whipping up hatred and the passion of revenge among their own peoples. Arthur Ponsonby, one of the promoters of the Union of Democratic Union and in the twenties and early thirties a chief adviser to the Labour Party on foreign policy, concluded a carefully documented study of the wartime press and propaganda by dramatically asking his readers: "Is further proof needed that international war is a monster born of hypocrisy, fed on falsehood, fattened on humbug, kept alive by superstition, directed to the death and torture of millions, succeeding in no high purpose, degrading to humanity, endangering civilization and bringing forth in its travail a hideous brood of strife, conflict and war, more war?" [14] Many people indeed, and not only pacifists, nursed a sense of having been tricked by the wartime politicians: they felt tricked both as to the war's origins and as to its outcome.

The Utilitarian Approach

The postwar world appeared neither a world fit for heroes to live in nor one in which liberal democracy had securely triumphed. Only in regard to the third battlecry of the victors—a war to end war—did there still remain the possibility of fulfilment. It, too, would prove a delusion, many argued, if militarism was not driven from the civilized world. Two methods were offered for achieving this result: the internationalist and the pacifist solution. During the twenties, allegiance to the League of Nations and advocacy of war resistance did not seem incompatible. In the next decade the rise of the Fascist dictatorships eventually forced a choice between the two. Both internationalists and pacifists, however, made use of roughly the same general case against war. Their opponents, too, were the same: protagonists of national power and prestige.

The enormous cost and wastefulness of modern war—one of the most frequently used arguments in the pacifist press—was one that could be expected to carry weight in an era of economic crisis and rising unemployment. Publicists tended to attribute to the aftermath of war much that was, in fact, due to other causes: increased taxation, for instance, or the depression itself. Villard wrote in 1934: "People are aware that our going to war . . . was a useless crime against America, that we got nothing out of it but misery, and that it nearly ruined the Republic we love." [15] As evidence of the "futility" of war, publicists like Villard liked to cite not only the world's economic plight but the host of dictatorships, small and large, which had sprung up after the Paris peace settlement. The settlement itself—the Versailles *Diktat*—was a favorite target of pacifist (and other) writers. Its denial of the right of self-determination to millions was particularly painful to those who had taken the Wilsonian doctrine seriously. Aggressive tendencies on the part of countries like Germany and Italy, which claimed to have been victimized in varying degrees in the settlement, came to be explained as the psychological outcome of their treatment in 1919.

Political pacifism drew strength from the researches of the revisionist school of historians, who, correctly challenging the thesis of the exclusive war guilt of the Central Powers as contained in Article 231 of the Treaty of Versailles, on which the peace settlement seemed to rest, went on in some instances, more controversially, to absolve the ex-enemy countries of any major responsibility for bringing on the recent war. The leading revisionists—Sidney B. Fay and Harry Elmer Barnes in the United States; G. P. Gooch, G. Lowes Dickinson and Raymond Beazley in Great Britain, to cite the most outstanding—were not pacifists, though some of the school's British representatives had been vocal wartime critics of allied diplomacy. (In postwar Germany, on the other hand, interest in the war guilt question, *Kriegsschuldfrage,* and the desire to minimize Imperial Germany's part in causing the outbreak of war were strongest on the right, with exponents of Germany's exclusive guilt located on the extreme left and in pacifist circles.) If, however, all the participants in the war had been more or less equally responsible—or equally innocent: it came to roughly the same thing—and if it was in the system of alliances, the ever-increasing armaments, the imperialist rivalries (as the more moderate revisionist historians were arguing with great cogency) that the blame for the war lay, then it was not illogical to conclude that, since even with the League of Nations, the system still remained basically almost intact, only a total repudiation of war would suffice to bring about the diplomatic revolution needed to establish peace on firm foundations.

Secret diplomacy, excessive nationalism, the struggle for overseas markets, and the arms race had really been the responsible factors in bringing about the last war. If there were guilty men in addition to such impersonal forces driving to war, pacifist writers sought them not so much in the politicians, who were more often than not mere cat's-paws unable themselves to shape events, as in the armament manufacturers. These men, it was believed (not without justification in some cases), were ready to foment wars in various parts of the globe in the pursuit of their private profit. Pacifists disagreed as to the exact extent of the war guilt that should be assigned to members of this "Bloody International." To many pacifists the nationalization of the arms industry, the solution proposed by such writers as the nonpacifist English Quaker Philip Noel-Baker, though a step in the right direction, would not in itself banish war from the globe. Militarism, as developments in the Soviet Union were proving, was not a capitalist monopoly. The sinister machinations of armaments manufacturers remained, however, a favorite theme in popular expositions of pacifism,[16] though it was also the subject of learned tomes and Congressional investigations.

The utilitarian case against war rested very largely on economic foundations. Liberal pacifists, like the American Villard, united with pacifist socialists, like the British Labour Party leader George Lansbury, in seeing the contemporary world divided into "have" and "have-not" powers. Among the latter were Germany, Italy and Japan. France, Great Britain and, though to a lesser extent, the United States were regarded as sated powers clinging desperately to their imperial supremacy. The not unnatural claims of the "have-nots" for a greater share in the booty thus led to the possibility of renewed war—or at least to the perpetual military preparedness of the "have" powers against attempts at dispossessing them. Among the many pacifists who were also socialists, the belief prevailed that war was inherent in the capitalist system and could only be finally eliminated by the expropriation of the capitalists (a view that led some to abandon nonviolence in the class struggle).

Utilitarian pacifists—and religious pacifists when using utilitarian arguments against war, as they increasingly tended to do— were not so much relying on the basic goodness of man as on his essential teachability. Their faith was one "in the ultimate reasonableness of mankind." [17] If man could once be convinced that arms did not give a nation lasting security and that armed conflict in the modern world would ultimately be disastrous for all, he could ultimately be persuaded to abandon the war method in favor of other means of solving disputes. In the age of the bombing plane, bacteriological warfare and poison gas, the individual could further the realization of the utilitarian principle of the greatest happiness of the greatest number only by an unequivocal renunciation of war. In the twentieth century, pacifism rather than militarism was the means for the survival of the fittest.

Pacifist Proposals for Peace

There was no consensus among pacifists on methods for achieving peace, if we disregard their fundamental agreement on the moral imperative of war resistance. Some pacifists saw salvation in a reformed League of Nations which, no longer representing mainly the interests of the chief victors of 1918, would strive to act impartially in promoting the welfare of all (others put their faith in schemes for world government or federal union under which the nation states of the past would gradually wither away). In the United States the "outlawry of war," a slogan that became popular toward the end of the twenties, had its supporters too in the pacifist movement. Pacifists, however, were more inclined to dismiss it as a blind alley which would lead the movement away from its main tasks.

Disarmament gained the enthusiastic support of almost all pacifists for they believed that the very existence of armaments threatened the peace; they entailed the danger of a renewed arms race and contributed indirectly to war by increasing the world's economic *malaise*. Unilateral disarmament, which would both act by force of example as a powerful factor in favor of peace and lessen the likelihood of invasion by removing any pretext for it, was certainly much preferable to no disarmament at all. Most pacifists, however, welcomed efforts to achieve multilateral disarmament by graduated stages. In the United States, for instance, they supported in large numbers the activities of the National Council for the Prevention of War which, under the able leadership of the Quaker Frederick J. Libby, worked for a step-by-step reduction of armaments. A few approved, as a compromise solution in a world where nonviolence hitherto had made little headway, the pooling of arms in an international police force, which would act only on the orders of an impartial international tribunal against those actually offending instead of against whole nations. Pacifists for the most part did not approve attempts merely to ban the most fearsome weapons of war—bombers, submarines, poison gas, etc.—while leaving more conventional weapons intact. The attack should be against war itself.

American pacifists called for the renunciation by their country of the alleged right to intervene in such areas as Central and South America in order to protect its citizens and their property rights. At a time when the achievement of international agreement to its abandonment seemed possible, British pacifists severely criticized the retention by their government of the bombing plane on the pretext that the bomber was essential for maintaining order in the outlying parts of the British Empire. In urging treaty revision in Europe and the abolition of tariff barriers, and the sharing of the world's raw materials and markets overseas on a basis equitable to all nations and by means of periodically held international conferences, British and American pacifists combined forces once again with the rest of the peace movement which did not share their belief in total war renunciation. They joined forces, too, in combating the various manifestations of militarism in national life—"from the sale of military toys to army and navy appropriations." [10] Officers' training corps and cadet corps were denounced, for the military training of youth ran directly contrary to the pacifist desire to educate the young in a spirit free from narrow nationalism. Pacifists led the struggle against conscription in lands which retained compulsory military service.

However, the one aspect of pacifist tactics that was unique to their movement and not shared by any other nonpacifist political group was individual war resistance, a personal pledge to refuse participation in any future war. Many who gave this pledge, especially during the 1920s and early 1930s, believed that they were thereby giving their allegiance to a mass movement that could successfully sweep away any government that attempted to commit a country to war. Many pacifists, especially in the United States, were convinced that the man in the street was basically in favor of peace and had a natural inclination toward the war resistance movement—this, despite pacifists' belief in the need for extensive peace education to eradicate militarist preconceptions in the populace. The great scientist, Albert Einstein, argued that if no more than 2 percent of the male population of the globe refused to fight this fact alone would stop all future wars, since there would not be prisons enough to hold so many conscientious objectors. No government, moreover, would dare to launch a war with so large a section of the men of military age in opposition.

Pacifists everywhere, whether regarding Einstein's proposal as feasible or not (and there were some like Romain Rolland who felt such a gesture ineffectual in the age of the bombing plane and bacteriological warfare and put their faith instead in a nonviolent social revolution), considered the organization of a war resistance movement as in itself an important, if not the decisive factor in preventing war. Governments, being uncertain of their citizens' readiness to fight, would be forced to pursue peaceable policies and to abandon war as a permissible method in the last resort; a renunciation that even the most peace-loving national administration had been most unwilling to make hitherto. In the second place, pacifists saw in public declarations of war resistance a valuable means for publicizing their cause and furthering its development. Only in this way could the state's control—directly or indirectly—of the major communications media be counteracted to some degree. Thirdly, they argued on the basis particularly of the 1914 experience that, at least in regard to modern war, it was impossible for the ordinary citizen to judge the pros and cons of the situation immediately prior to the outbreak of war. Each side emitted such a smoke barrage of propaganda that it was impossible to see through to the truth until long after the war situation had passed; this alone served to destroy what the French antimilitarist writer Georges Demartial called "the myth of wars of legitimate defence." Lastly, of course, the case for war resistance rested on the moral objection. This objection was fundamental to it, whether the moral impulse derived from religion or from reason.

Adherence to pacifism did not necessarily entail allegiance to political or social reform, let alone nonviolent revolution. In England Quakers were by tradition supporters of the Liberal Party; in the United States they had been in many areas firmly Republican. Many religious pacifists eschewed all political activity; even among the nonreligious there were some who expressed disinterest in politics and felt that they could join effectively in the struggle against war without the need to wrestle with other social evils. In the interwar years, however, pacifists outside the sects mostly gave some degree of assent to the ideas of the left: we have already seen this pattern emerging in our survey of conscientious objection in World War I.

Capitalism is based on competition—thus ran the argument linking pacifism with the need to remold the social order—and its motive force is the exploitation of man by man. The competitive society merely reproduces the life of the jungle in more sophisticated terms. It is not sufficient for pacifists to say that they refuse to participate in war. They must go further and work for a classless society in which cooperation replaces competition as the goal of men's actions. The struggle to win overseas markets for the surplus products of the developed capitalist countries had led to the recent war and would once again end in a similar holocaust if steps are not taken to counter this drive to war. Without tackling the roots of war in a faulty economic system, moral protest remains an empty gesture. "Only when countries adopt a Socialist form of government will the world be finally secure for peace." Pacifists like Lansbury argued that, just as a failure to eliminate capitalism would in the long run frustrate efforts to abolish war, so war and preparation for war would undermine the conditions for a socialist order both through the enormous waste of material resources for purposes of destruction and by the annihilation of the moral values for which socialism stood. Most socialist pacifists withheld assent from the Marxist prognosis of the inevitability of war under capitalism—or at least they believed that war might be indefinitely postponed, thus giving time for the transformation of the political structure in a socialist direction. Lansbury expressed this pacifist revisionism when he wrote: "Just as capitalism had been compelled for its own safety to make concessions to the workers, so I believe it is not unreasonable to expect that the same system will be compelled to make concessions to the cause of world peace." [19] Such concessions would include a more equitable sharing of the world's economic resources by means of international control of colonies, removal of trade barriers and periodic world conferences to discuss political and economic issues threatening the peace.

Pacifists remained suspicious, however, of the etatist tendencies in socialism. The decentralized cooperative commonwealth was their ideal and not the monolithic workers' state.[20] Nurtured in Britain on the traditions of guild socialism and based in the United States on the moral conscience as exemplified in the social gospel, the pacifist movement in these two countries tended to regard a society which retained a vital local democracy alongside a developed system of communal welfare as the best guarantee for a peaceable world. On the European continent pacifists were often drawn from circles influenced by the libertarian anarcho-syndicalist tradition. They stressed in even bolder form the role of the individual and of local self-government in maintaining a pacifist society.

Finally, mention must be made of the not inconsiderable number of pacifists who rejected political action of any kind in favor of what has aptly been called "the politics of the unpolitical." One of the most gifted spokesmen of this school of pacifist thought has defined it as "the politics of those who desire to be pure in heart: the politics of men without personal ambition; of those who have not desired wealth or an unequal share of worldly possessions; of those who have always striven, whatever their race or condition, for human values and not for national or sectional interests." "The Sermon on the Mount is the source of all the politics of the unpolitical." [21] This view derived much of its inspiration from Tolstoy; in the contemporary world Gandhi was its patron saint. It leaned towards a renunciation of this world, or at least of its materialism and its hedonistic culture. It did not usually follow Tolstoy or Gandhi, however, in their downgrading of artistic creativity. Indeed, for the artist and the man of letters it provided a faith that expressed both their repugnance for a world that appeared to reject the aesthetic values they cherished most and their revulsion from the institution of war that threatened with destruction, and even total extinction, the creative impulses of man.

One variant in the pacifist politics of the unpolitical was provided in the second half of the thirties by the English novelist, Aldous Huxley, who, with his colleague the publicist Gerald Heard, then transplanted it just before World War II to the sunnier climate of California. The Huxley-Heard thesis was also an outgrowth of the Tolstoy-Gandhi symbiosis. For Huxley and Heard "non-attachment" should be the human ideal: non-attachment to worldly things, whether to persons (e.g., love) or to objects (e.g., greed or ambition) or to emotions (e.g., lust or anger or envy). It was not merely the goals men pursued which should be in consonance with this ideal, the means must be in line with it, too. For good ends can never emerge through the use of evil means. This proposition was argued by Huxley with considerable force and with an impressive wealth of illustrative documentation. He applied it in particular to war to prove war's incompatibility under any circumstances with the ends of a humane and democratic society (a society which he sought in the small community and the self-governing workshop). Huxley's theories were widely discussed at the time and undoubtedly exercised a considerable influence on pacifist thinking in Britain and America.[22] Yet there were few ready to accept them whole: non-attachment for Huxley and his disciples entailed the practice of meditative union with the Ultimate Reality and the cultivation of asceticism along the lines laid down by Indian Yoga—practicing pacifists in small, self-contained communities, sealed off in this way against the inevitable doom of Western civilization, and the conversion of the pacifist movement into an ascetic—but not necessarily celibate—order of gurus and their followers. A movement that had in the past striven to bring the Kingdom of God down onto earth and to realize the Brotherhood of Man found it difficult to swallow in its entirety so otherworldly a doctrine.

Nonviolent Resistance

There was indeed a certain contradiction in Huxley himself. Just as socialist pacifists appeared at times to believe war to be inevitable under capitalism and yet to advocate pacifism as a method of avoiding it even while capitalism remained intact, so Huxley posits a total reorientation of Western man towards a philosophy of non-attachment as the only method of eliminating the evil of war and at the same time preaches nonviolence as an effective resistant to war within a world order still given over to nationalism and "mechanomorphism." We have here perhaps just one further example of the tendency of a political philosophy dedicated to a radical transformation of society unconsciously to accept at times piecemeal reforms as a surrogate for total change.

In his exposition of nonviolent resistance as not only a moral equivalent of war but an effective instrument for preserving the values war was supposed to defend, should a nation decide to abandon its arms, Huxley emphasized the need for training nonviolent cadres. If, he argued, the making of an efficient soldier normally took some three or four years, then the creation of an equally efficient nonviolent resister would require no less a period. "Though mainly preventive," pacifism was also "a technique of conflict—a way of fighting without violence." Therefore, only "trained troops . . . soldiers of peace" could successfully undertake nonviolent resistance.[23] Like Gandhi, Huxley was prepared to concede that these soldiers of peace did not have to be saints or mystics to wage successful nonviolent resistance; they did need, however, training in their technique of struggle.

Huxley's ideas on nonviolent resistance were derived in some measure directly from Gandhi. Even more, they were influenced by the writings of two Western exponents of nonviolence: the Dutch ex-pastor and convert to anarchism Bart de Ligt and the American ex-lawyer and convert to Quakerism Richard B. Gregg. De Ligt strove to make from Gandhian nonviolence an instrument of revolutionary social change: the nonviolent equivalent of the class war. He developed a detailed program for mobilizing the antiwar forces behind a general strike in case war threatened, including a complete boycott of the functions of the warmaking government. De Ligt hoped that the general strike against war would quickly merge into a nonviolent social revolution.[24] In 1920, it is true that British workers had averted Great Britain's entry into the Russo-Polish war on the side of Poland by threatening a general strike and since then organized labor in several countries had toyed with the idea of a strike against war. The situation in the late thirties, however, was entirely different and Huxley himself was sceptical of the war resistance movement's ability to prevent war once any government had embarked on it.

Gregg, in his book *The Power of Nonviolence* (1934), interpreted Gandhi's *ahimsa* as a kind of "moral jiujitsu," which might be effectively substituted for armed violence in both domestic and international relations. He attempted to trace the practice of nonviolence in the history of modern Western civilization, pointing to such incidents as the Magyar struggle against Hapsburg autocracy in the 1860s to back up his point that nonviolence was something more than a peculiarly Hindu custom. Though Gregg, like Gandhi, favored a decentralized, grass roots democracy and a society in which man and not technology set the tone, his writings lacked the revolutionary passion of de Ligt.

Most European and American pacifists looked for inspiration, if not always with complete agreement, to Gandhi's nonviolent struggle in British India. They admired the moral superiority of nonviolence as a means of defense against external attack. In the domestic struggle for social justice it offered to left wing pacifists a technique which appeared to avoid the danger of replacing capitalist oppression by Red totalitarianism. With the day of the barricades now over, nonviolence gave the workers a new weapon. Nevertheless, at this time, pacifists seldom thought seriously of initiating nonviolent campaigns of their own. The idea of a "Peace Army," recruited from volunteers ready to stand without weapons between the opposing forces, appeared in 1932 at the time of the Sino-Japanese conflict over Manchuria. The project, largely the brain child of two prominent British pacifists, A. Maude Royden and A. Herbert Gray, proved abortive. Many pacifists, though sympathetic, felt that the time was not yet ripe for implementing Gandhi's technique on such an ambitious scale. To some religious pacifists, moreover, the Gandhian method seemed to be too like war with only the bloodshed left out. They felt that conciliation was the true task of the peacemaker and not the waging of nonviolent war. There were, too, nonreligious pacifists, like the popular English philosopher C. E. M. Joad, who were sceptical of the more far-reaching claims of the proponents of nonviolence. They felt that whereas nonviolent resistance had a role to play under the present conditions of international anarchy the best solution would be the creation of a genuine world authority backed by overwhelming force.

In general, there was much uncertainty within the pacifist movement concerning the relationship between nonviolence and a morally legitimate use of physical force. Might one, for instance, advocate the use of nonviolent means against external attack while supporting a degree of coercion in the internal arrangement of the state? Was there indeed a distinction in kind rather than merely in degree between loving persuasion and nonviolent coercion? In the idea of nonviolent resistance, it was widely felt, the pacifist movement now possessed a tool that might help to give positive content to what had previously seemed to outsiders a negative creed. The idea of nonviolence brought the pacifist philosophy down to earth, changing it from a counsel of perfection to a more perfect method of maintaining terrestrial values than the way of armed force. But when world war broke out again in 1939, for Western pacifists nonviolence still remained untried, still hung high in the realm of theory.

PACIFISM AND THE GROWTH OF TOTALITARIANISM

The 1920s

During the decade and a half that followed the Armistice of 1918 the chances of eventually establishing a peaceable world looked promising. Germany was disarmed; the former Austrian Empire lay in fragments; the United States and Soviet Russia had retreated into isolation; Italy and Japan had not yet clearly revealed expansionist designs. With Great Britain economizing radically on its armament expenditure, the only important power suspected of nurturing an aggressive militarism was France—and suspicions on this score were in fact considerably exaggerated. Moreover, that old dream of Europe and America's internationalists—a League of Nations—was in being: it needed reform and even reconstruction, many thought, but its very existence seemed to indicate that law was at last taking the place of anarchy in international relations. In 1932 the opening of the international disarmament conference momentarily raised hopes that a warless world was about to be brought into being. And for those who despaired of peace being established so long as economic exploitation held sway, the Soviet experiment in Russia combined with the imminent collapse of capitalism elsewhere offered the prospect of a new and more just international order in the not too distant future.

Pacifists shared in these various rosy dreams. Many indeed became pacifists in this period because war seemed unlikely and a pledge of war resistance, like an incantation against sickness, would itself remove the possibility of the occurrence of the evil. This did not mean that pacifism overnight became everywhere equally popular. In the conscriptionist countries of the European continent, as we have seen, the lot of the conscientious objector remained extremely hard; although in a few countries alternative civilian service now became permissible, the pacifist movement made little headway in this area. Even in the United States the wartime mood changed slowly. In November 1920, for instance, we find the editor of the *Christian Century,* Charles Clayton Morrison, writing to the prolific pacifist publicist, Kirby Page: "Your book will be read by the esoteric few. The mood of the time is anything but congenial with pacifist doctrine." [25]

It was in Great Britain that postwar pacifism first gained momentum. It drew its adherents largely from the labor movement, the leaders of which had in many instances opposed the recent war, and from left wing intellectuals. In October 1925 Arthur Ponsonby, a convert from Liberalism who had held the post of Under-Secretary of State for Foreign Affairs in the Labour government of 1924, wrote a letter to the press in which he called for signatures to a declaration of war resistance. Signatories were to pledge themselves to withhold support of any kind, including war service, to a belligerent government. In the civilized world, aggression was not the real cause of war, said Ponsonby: either direct negotiations or some form of arbitration could resolve all disputes between nations.[26] By the following December 40,000 pledges had been received. A year later Ponsonby and his associates organized a mammoth rally at the Albert Hall in London at which the trade union leader Ernest Bevin, among others, declared their allegiance to pacifism.

The thinking behind the movement is best illustrated by quoting from an article entitled "The Prevention of War," which Bertrand Russell wrote in 1922 for the organ of the British No More War Movement. Russell did not envisage the abolition of war being reached "by the world in general adopting the pacifist theory." The role of pacifists was to be a leavening one, the influencing of opinion. Russell wrote:

Men who are convinced that the prevention of war is the most pressing problem facing civilization should, it seems to me, publicly and solemnly pledge themselves to take no part in war, no matter what the issue may be. It is not implied logically that all war, always, is on the balance harmful. What is implied is (a) that most wars are harmful; (b) that the outbreak of war produces an excitement that clouds people's judgement as to whether this particular war is harmful; (c) that no one can know that a war which is in progress will not be harmful on the whole; (d) that therefore it is better to make a rule of abstaining from war, to guard against war hysteria.[27]

Modern war, it is implied, is fought mainly for prestige between contestants whose alleged reasons for going to war were equally fictitious and whose peoples could only be persuaded to fight if whipped up by war propaganda into a state of hysteria. As A. J. P. Taylor has remarked, "the principle of resistance to aggression was passed over so lightly in the twenties that the phrase 'collective security' was not used until 1932." [28] This attitude explains the fact that in this period many in Britain and America rallied to the pacifist movement without having fully considered the implications of their stand. In the pacifist ranks stood supporters of the class war and apologists for the military power of the Soviet Union as well as advocates of League sanctions and spokesmen for an armed international government, alongside believers in the gospel of reconciliation and in the practical power of nonviolence. Only during the thirties did the various positions become clearly demarcated from each other.

The end of the twenties saw a great upsurge of pacifistic feeling. A whole spate of popular antiwar novels, plays and memoirs appearing in the years 1928–30 illustrated rather than caused this tendency. Their authors were former combatants, who shared the prevailing disillusionment with the course and outcome of the recent war: E. E. Cummings and Ernest Hemingway in the United States; Edmund Blunden, Siegfried Sassoon, R. C. Sherriff and Richard Aldington in England; Erich Remarque and Arnold Zweig in Germany. Several of these writers—Blunden and Sassoon, for instance—became for a time complete pacifists. The work of all helped to bring new recruits into the pacifist movement, especially among the younger generation. Their moral in respect to war was the same: "Never again." In contrast to much literature in earlier periods that had glorified war, these writers stressed the darker side of war which the undoubted heroism of the ordinary soldier, often a conscript dragged unwillingly from his home and family, could not ameliorate.

The young people who grew to maturity in the years after 1918 were often drawn to pacifism. In part this trend reflected the perennial revolt of youth against an older generation, which in this case was held responsible for the recent holocaust and for creating the conditions for a new one. In the United States the student groups which pledged themselves to refuse to fight in another war were partly motivated by isolationist sentiment. However, while some of this antimilitarism was superficial, many young men and women—especially in the English-speaking world—saw in the pacifist movement an instrument through which they could work for a more decent world without resort to the degrading violence of modern war.

In the Oxford Union resolution of February 1933, youthful pacifism produced its *cause célèbre*. At the time, as well as later, much that was misleading was written concerning this incident. Winston Churchill, for instance, has referred to it as an "ever-shameful resolution" passed by "foolish boys," an example of "the basest sentiments" receiving acceptance "in this dark time." "It was easy to laugh off such an episode in England," he goes on, "but in Germany, in Russia, in Japan, the idea of a decadent, degenerate Britain took root and swayed many calculations." [29] In fact, no evidence has ever been produced to show that it was taken abroad as a sign of England's degeneracy. It is true that the formal wording of the motion passed by this student debating society by a vote of 275 to 153 (and repassed by a number of such societies at other British universities) was pacifist: "That this House will in no circumstances fight for King and country." The guest speaker for the motion, Dr. C. E. M. Joad, considered himself a pacifist at this time. But the students who passed it were voting in most cases against imperialist wars, against obsolescent jingoism inherited from previous centuries and against the identification of patriotism with a declining military caste. Armed sanctions under the League of Nations or resistance against totalitarian aggression were not points at issue in the debate. The last war in which Britain had been involved, it may be pointed out, too, was the war of intervention against Soviet Russia, the "nice new war" (to use the ironic phrase of the poet Osbert Sitwell), which Churchill himself had done so much to promote: this was the kind of war against which his "foolish boys" were protesting.

The Great Divide

Two events in the 1930s contributed more than any others toward finally separating pacifism from its temporary allies among League of Nations internationalists and left wing militants: the accession of Hitler to power in 1933 and the outbreak of the Spanish Civil War in 1936. The one raised the challenge of Fascist aggression (together with the menace of antisemitism); the other presented a threat of extinction for all left wing groups in a newly established democracy. Pacifists were forced to reconsider their position. The successive departure of all who now considered that in the last resort war might be justified in repelling expansionist dictatorships, in preserving democracy and social progress against their internal foes, or in maintaining humane values against an upsurge of barbarism, left the pacifist movement much weakened. Its political relevance appeared to have dwindled; by 1940 it had contracted once more within the confines of a quasi-religious sect. However, the increased cohesion that resulted from this ordeal may have proved ultimately of some advantage. It permitted concentrated attention on developing the idea of nonviolence and its application to society. This might not have been possible if the movement had remained a mishmash of conflicting attitudes in regard to the central issue of violence.

We may take the case of Albert Einstein to illustrate the effect the Hitlerite challenge could have even on one who had only recently come out in favor of uncompromising war resistance. Einstein's commitment to pacifism, though its roots went back before 1914, became explicit in 1928. "I am convinced that the international movement to refuse participation in any kind of war service is one of the most encouraging developments of our time," he declared in that year. "Every thoughtful, well-meaning and conscientious human being should assume, in time of peace, the solemn and unconditional obligation not to participate in any war, for any reason." For the next five years he was actively associated in the work of the WRI and made many public statements in support of imprisoned conscientious objectors. He pleaded with conscriptionist governments to permit objectors to choose some form of civilian work in place of military service. His 1930 "Two-Percent-Speech," as it became known, has already been mentioned in this chapter. In the early thirties Einstein was internationally the best known figure on the roster of the war resisters' movement.

The coming of the Nazi regime in Germany brought about a radical alteration in Einstein's thinking. As a liberal and a Jew, Einstein was forced into exile. After a few months we find him writing: "Conditions, unfortunately, have changed." Though he did not advocate a preventive war, he felt now that only "vigilance" on the part of strongly armed and united democracies would stem the expansion of Nazi Germany. Answering a plea to speak out on behalf of two conscientious objectors awaiting trial in Belgium, he said: "Were I a Belgian, I should not, in the present circumstances, refuse military service; rather I should enter such service cheerfully in the belief that I would thereby be helping to save European civilization." He continued to assert that a time might come again in the future when he would be ready to uphold the stand of the objector to war. But for the present only armed strength on the part of the democracies, however odious such means might still seem to him, could serve to maintain peace. To Arthur (now Lord) Ponsonby who, as chairman of the WRI, had tried to expostulate with Einstein, the latter replied: "I am sure, that if you were [a] responsible Minister in France, you would change your view [on] this point, as long as this threatening condition lasts."

Pacifist reaction to Einstein's renunciation of pacifism varied from angry outrage to pained disappointment. The Secretary of the WRI confided to the International's leading supporters: "I am afraid that this will do our Movement considerable harm. I think that the less publicity given to it, the better. You will notice that I have removed reference to Einstein in the *War Resister* which is about to be published and I shall drop the term "Einstein Fund" from our notepaper as soon as possible." To Einstein's old friend and fellow pacifist, Romain Rolland, the former's present stance smelled of apostasy. "Such weakness of spirit is indeed unimaginable in a great scientist." Rolland complained. "Had it never occurred to him that circumstances might develop, circumstances such as those that prevail today, which would make it dangerous to practice [the] conscientious objection which he espoused?" He accused Einstein of having been guilty of playing "a kind of intellectual game"; he had urged Europe's youth to refuse military service without considering responsibly the full implications and all the risks of such a stand. There was much force behind this critique, yet Rolland himself a few years later followed the same path as Einstein had done.

In several ways Einstein's pacifism had been typical of much of the antiwar sentiment of the postwar era. In the first place it was largely an emotional response, a repulsion against the horrors of modern war and an expression of the disenchantment that had followed World War I.[30] Einstein did not hide this fact. "My pacifism is an instinctive feeling," he wrote in 1929. "My attitude is not the result of an intellectual theory." There was indeed nothing shameful in an emotional antipathy to the hatred and cruelty involved in war such as swept Einstein in these years. A purely intellectual pacifism based on a fine calculation of advantage and loss is likely to prove sterile in the long run. But just as in 1914 the promptings of his heart had brought the American Clarence Darrow in the twinkling of an eye to exchange his belief in Tolstoyan nonresistance for an equally compulsive faith in the need to resist the German invasion of little Belgium, so Einstein and many others found that the same emotional impulse that had made them espouse war resistance now propelled them into the camp of those who urged armed resistance. For Einstein the path that conducted him away from pacifism led him (to his shocked horror, let it be added) toward the creation of the atom bomb.

A second point at which Einstein's pacifism coincided with that of many others among the movement's adherents was in his belief that arms could be dispensed with only in the civilized world. He was not prepared to urge unilateral disarmament on "a native African tribe" as a remedy for war, he declared, "for the patient there would have died long before the cure could have been of any help to him." But what if in Europe itself a reversion to the law of the jungle should ensue and the painfully gained achievements of humanist culture were to be abandoned throughout large areas of that continent? Would not disarmament and conscientious objection be as out of place there as on the dark continent? That they were indeed no longer feasible was the understandable conclusion drawn from the state of Europe from 1933 on by Einstein, and by countless others who had previously sympathized with the war resistance movement.[31]

At first, however, many pacifists, as well as many politicians and ordinary citizens outside Germany, believed that negotiation combined with treaty revision would preserve the peace and satisfy the claims, some of them not unjustified, of the dictators. The English novelist, A. A. Milne, in one of the most popular expositions of utilitarian pacifism published in the interwar years, was typical of this way of thinking. In 1934 he wrote: "I shall assume that Germany is as amenable to reason as Italy (or any other nation), and that within certain limitations imposed on her by the Versailles Treaty, she is as anxious as any other nation for the security of peace." [32]

It was Italy's attack on Abyssinia in October 1935 that finally precipitated the division and brought subsequent hostility between the pacifists, on one hand, and those internationalists who were prepared to support collective security under the League of Nations' auspices to the point of military sanctions, on the other. According to the privately organized Peace Ballot[33] of the previous year, in which 1.5 million Britishers took part, an overwhelming majority had voted in favor of applying sanctions against any power found guilty of aggression. "The Peace Ballot," it has been pointed out, "was an appeal for militant resistance to aggression, not a manifesto of appeasement." [34] But the lines were still not yet clearly drawn. While a substantial minority of over two million came out against military sanctions, the vote in favor of economic sanctions was well over three million stronger than the vote for military sanctions. Among both nonpacifists and pacifists who participated in the balloting there was still a feeling that some measure of support for League action was not incompatible with an unwillingness to commit the country to full-scale war under the banner of the League.

There were pacifists who were not opposed to the application of an economic blockade when Italy began its conquest of Abyssinia. In the Quaker community, especially in the United States, opinion

was divided on this issue with a vocal minority in favor of supporting League action. In Great Britain, Clifford Allen (now Lord
Allen of Hurtwood) pleaded for pacifist support of even military
sanctions, since the practical alternative then facing the world was
not one between a nonviolent way to peace, however theoretically
desirable, and collective security but between collective security
and a reversion to the international anarchy of pre-League days.
In his view, opposition to League action on the part of the pacifist
movement meant lining up in practice with the believers in old-
style power diplomacy and with the isolationists. While still reserving their personal renunciation of violence, war resisters could
best further the cause of peace by supporting collective action for
its preservation based on the rule of law, which, according to Allen,
approximated more closely police action than the intra-national
warfare of the past. But Allen's agile balancing trick between personal repudiation of war and support for armed action by the
League found few imitators. Those who approved the latter course
inclined to lose their belief in the efficacy of nonviolence altogether.[35] On the other hand, pacifists tended to repudiate sanctions,
especially military sanctions, as merely war under a new name.

At the beginning of October 1935, on the very eve of Mussolini's
onslaught on Abyssinia, a showdown took place within the British
Labour Party between Ernest Bevin, representing the majority
which supported the League action against Italy even at the risk of
war, and George Lansbury, the party leader and a convinced
Christian pacifist. The scene of this confrontation was Brighton
where the party was holding its annual conference. Lansbury, whom
Taylor has well described as "the most lovable figure in modern
politics," later admitted to having experienced increasing difficulty
in "squaring my pacifist principles with the policy of my party"
after he became its leader following Ramsay Macdonald's defection
in 1931. At the conference, Bevin, alarmed by the impression
rumors of a divided party leadership would create in the country
just before a general election due in November and angry at what
he considered Lansbury's prevarication hitherto on the issue of
sanctions, attacked him in a harsh, even brutal speech. After appealing to the delegates to be influenced neither by sentiment nor
personal attachment Bevin had turned to Lansbury and said: "It
is placing the Executive and the [Labour] Movement in an abso-

lutely wrong position to be hawking your conscience round from body to body to be told what you ought to do with it." Despite considerable personal sympathy for Lansbury the conference voted in favor of sanctions by an overwhelming majority.[36] With organized labor in Britain firmly committed to collective security (though not yet ready to back rearmament under the National Government), British pacifism's connection with official labor was severed. Though the two movements had never been identical, the post-1918 war resistance movement in Great Britain had derived, as we have seen, considerable impetus and widespread support from the connection. After their ways had parted, British pacifism was left without representation in parliament, except for a solitary bishop, a Quaker independent, and a handful of Labour pacifists in the two Houses.

In the summer of 1935 Bertrand Russell, in answer to a prominent supporter of collective security who now urged that League action was equivalent *mutatis mutandis* to the beneficial measures taken by medieval kings to quell their turbulent barons, had replied: "I am against a League war in present circumstances because the anti-League powers are strong. The analogy is not King *v.* Barons, but the Wars of the Roses." [37] Whether collective security, if firmly applied, would have been successful in stemming the expansionist powers of the thirties without war is a question to which no conclusive answer can be given, since, in fact, the policy was never followed with any measure of consistency. Most pacifists by this time, however, believed that collective security meant war. It can well be argued that any alternative policy involved equal risk of war, as well as the likelihood that war if it did come would be fought in much less advantageous circumstances for the anti-aggressor powers. The political policy that large sections of the pacifist movement in Britain and America, rejecting not only collective security but also isolationism and national preparedness, promoted now was that of unilateral disarmament.

Unilateralism was urged in many cases not so much because its proponents put forward some form of nonviolent resistance as an alternative way of defending humane values—the question (to quote from Russell again) was considered to be "quantitative." In addition, the unpleasantness which the possibility of enemy occupation might entail was found to be "infinitely less terrible than

the consequences of a war, even if it ended in complete victory." [38]
Like most of the military experts in the thirties, pacifists over-
estimated the effects of air warfare and underestimated the effectiveness of defense against the bomber which, it was believed, would
always get through. Mass destruction of cities, millions killed by
bombs and poison gas, largescale disorganization of the civilian
population, and even the total extinction of civilized life and a
reversion to barbarism in belligerent countries: this was the
picture painted of the outcome of a future war. We cannot be
sure today, in the age of nuclear warfare, if it was not the time-
table rather than the prognostication itself, which was incorrect.
Yet it certainly proved an exaggeration in respect to World War
II, despite the terrible moral and material damage wrought by that
conflict.

The mistake made by the pacifist movement in the half-decade
before World War II was in trying to sell pacifism as an immediately
viable political program without imparting sufficient insight into
what its adoption would require or attempting to develop in any
detail the positive aspects of nonviolent action as an alternative
to military power. Fear of war was not by any means the only
important factor leading to the rapid expansion of pacifism in the
English-speaking world in the thirties (as some critics of pacifism
have implied); it is true, however, that in its propaganda the movement did play unduly on the widely spread feelings of horror at
the prospect of another world war. Understandably, pacifists, like
most other people in the West, found it hard to comprehend the
potentiality for evil of the Nazi and other totalitarian regimes and
their capacity to dupe their own peoples by the mass communications media. Pacifists almost to a man condemned both antisemitism
and the repressive aspects of Fascist ideology and practice. They
rejected any suggestion of supporting Hitler and Mussolini as a
bulwark against Communism. But they failed to consider properly
the implications of pacifism and nonviolence in relation to a totalitarian dictatorship equipped with all the means of suppression
provided by modern science.

If 1935 had at last sorted out the supporters of collective security
from the pacifists proper, 1936 brought the beginning of the Civil
War in Spain and a rift between pacifism and the antimilitarism
of the radical left, which had been foreshadowed earlier in the

debates within the peace movement following the Russian Revolution. What attitude should pacifists adopt if, as in Spain, right wing elements supported by the military attempted to overthrow a democratically elected government by force? Was it possible to urge nonviolent resistance in these circumstances? Or might pacifists make a distinction (as, for instance, the American peace movement had done at the time of the war for the Union) between international war and civil war, maintaining a testimony against the one while regarding the other merely as an extension of the legitimate police functions of the state? Even the anarchists in Spain were supporting the Republican government. As the fighting ground on, however, it became increasingly hard to regard it as anything else but war.

As in the not dissimilar question of military action under the League, war resisters who actively supported the Loyalist war effort tended to entirely abandon their belief in pacifism: Fenner Brockway, the founder of the British No-Conscription Fellowship in 1914, and the American socialist leader, Norman Thomas, who had played a leading role in the Fellowship of Reconciliation, are two such cases. The continuance of the war caused pacifists increasing uneasiness and generated a rising tension, which sought outlet in such activities as the relief of the victims of war, for pacifists' emotions were largely committed on the Loyalist side.

In regard to the Munich crisis of 1938 the pacifist dilemma expressed itself in different terms. A revision of the Versailles settlement and the claims of national self-determination had both long been planks in the pacifists' political platform. The demands of the Sudeten German minority in Czechoslovakia and Hitler's backing of these demands appeared at first sight by no means unreasonable. In themselves the demands provided no justification for unleashing another war, this time in defense of Czechoslovakia's integrity. These sentiments were widely held in Western countries: in fact they formed the intellectual superstructure erected by the architects of appeasement. For pacifists, Czechoslovakia (still less Poland in 1939) did not supply the emotional associations of Spain. Thus in the months before Munich, the pacifist press, as a perusal of the files of the English pacifist weekly *Peace News* for that period reveals, differed little in tone or in the nature of its comment on the Czechoslovak crisis from the organs of

appeasement. Lacking much knowledge of the historical background of Central Europe, its publicists only too often served up
the German viewpoint and pleaded for its consumption on grounds
of moral principle. In a not ignoble desire to avoid war they
confused a principled pacifism with the politics of surrender. As
a friendly critic has remarked, Munich "finally exposed the weakness of pacifist political propaganda." [39]

The same weakness was exemplified across the Atlantic in many
of the utterances and activities of American pacifists, especially
among the more politically involved. The Emergency Peace Campaign, which was started in 1936 as a result of Quaker initiative
and was led largely by pacifists, endeavored to find a middle way
between isolationism and collective security. In striving to ensure
American neutrality in case of European war, the Campaign was
eventually driven into alliance, however unwillingly, with the
isolationist forces, whose creed was basically opposed to the internationalism of the pacifist movement. This trend was accentuated
after the actual outbreak of war in September 1939. Politically
minded pacifists for the most part felt that the conflict was the inevitable outcome of the unrectified mistakes of the past, that
essentially it was being fought to maintain an unjust *status quo,*
that whatever the war's outcome, decency and democracy would
disappear in Europe, and thus only a neutral, noncombatant
America would be able to preserve the humanity and freedom
for which the Western powers claimed to be fighting. "Somebody
ought to be left the means to put the world together again if that
is possible," wrote Villard. A desire to prevent at any cost America's
entry into the war led Villard, the veteran liberal, who genuinely
abhorred everything that smacked of Fascism or dictatorship, into
virtual alliance with such right wing, isolationist groups as the
America First Committee. In 1941 we even find him praising the
pro-Nazi and antisemite Colonel Charles A. Lindbergh and calling
his stand against American involvement in war "magnificent." [40]
As in Britain, tactical collaboration with political elements basically
hostile to everything for which pacifism stood, solely because of
their opposition to the current war, aroused intense misgiving
and a strongly negative reaction in some sections of the pacifist
movement. This was especially true of those pacifists who stressed
the moral and religious case against war.

The Peace Pledge Union

The years which witnessed the exodus first of the League internationalists and then of the social militants from the pacifist movement saw in Great Britain the genesis of a new organizational center for pacifist activities: the Peace Pledge Union. For half a decade the PPU infused new life into the British pacifist movement. The hundred thousand or more members whom it recruited within a short time were mostly new to the movement; few of them had joined an antiwar society before, many were young people in their late teens or in their twenties. Never before had an organization pledged to complete pacifism enlisted such enthusiastic support; never again were so many potential conscientious objectors to war enrolled under one banner. Historians of Britain in the 1930s have mostly either ignored the PPU altogether or dismissed it as a front for appeasement—or at best a collection of naive "do-gooders." Both verdicts are unjust. The PPU was a typical example of the moral impulse of the time. For all its shortcomings, it represented a genuine and significant protest against the evils of modern war.

The Union originated in a letter which Canon "Dick" Sheppard sent to the press in October 1934 asking for the names of those ready to sign a declaration renouncing war and expressing their determination not to support another conflict. He modeled his pledge on one devised a year earlier by the equally popular American pacifist preacher Harry Emerson Fosdick for an Armistice Sunday sermon. At the beginning Sheppard had not intended to found a new organization; the response to his appeal, however, even though it was confined at first to men, was so large that he soon took steps to set up a permanent body of war resisters. The PPU came formally into existence in 1936. Sheppard was a clergyman of the Church of England, a popular preacher and broadcaster, and a talented organizer. One of his early collaborators, the novelist Rose Macaulay, has written: "He had every gift for running a mixed team, and a very mixed team his Peace Pledge Union members were; . . . he was probably the only person who understood all their various points of view and angles of approach. A Christian [pacifist] himself . . . so far from regarding this as the only creditable or genuine approach, he said that it made pacifism simple and easy for him, as compared with that of his non-Christian friends." [41] Anyone prepared to say no to modern war was welcome in the PPU.[42]

The PPU had a formidable array of sponsors including a retired general ("a lifetime of professional soldiering has brought me, by painful ways, to the realization that all war is wrong, is senseless," he confessed[43]), a number of persons prominent in the literary and artistic worlds, an array of dignitaries from both the established church and the nonconformist bodies, and leading representatives of the World War I generation of war resisters alongside veterans of that conflict, like Dick Sheppard himself, who had subsequently become pacifists. The Union possessed not only well-known names, but was able to harness the enthusiasm of the young to create a crusade of formidable dimensions. Local PPU groups sprang up throughout the country; there were as many as 800 functioning at the height of the campaign. A lively weekly newspaper, *Peace News,* commenced publication in 1936. Bookshops and open-air meetings, study groups and traveling peace-caravans helped to spread the message.

The only snag was that, beyond a negative pledge of war renunciation, the message purveyed was exceedingly nebulous. We find a Tory pacifist (a very rare bird, it must be admitted) castigating the PPU for its left wing sympathies.[44] Others criticized it for its alleged connection with extreme right wing groups like the British People's Party and even for harboring crypto-Nazi tendencies. It is true that most PPU members belonged, often rather vaguely, to the left; but it is also true that many of them approved, with considerable reservations, the Conservative-backed policies of appeasement that found their climax in Munich. The average PPU member probably felt that peace-pledging was the surest way to prevent war from again breaking out. After September 1939, since this hope proved to be an illusion, many at once abandoned pacifism for support of war. This fact alone would account for the decline in numbers that ensued after the declaration of hostilities. In addition, as in similar undertakings, many signatures to the peace pledge were purely nominal; in such cases those signing did not feel it incumbent on them to take any further part in the Union's activities.

The PPU faced the dilemma with which every mass movement of reform is confronted. Its promoters had to decide whether, on the one hand, to agitate on a broad platform and thus in all likelihood limit the number of its adherents through the difficulty of reaching consensus on a wide number of issues or, on the other, to base their campaign on a single demand and risk reducing its program to meaninglessness by the need to accommodate all. At various times in the past, great moral crusades have achieved success by a single-minded concentration on one issue: antislavery, for instance, or temperance, or women's rights. The PPU in its campaign against war had one great disadvantage: it had no control over time or circumstance. It could neither bring sufficient influence to bear on those in whose hands the issues of peace or war then lay, nor could it win time to slowly sway opinion toward the adoption of non-violent techniques and attitudes. Despite its errors in tactics and in judgment, however, the prewar PPU expressed a sincere attempt to create from the widespread, but hitherto amorphous sentiment for peace, an unambiguously pacifist movement.

POLITICS AND THE GOSPEL OF RECONCILIATION

Pacifism presents in most acute form perhaps the problem of the place of morality in political life. This is particularly true of Christian pacifism. Hans J. Morgenthau has spoken in this connection of "an element of tragedy," for "it is the very function of Christian ethics to call upon man to comply with a code of moral conduct with which, by virtue of his nature, he cannot comply." [45] True, in the twentieth century many religious pacifists have shared the tendency of liberal Christianity to regard man as perfectable; modern Quakerism has frequently interpreted the Society of Friends' belief in "that of God in every man" as implying humanity's essential goodness. Yet, even outside the Mennonite communities, there have still been in this century many pacifists who view war as sin, as the result of man's sinfulness. For liberal Christians, too, both pacifist and nonpacifist, the problem remains of accounting for the continuing presence of violence in domestic and international life.

Have the injunctions of the Sermon on the Mount relevance outside the sphere of purely personal relations? The majority view within the Christian churches through the centuries has, of course, been that, in preserving order within the state and repelling attack from without, Christian authorities are not required to interpret the Beatitudes too literally. Many Christians have also maintained that when at the behest of the magistrate the Christian citizen is obliged to gird on his sword, the responsibility for bloodshed rests upon his rulers. In the interwar years two aspects of the problem, above all others, exercised the minds of religious pacifists. In the first place, what was the relationship between violence as expressed in international war and violence as revealed in the existing capitalist economic order? Could the former be repudiated so long as the latter remained intact? And, secondly, was it possible for Christians to isolate one evil—war—if, as social beings, they were also implicated in an unchristian society, from which it was impossible to escape. Both questions revealed the increased interest in social affairs manifested widely throughout the Christian churches in the twentieth century.

In our discussion of the political program of the interwar pacifist movement we have drawn most heavily on Great Britain for illustrative material. Now the process will be reversed. It is to a consideration of the American section of the FOR that we must turn for insight into the political outreach and the political dilemmas of the gospel of reconciliation.[46]

The American Fellowship of Reconciliation

The American FOR in the interwar period, though in 1930 it had opened its doors to all with "faith in love and non-violence," remained overwhelmingly Protestant in membership. What is more, it drew its main inspiration from one particular stream in modern American Protestantism: the "Social Gospel." The founder of the Social Gospel movement, Walter Rauschenbusch, had associated himself with the work of the FOR shortly before his death in July 1918. The three major denominations most strongly impregnated with the ideas of the Social Gospel—Methodists, Disciples and Congregationalists—were also those in which the pacifist minority was largest. From the outset most FOR members, and especially the leadership which came to include such socially committed persons as Norman Thomas, Reinhold Niebuhr, Jane Addams, John Haynes Holmes, etc., felt that objection to war must be buttressed by an effort to transform society. They shared the hopes of the protagonists of the Social Gospel to be able so to transform human society that it approximates the Kingdom of God. The coming of the Kingdom was for them no Utopian dream but a real possibility open to all men on this earth. The elimination of war between nations and the ending of economic exploitation within society were merely different aspects of one struggle: the struggle for the realization of Christ's Kingdom.

Pacifism and the Social Gospel were not necessarily identical. In fact, before 1917 the Social Gospel movement was little, if at all, concerned with issues of war and peace, while religious pacifists had not been greatly interested in the labor question. After World War I, however, members of two of the three historic peace churches on which religious pacifism had been hitherto based, the Quaker Society of Friends and the Church of the Brethren, were influenced in considerable numbers by the Social Gospel. (Mennonites, on the other hand, were almost entirely untouched by this movement.) They began to advocate varying degrees of social reform as an integral part of their peace testimony. In addition, during the interwar years, churchmen in nonpacifist denominations were drawn by their sympathy for the Social Gospel to repudiate war as an obstacle to the fulfilment of their social aspirations. By 1928, when it merged with the FOR, the Fellowship for a Christian Social Order, which Kirby Page and Sherwood Eddy started in 1921, had succeeded in winning over to pacifism many members whose first endeavor had been the changing of the social order. For both socialistically inclined Christian pacifists and antimilitaristic Christian socialists, the FOR acted as a fulcrum on which they could base their strategy for defeating both capitalism and war.

Since capitalism now appeared as a primary cause of human conflict, pacifists affiliated to the FOR increasingly sought the seeds of war in the domestic scene. They detected them in the exploitation of labor by capital and in the brutal suppression of the workers' efforts to organize, a suppression carried out by capital backed by a state which it dominated. "Capitalism is based upon coercion and violence," wrote John C. Bennett in 1933, "it is destructive of human life and human values on a colossal scale . . . a ruthless system which results in starvation, disease, death, warped bodies and souls for millions." [47] As the depression and its aftermath closed down on the country, it seemed clearer than ever to many FOR members, despite their middle-class origins and status, that the fight against war could, paradoxically, be pursued only by means of the class war. But could the class war be waged with the weapons of nonviolence alone? This was the question that continually haunted the FOR from the late twenties onward.

The FOR stand had thus ceased to be an inward-looking sectarian witness against war such as the historic peace churches had upheld for many centuries. For the FOR now the rationale for the organization's pacifism, as a historian of the Social Gospel has well remarked, became "its effectiveness as a social technique adapted to every social problem . . . the drive of energy was outward." [48] FOR members regarded themselves no longer as an elect minority leavening the world, but as the nonviolent vanguard of those political forces whose task it was to inaugurate the classless society. From this new Christian social order, capitalist exploitation would be banished along with international war. In the twenties and early thirties at least, the main dynamic of the FOR's thinking came to be directed, therefore, toward exploring the relationship between violence and an unjust domestic order. It was the use of physical force in the class war that aroused the most heated debates in the Fellowship. It was not the problem of the magistrate's sword turned against a foreign aggressor that generated the first major schism in its ranks, but that of the policeman's baton raised against workers struggling to throw off the yoke of capitalism.

"I am determined to take the position of a conscientious objector in the labor movement, if the issue of a violent class war is ever clearly drawn, but I hope that this time may never come." So wrote a young minister Harold Rotzel, who was active at the time in labor organization, in the March 1926 issue of the FOR's lively unofficial journal, *The World Tomorrow*. A few years later came the depression accompanied by a steep rise in labor unrest and a heightened sense of class antagonism, even the threat of civil war. Many in the FOR had joined the organization in the belief that their ideal ends—social justice and a classless society—might best be achieved through peaceful means. The modern state in any case was in possession of such overwhelming physical power as to make the barricades appear an outmoded method of waging the social war. Violence appeared pragmatically a useless weapon in this struggle. "But," as the theologian H. Richard Niebuhr wrote, "the realistic purpose dominated. It was not the pacifism of non-resistance but the pacifism of non-violent aggression." [49] Once the efficacy of nonviolent means in bringing the Kingdom appeared doubtful, hesitancy appeared, too, concerning continued adherence to an abstract nonviolence. And even before this, FOR members were already to be found on both sides of the Atlantic,[50] who reserved the right of the Soviet Union, the worker's state, to use violence against the threat of capitalist aggression.

A. J. Muste, who in 1919 had been Rotzel's colleague in leading a strike of textile mill workers at Lawrence, Massachusetts, was one of those whose attempt to face the dilemma led him temporarily to repudiate pacifism altogether and to espouse the Trotskyite variant of Marxism.

> I came to embrace the view [he has written] that only revolutionary action by the working class and other elements under the leadership of a vanguard party could bring in a new social order, and that revolutionary action did not in principle exclude violence. Violence in taking over power would almost certainly be necessary and hence justified. . . . For a time I tried to reconcile my Christian pacifism with involvement in the struggle as it was then taking place. Gradually . . . I came to feel that I was more and more a caricature of a Christian pacifist and only a half-baked revolutionary, and that I had to choose. I chose revolution, recognizing that it might involve violence. I did not, having given up my pacifism, think that I could remain a Christian.[51]

In the late twenties and early thirties, many FOR activists were asking themselves the same questions as Muste was doing. They had already shown their readiness, indeed their anxiety, to join the picket line in industrial disputes and to act as labor organizers where worker leadership was still weak. They were prominent in the counsels of the Socialist Party; they took part in such lively experiments in working class education as the Brookwood Labor College. But was this commitment sufficient? Could the Kingdom of God ever be ushered in, and righteousness established, if Christians relied only on conversion and persuasion vis-à-vis "a privileged class which . . . may be described as the aggressor in the class-war." [52] Is there after all, as Reinhold Niebuhr enquired with repeated insistence, any absolute difference between nonviolent and violent means of coercion, which should lead one to exclude the latter under all circumstances as an instrument for changing society? [53] If a Christian is presented in politics with a choice between justice and love, on which side should his choice lie?

Though some FOR members denied that a decision of this kind was ever necessary, many were troubled. At last, in 1933, came a crisis within the organization on this issue.

When, in the last quarter of that year, a questionnaire was circulated among the membership, about 10 percent of those who answered (996 replying out of an active roll of 6,395) agreed—with varying degrees of enthusiasm—to the employment of violence by the workers to overthrow capitalism. In this number, however, were included three of the four secretaries of the FOR. And the statement which gained greatest assent was the fourth: that "in case the legal owners of the essential industries resort to armed force in an attempt to maintain or to regain control of their property, [members would] refuse to use violence against them, but offer to serve the workers as a social worker among their families, as a maintainer of food supplies, as a nurse or stretcher bearer, or in other nonviolent ways." [54] Despite the small percentage of members who participated in the poll it seemed clear that the Fellowship was still overwhelmingly in favor of nonviolence in class as well as in international war. In regard to the former, however, many members now took up a position of sympathetic nonbelligerency ready to support the proletarian side in every way short of combatant service. The Fellowship, then, was not against coercion, provided it were nonviolent coercion and exercised on behalf of the proletariat.

Publication of these results in December 1933 led to the resignation of the executive secretary, Joseph B. Matthews, who had been foremost in espousing militancy in the workers' cause. Matthews in fact was at this time collaborating closely with Communist front organizations and wished to harness the FOR to the Communist sponsored peace movement. He accused "the pure pacifists" within the FOR, despite their "political innocence" vis-à-vis "the class struggle," of rigging the questionnaire so as to produce the results they desired. "The larger the unearned income, the greater the faith in love, moral suasion and education," he exclaimed sarcastically (without, however, producing evidence for this thesis). "An almost perfect demonstration," he called the results of the poll, "that those who have a vital stake in privilege are to be found arrayed against the only methods which, according to history, promise the slightest success in overthrowing the rulers of a parasitic order." [55]

Among those who soon followed Matthews out of the FOR was Reinhold Niebuhr. "I share, roughly speaking, the political position of Mr. Matthews," Niebuhr wrote at the beginning of 1934 in the *Christian Century*,[56] "as a Marxian and as a Christian" (though without Matthew's bitterness against the pure pacifists or his unqualified ardor for Soviet communism). For Niebuhr neutrality in the class struggle was impossible. Christians, who stood—as did most people in the FOR—for a more just social order than the existing capitalist one, could not reasonably stand aside if violence were needed to establish the new order. Violence indeed was implicit in capitalism: either negatively in the form of starvation and economic pressures on the working class or positively as in the case of police brutality. To maintain that one could escape implication in violence was a form of "ethical perfectionism." To refuse to choose between two inevitable species of violence was to shirk social responsibility. "There is no choice except between more and less violence. One cannot distinguish between violent and nonviolent coercion in our social system." Since love cannot be perfectly incarnated in men, Christians must recognize "the tragic character of man's social life" and, while still acknowledging a degree of imperfection in the course chosen, opt for "the devil of vengeance," which offered the chance of creating a more just society, in place of "the devil of hypocrisy," that is, a formal nonviolence cloaking the realities of class war. Reconciliation would come not from ignoring the violence endemic in capitalist society, but from so transforming society, if need be by violent means, that the seeds of violence would be removed from its midst.

With the departure from the FOR of the Christian Marxists, and the consequent cooling of relations between the main body representing American pacifism and the Communist sponsored peace movement, the way was open for the FOR to explore the implications of a nonviolent alternative to class war, to which the majority was wedded. In fact, little was done in the period prior to America's entry into the war in 1941 to investigate the practical possibilities of nonviolent struggle on the domestic scene. The publication in 1934 of Gregg's book on the *Power of Nonviolence* certainly

stimulated interest in the subject, which had already been awakened
by Gandhi's civil disobedience campaigns in British India. In 1936,
in the course of a strike, several FOR members active in the
trade union movement, who had been studying Gregg's work,
organized a "lie-down" in an effort to prevent strike-breakers
from entering the plant. But this remained an isolated instance.
Though many FOR members showed interest in Gandhian techniques, others cleaved to the older concept of the pacifist's role in
society as one of mediation between two conflicting positions without actually taking sides.

In fact, from the mid-thirties the FOR's attention had begun to
turn from the domestic to the international scene. Whereas the
debate hitherto had been concerned primarily with the relationship
between nonviolence and social revolution, interest moved over now
to the problem of war itself. Here Christian pacifism's most
trenchant critic was the FOR's one-time chairman, Reinhold
Niebuhr, writing no longer in the role of a Marxian Christian
anxious to greet the coming of the Kingdom but as the disciple of
the pessimistic school of Neo-Orthodoxy associated in particular
with the name of the Swiss theologian, Karl Barth.

For Niebuhr pacifism still retained *raison d'être* within the church
if it eschewed all attempts to claim political relevance. The otherworldly defenselessness of groups such as the Mennonites witnessed
indeed to a legitimate striving for perfection in a fallen world; it
represented "a genuine impulse in the heart of Christianity." Jesus
himself had taught "an absolute and uncompromising ethic" of
love and nonresistance: Niebuhr found the efforts of nonpacifist
theologians to deny this "futile and pathetic." But the kind of
pacifism represented by the FOR was a heresy. Rejecting "the
Christian doctrine of original sin as an outmoded bit of pessimism,"
its protagonists had asserted the possibility of overcoming evil in
this world by means of all-conquering love. This, in Niebuhr's
view, was a dangerous illusion. It derived, as did liberal theology
itself, not from the New Testament but from the humanist view
of man which had emerged with the Renaissance. There was no
such thing as "non-violent politics," for politics was the realm
of sin. Political goals could never be pursued with wholly moral
means. "It is because men are sinners that justice can be achieved
only by a certain degree of coercion on the one hand, and by

resistance to coercion and tyranny on the other hand." Where the objective situation presented only a choice between submission to injustice or war (both admitted evils from the Christian point of view), war might be less inconsistent with the law of love than not to fight. Why, asked Niebuhr, did pacifists isolate war from a number of social evils? Why did they pretend that by sacrificing justice to nonviolence they were absolving themselves from guilt?

The pacifist witness, Niebuhr thought, so long as it did not confine itself within the limits of a purely vocational framework, was usually "corrupted by self-righteousness." It failed to acknowledge the necessity of making imperfect choices in a sinful world. Again, because all men were sinners, Christians were not thereby exempt from the obligation of resisting evil in others, or else no human action would be possible.

In answer to Niebuhr's critique, pacifists maintained that, despite the reality of human sin, his pessimism was out of tune with the New Testament. "Jesus," wrote the Scottish theologian Professor G. H. C. Macgregor, perhaps the most cogent spokesman on the FOR side, "saw the world always and everywhere as God's world." Christians, therefore, did have the obligation to strive to apply Jesus' ethic in politics as well as in personal relations. True, tension would always exist between the demands of the law of love and the exigencies of the political situation. But, wrote Macgregor cleverly paraphrasing Niebuhr's own words, an ethical ideal is not made politically irrelevant by the impossibility of its perfect fulfilment here and now. In the modern world, moreover, war presented the most pressing moral problem; it was "the test case" for Christianity, the most obvious denial of the redemptive means which Jesus had postulated and of the active outgoing love from which alone reconciliation could flow.[57]

Niebuhr once called the FOR "a kind of Quaker conventicle inside of the traditional church." And indeed the pacifism of the FOR, like the traditional peace testimony of the Quakers, was an essay in moralizing politics. It aimed, as it were, at recreating the seventeenth-century Quaker experiment in Pennsylvania but on an extended scale. The United States, the whole world, must be molded into a Quaker-like peaceable kingdom because the Kingdom of God on earth was a realm of peace. But with the rise of the dictatorships and the deteriorating international situation of the late thirties and early forties, it became increasingly difficult to present pacifism as an immediately viable and responsible political policy. The peace witness of the FOR, which originated in the Social Gospel's endeavor to realize the Kingdom of God on the international as well as the national plane, reverted more closely to an earlier type of pacifism and began increasingly to take on the coloring of a sectarian creed. In the years before Pearl Harbor, with the exception of A. J. Muste who, after his return to the pacifist fold, had continued to argue for a national acceptance of pacifism as the sole realistic way out of the impasse and to plead for nonviolence as an empirical technique for achieving social objectives, the FOR leaders stood for a pacifism that now judged more and more by standards other than political realism. It largely discarded the utilitarian arguments and the pragmatic justifications. The Kingdom of God on earth remained its goal but the politics of the Kingdom might lead by way of the Cross.

NOTES

1. Roger N. Baldwin, *Liberty under the Soviets* (New York: Vanguard Press, 1928), p. 268. See Chap. XVIII for his survey of "Conscientious Objectors and Pacifist Propaganda" in Russia.

2. Bart de Ligt expounded such ideas in his book *The Conquest of Violence*, translated from the French (London: George Routledge & Sons, Ltd., 1937).

3. See Martha Steinitz, *Die englischen Kriegsdienstverweigerer* (Berlin: Verlag "Neues Vaterland," 1921), Appendix: "Klassischer Pazifismus und Kriegsdienstverweigerung," pp. 27–32.

4. Rennie Smith, *Peace Verboten* (London: Hutchinson & Co., Ltd., 1943), pp. 45–53.

5. Detailed information concerning the interwar peace movement in Great Britain (as well as in other lands) may be found in successive issues of the *Peace Year Book* (London: National Peace Council).

6. *The Christian International* (London), no. 1 (April, 1920), p. 9.

7. Quoted in Grace M. Beaton, *Twenty Years' Work in the War Resisters' International* (Enfield, Middlesex: WRI, 1945), p. 5.

8. See Gertrude Bussey and Margaret Tims, *Women's International League for Peace and Freedom 1915–1965* (London: George Allen & Unwin Ltd., 1965).

9. Leslie D. Shaffer, "Conscription and European Quakerism," *Friends Intelligencer* (Philadelphia), vol. 101, no. 46 (November 11, 1944), pp. 738, 739. See also Willis H. Hall, *Quaker International Work in Europe since 1914* (Chambéry, Savoie: Imprimeries Réunies, 1938).

10. *Modern Martyrs: Documents Collected by the War Resisters' International* (Enfield: WRI, 1927), opposite p. 1. In Eastern Europe conscientious objectors in the interwar years were drawn almost exclusively

from such sects as the Nazarenes, Seventh-Day Adventists or Jehovah's Witnesses or from isolated Tolstoyans. The influence Tolstoy's writings could still exert on religiously minded Slav peasants is shown in the following letter dictated by the illiterate mother of a young Polish country boy imprisoned for refusing to undergo military training: "Five years ago there appeared what was at first a remarkable but joyful change in him. He was constantly reading. At my request he formed the habit of telling me what he had been reading, or he read it to me—and then I became convinced, to my great joy, that he was reading religious books. So that the name of Leo Tolstoy became known to me. . . . My son, who was then a lad of 17 or 18, began more to be sharply distinguished from others of his age. When he was 21 he appeared before the Recruiting Commission and explained straightforwardly and plainly that he would not serve as a soldier because he loved his neighbour and therefore could not learn to murder him." From a leaflet (1937) in Archives, Swarthmore College Peace Collection: War Resisters' International, DG 39, Box 5.

11. Dr. Hans Kohn in *War Resisters in Many Lands* (Enfield, WRI, 1928), pp. 34–36. From the 1930s Kohn became a severe critic of pacifism as a political movement. See for example his book *The Twentieth Century: A Mid-way Account of the Western World* (New York: The Macmillan Company, 1949), pp. 204, 205.

12. Ethelwyn Best and Bernard Pike, *International Voluntary Service for Peace 1920–1946* (London: George Allen & Unwin Ltd., 1948), Appendix IV.

13. Quoted in John K. Nelson, *The Peace Prophets* (Chapel Hill: The University of North Carolina Press, 1967), p. 45. I owe much that follows in this section to Nelson's book.

14. Arthur Ponsonby, *Falsehood in War-time* (London: George Allen & Unwin Ltd., 1928), p. 192.

15. Quoted in Nelson, *op. cit.,* p. 55.

16. A good example is to be found in the bestseller by Beverley Nichols, *Cry Havoc!* (London: Jonathan Cape, 1933).

17. C. E. M. Joad, *Why War?* (Harmondsworth, Middlesex: Penguin Books Limited, 1939), p. 231.

18. Nelson, *op. cit.,* p. 122.

19. George Lansbury, "Why Pacifists Should Be Socialists," *Fact,* no. 7 (October, 1937), pp. 37, 38.

20. Aldous Huxley, ed., *An Encyclopaedia of Pacifism* (London: Chatto & Windus, 1937), pp. 100, 101. Cf. p. 41: "Co-operation is applied pacifism."

21. See Herbert Read, *The Politics of the Unpolitical* (London: Routledge, 1943), pp. 1–12. Much the same thought is expressed in a letter from Aldous Huxley to Kingsley Martin, dated 30 July 1939 (printed in Martin's *Editor: A Second Volume of Autobiography 1931–45* [London: Hutchinson, 1968], p. 204): "Religion can have no politics except the creation of small-scale societies of chosen individuals outside and on the margin of the essentially unviable large-scale societies, whose nature dooms them to self-frustration and suicide."

22. Huxley's *Ends and Means* (London: Chatto & Windus, 1937) was quite recently described by Kingsley Martin in *War, History, and Human Nature* (Bombay: Asia Publishing House, 1959), p. 79, as "the most logical statement of the pacifist case yet made by a Western author."

23. A. Huxley, *What are you going to do about it? The Case for Constructive Peace* (London: Chatto & Windus, 1936), pp. 14, 17.

24. de Ligt, *op. cit.*, pp. 281–285.

25. Letter quoted in Earl Charles Chatfield, Jr., "Pacifism and American Life: 1914 to 1941" (Ph.D. diss., Vanderbilt University, 1965), p. 227.

26. Cf. A. Ponsonby, *Now is the Time: An Appeal for Peace* (London: Leonard Parson, 1925), pp. 109, 129.

27. *No More War* (London), vol. I, no. 5 (June, 1922), p. 5.

28. A. J. P. Taylor, *English History 1914–1945* (Oxford: The Clarendon Press, 1965), p. 299, n. 3.

29. Winston S. Churchill, *The Second World War*, Vol. I: *The Gathering Storm* (London: Cassell & Co. Ltd., 1948), pp. 66, 67.

30. For a brief but not unperceptive analysis of this "emotional pacifism," see R. G. D. Laffan, *Survey of International Affairs 1938*, Vol. II, revised ed. (London: Oxford University Press for the Royal Institute of International Affairs, 1951), pp. 165, 166.

31. I have based my discussion on Einstein's pacifism mainly on Otto Nathan and Heinz Norden (eds.), *Einstein on Peace* (New York: Simon and Schuster, 1960), esp. pp. 91, 98, 100, 101, 117–119, 124, 232, 233, 239, 246; WRI International Council Communication No. 161 (5 September 1933), in Archives, Swarthmore College Peace Collection. See also Harold F. Bing, "Einstein and the WRI," *War Resistance* (London), vol. 2, no. 23 (1967), pp. 10–15, 19.

32. A. A. Milne, *Peace with Honour: An Enquiry into the War Convention* (London: Methuen & Co., 1934), p. 144.

33. The official history is given in Adelaide Livingstone *et. al., The Peace Ballot* (London: Victor Gollancz Ltd., 1935).

34. *The Role of the Peace Movements in the 1930's: Who Was for Munich?* Pamphlet No. 1 (London: University Group in Defence Policy, 1959), p. 15.

35. For one example of this tendency out of many, see Sherwood Eddy, *Eighty Adventurous Years: An Autobiography* (New York: Harper & Brothers, 1955), p. 104.

36. Taylor, *op. cit.*, p. 142; G. Lansbury, *My Pilgrimage for Peace* (New York: Henry Holt and Company, 1938), pp. 6, 7; Alan Bullock, *The Life and Times of Ernest Bevin,* Vol. I (London: Heinemann, 1960), pp. 565–571.

37. Letter dated 7 August 1935, in Martin, *op. cit.*, p. 194.

38. Bertrand Russell, *Which Way to Peace?* (London: Michael Joseph Ltd., 1936), p. 139. Cf. Alan Wood, *Bertrand Russell: The Passionate Sceptic* (London: Unwin Books, 1963), pp. 163–165.

39. Wolf Mendl, "British Pacifist Policy: A Study of Pacifist Attitudes to Some International Problems, 1919–1938" (1954), typescript in Archives, Swarthmore College Peace Collection, p. 46.

40. Quotation from Nelson, *op. cit.*, p. 58; Michael Wreszin, *Oswald Garrison Villard: Pacifist at War* (Bloomington: Indiana University Press, 1965), p. 268.

41. Quoted in R. Ellis Roberts, *H. R. L. Sheppard: Life and Letters* (London: John Murray, 1942), p. 277.

42. Sheppard was the author of *We Say "No": The Plain Man's Guide to Pacifism* (London: John Murray, 1935), not, however, one of the best expositions of Christian pacifism.

43. Brigadier General F. P. Crozier, *The Men I Killed* (London: Michael Joseph Ltd., 1937), p. 23. Crozier is not the only general to be converted

to complete pacifism in the twentieth century. In France, Percin and Verraux; in Germany, von Deimling and von Schönaich are other examples.

44. H. W. J. Edwards, *Young England* (London: Hutchinson & Co., 1938), Chap. VII.

45. In his Foreword to Robert O. Byrd, *Quaker Ways in Foreign Policy* (Toronto: University of Toronto Press, 1960), pp. vii–ix.

46. For Christian pacifism in the interwar United States, see in general Vernon H. Holloway, "A Review of American Religious Pacifism," *Religion in Life* (New York), vol. 19, no. 3 (Summer, 1950), pp. 367–379. This is drawn from his Yale University Ph.D. dissertation (which I have not consulted), "American Pacifism between the Two Wars, 1919–1941" (1949). There is unfortunately no adequate study of the American FOR; John Nevin Sayre, *The Story of the Fellowship of Reconciliation 1915–1935* (New York: FOR, 1935) is only a pamphlet.

47. Quoted in Nelson, *op. cit.*, p. 84.

48. Donald B. Meyer, *The Protestant Search for Political Realism, 1919–1941* (Berkeley and Los Angeles: University of California Press, 1961), p. 51.

49. Quotations from *ibid.*, pp. 95, 439.

50. For example, the Englishman John Lewis, *The Case against Pacifism* (London: George Allen & Unwin Ltd., 1940), p. 5: "Although a member of the Fellowship of Reconciliation and the No More War Movement, it had never been possible for me to criticize the Russians for their defensive policy." Cf., though, his article in *No More War*, vol. 4, no. 1 (February, 1925), p. 5: "Why a Christian Church Must Oppose All War," which he appears to have forgotten.

51. Nat Hentoff, ed., *The Essays of A. J. Muste* (Indianapolis, New York, Kansas City: The Bobbs-Merrill Company, Inc., 1967), p. 75. See also Hentoff, *Peace Agitator: The Story of A. J. Muste* (New York: The Macmillan Company, 1963). The most recent study is by Noam Chomsky, "The Revolutionary Pacifism of A. J. Muste," *Gandhi Marg* (New Delhi), vol. 12, no. 2 (46) (April 1968), pp. 156–179.

52. *Christ and the Class War* (London: International FOR, 1929), p. 2.

53. See, for example, Reinhold Niebuhr, *Moral Man and Immoral Society* (New York and London: Charles Scribner's & Sons, 1932), p. 251.

54. Quoted in Nelson, *op. cit.*, p. 75.

55. J. B. Matthews, "Is Pacifism Counter-Revolutionary?" *New Masses* (New York), 2 January 1934. See also his *Odyssey of a Fellow Traveller* (New York: Mount Vernon Publishers, Inc., 1938), pp. 69, 70, 72, for a not very illuminating account of his connection with the FOR. After traveling with the Communists for a time, Matthews ended up as Senator Joseph McCarthy's henchman for "exposing" Reds among the Protestant clergy.

56. "Why I Leave the FOR," reprinted in D. R. Robertson, ed., *Love and Justice: Selections from the Shorter Writings of Reinhold Niebuhr* (Philadelphia: The Westminster Press, 1957), pp. 254–259. See also Niebuhr's contribution in *Economic Justice* (New Haven, Conn.), vol. 1, no. 9 (November, 1933).

57. Niebuhr's polemics against pacifism are to be found scattered among his later writings. Perhaps his most succinct exposition is in *Why the Christian Church is not Pacifist* (London: Student Christian Movement Press, 1940). G. H. C. Macgregor's *The Relevance of the Impossible* was first published by the British Fellowship of Reconciliation (London, 1941).

V. The Pattern of Conscientious Objection: World War II

ON THE OUTBREAK OF WAR IN SEPTEMBER 1939 A PROMINENT English Quaker theologian said of his two sons, both of military age: "They might feel they had to serve with the Friends' Ambulance Unit or in any relief service Friends might organize; they might feel called to take the absolute position and suffer imprisonment if need be for conscience sake, or they might feel they had to serve with the armed forces. Whatever their decision, they would have my full support. But I told them however they might choose, they would never be entirely happy, and would always have a guilty conscience." [1] They would retain a sense of guilt, he said, because of man's collective responsibility for the sin from which the war had sprung.

By no means all pacifists, either in Britain or America, shared in full this almost Niebuhrian view. In World War II, however, the pacifist movement in both countries shed something of its previous optimism and took on a sectarian, a quasi-vocational coloring to a much larger extent than had been the case in the First World War. In 1914–18 the pacifists who gave the movement its tone had looked forward, despite the discouraging present, to the speedy inauguration of a peaceable world in the years ahead. A quarter of a century later such confidence appeared to many misplaced. Endeavor to slowly infuse society with the pacifist ethic now largely replaced the earlier hopes.

In Great Britain during the so-called "phony" war, that is, until the rapid German advances of the spring and early summer of 1940 culminating in the battle of Dunkirk, the Peace Pledge Union went on pleading the need for a negotiated peace. A slightly eccentric pacifist aristocrat, Hastings, Duke of Bedford, even undertook private efforts to this end. But after Dunkirk, as the PPU's chronicler wrote, "no-one who lived through those days would deny that to continue such a campaign [i.e., for a negotiated peace] was not only useless, but damaging to the pacifist cause." [2]

In beleaguered Britain there still existed a surprising degree of political freedom, even for pacifists. True, in the hectic summer of 1940, the PPU's journal *Peace News* had difficulty both in finding a printer and in circumventing an unofficial boycott of the wholesale news agents. Also, voices were raised demanding its suppression, while the government threatened to prosecute the organization's leaders for displaying an old poster urging men to refuse to fight. But in the end *Peace News* appeared regularly—and legally —throughout the war, although for a time in a much reduced format. As for the poster, the case against the PPU was withdrawn on its agreeing not to put copies on display. In 1940 a bulwark of English liberty, *habeas corpus,* was suspended by parliament. But "Regulation 18B," whereby those suspected by the authorities of sympathy with the enemy could be confined for an indefinite period of time, was employed (with a few exceptions) against Sir Oswald Mosley's British Union of Fascists and allied groups rather than against pacifists.

This moderation, especially if we compare it with the situation either in Britain or the United States in World War I, is indeed striking. It was due in part to the realization by the authorities that the pacifist movement, despite the fears of alarmists, scarcely represented a threat to the security of the country: most pacifists disliked Nazism as much as anyone. It stemmed, too, from the liberal attitude of both administration and general public, which will also appear later from our discussion of the treatment of conscientious objectors in World War II Britain. The fact that ex-pacifists sat in the coalition government formed by Winston Churchill in May 1940 and that a small group of convinced pacifists (mostly members of the Labour Party) existed in the two houses of parliament guaranteed that this minority view would be granted at least some understanding.

At the end of the war, in 1945, the PPU still had nearly 100,000 names on its membership list. There had been of course a number of defections, including several among its sponsors.[3] In the course of the war, as its younger and most active members were caught up in the draft, the Union's activities had slackened. Under the brilliant direction of John Middleton Murry, who took over as editor in July 1940, the Union's *Peace News* gave strong support to the growing movement among pacifists to form income-pooling communities. According to Murry, these cells of a new society were to perform the same task in the contemporary war-ridden world as the Christian monastic orders had done in the dark days following the fall of the Roman Empire. Not all pacifists, however, followed him in this plan, and the communitarian movement in fact proved a passing phase in the history of British pacifism. Equally controversial were other theses expounded by Murry on the pages of his weekly journal: his belief, for instance, that, although Nazism was *per se* a bad system, a *pax germanica* was preferable to the intra-national anarchy that had hitherto existed on the European continent, or his increasingly anti-Soviet stance and fear of Stalinist totalitarianism which eventually led him in 1947 to abandon pacifism altogether.[4] The PPU threw most of its energies into the support of conscientious objectors. Some members were active in the movement to get food relief through the allied blockade to the starving population of occupied Europe. Others backed the Bishop of Chichester's courageous campaign to stop the saturation bombing of German cities (the senseless cruelty of which is being increasingly recognized today).

For the United States, the Japanese attack on the American fleet at Pearl Harbor on December 6, 1941, played the same role as Dunkirk had done for the British in rallying the people behind war against the Axis powers. The prewar pacifist movement in America, as we have seen in an earlier chapter, had been organizationally weaker than its counterpart in Great Britain. Its orientation was in some respects more religious; its involvement in active politics—in the sense of party politics and not the struggle for the Kingdom of God on earth—had been less. Pearl Harbor found a single pacifist in Congress, the liberal Republican, Representative Jeannette Rankin, whose vote then was the only one cast against war. During the war years the American FOR concentrated its efforts on stating the case for Christian pacifism. The historic peace churches—Quakers, Mennonites and the Church of the Brethren—had their hands full in looking after the interests of conscientious objectors and in planning for the day when postwar relief activities would become possible. True, in mid-1943 a leading member of the secularly oriented War Resisters' League, Professor George W. Hartmann, launched a Peace Now Movement. This, however, did not succeed in enlisting the support of more than a fraction of the country's pacifists. By a negotiated settlement, so it was hoped, the Nazi extermination of the Jews, news of which was beginning to percolate through, might have been averted. But most pacifists remained suspicious of Hartmann's movement, especially on account of the support it sought to gain from extreme right wing elements.

In the United States, as in Great Britain, attempts to mount a political antiwar movement were regarded by most pacifists as mistaken. Pacifism remained for the duration an expression of private witness, however frustrating this might seem to some. In both countries, despite the greater threat from without, the violent antagonism aroused in the public mind by conscientious objectors and pacifists in World War I was largely absent. The attitude of the authorities, too, was more tolerant than it had been then; in the United States, freedom of the press remained intact. From the pacifist side there was a greater sense now of unity with their nonpacifist countrymen and a more widespread desire to witness to their faith by service to the community in its hour of need rather than by a merely negative protest.

BRITISH OBJECTORS: SERVICE *v.* WITNESS

Legislative Provision for Conscientious Objection

In 1932 a popular novelist, temporarily in the pacifist camp, had envisaged his appearance before a tribunal in a future war as follows: "I am in the presence of General somebody, a bunch of Colonels and a clerk. My entrance coincides with the renewal of an air-raid outside. It is all rather dramatic, for the air-raid punctuates our arguments quite effectively." [5] In actual fact, although bombs did indeed fall on London and other cities in Britain, the reality was considerably more mundane. The administration of conscientious objection, too, was kept firmly under civilian control throughout the war.

Conscription was reintroduced a few months before the actual outbreak of war on September 3, 1939. In the previous May, a Military Training Act had been passed by Parliament, applying to males reaching the age of 20. In the debates that preceded its enactment both government and opposition spokesmen had talked of the need to avoid penalization of genuine scruples against war. Prime Minister Neville Chamberlain expressed a wish to respect even the absolutist stand. He had served himself on a tribunal during World War I and from his experience then, so he now assured the House, he felt "that it was both a useless and an exasperating waste of time and effort to attempt to force such people to act in a manner which was contrary to their principles." [6]

On September 3 the previous act was replaced by a National Service (Armed Forces) Act, which made all men between the ages of 18 and 40 liable for military service for the duration of the war emergency. At the end of 1941 the age limit was raised to 51; in addition, single women between 20 and 30 were now made liable for the special women's branches of the armed services, which had been set up in the meantime.

Tribunals to deal with conscientious objectors were established under the conscription acts. These tribunals were bodies which, unlike their counterparts in World War I, were not required also to hear general cases of hardship: a duality of purpose which, as we have seen, had not contributed to their efficient functioning in the earlier war. Tribunal members now were, on the whole, well chosen and they attempted to be courteous and fair in most instances. Some were moderately sympathetic to the pacifist case, while not themselves pacifists; a few Quakers and pacifists were appointed to tribunals, but this was very rare. Every tribunal was required by law to include one trade union member, and the whole system was placed under the administration of the Ministry of Labour and National Service (whose head under Churchill's coalition government was the trade union leader, Ernest Bevin). If the application of a woman was being heard, the tribunal had to contain at least one woman member.

As in World War I, tribunals were entitled either to reject an application altogether, if they believed the applicant was insincere, or to give some form of exemption that would meet his conscientious scruples. This exemption might be unconditional, or it might be granted on condition that the applicant undertake some kind of alternative service under civilian control. A third possibility open to a tribunal was to require the applicant to do noncombatant service in the army: as in World War I, a special Non-Combatant Corps was set up within the army in April 1940, although a few objectors also served in the Royal Army Medical Corps or with Pioneer units. The decision of the local tribunal might be appealed either by the applicant or by the Ministry of Labour's representative.

Although the administration of the tribunal system in World War II normally allowed a far more fair hearing to objectors than they received in the previous war, the attempt to assess conscience did not fully succeed. In the first place, most tribunals in judging an applicant's sincerity put greatest reliance on supporting evidence: witnesses who would speak on the applicant's behalf, or letters of recommendation, or a past record of pacifist activity or of social work. Support from a minister of religion usually carried special weight. Those objectors, however sincere, who could not produce testimonials of some kind, were at a distinct disadvantage in presenting their case. Such persons were especially numerous among the youngest age groups called up. Again, many tribunal members experienced difficulty in understanding why most pacifists objected to noncombatant service. The former tended to regard such service as essentially humanitarian; while most objectors considered its basic aim, as with the rest of the army, to be the prosecution of war and not the saving of life. If an objector, asked whether he would help a wounded soldier, replied in the affirmative, he was quite likely to find himself directed by his tribunal to noncombatant duties, even if he had expressed his unwillingness to undertake them. (Objectors, usually through inexperience in argument, occasionally answered this question in the negative, and as a result were often given adverse publicity in the press.) Trouble would have been saved if tribunals had recognized that such applicants, whose objection to combatant service they had acknowledged to be sincere, had also genuine scruples concerning service in the NCC or RAMC. Finally, as the war dragged on and for several years the military situation continued to look extremely bleak, signs of strain began to appear among tribunal members as in the rest of the population. Less patience was shown toward unpopular attitudes; less understanding was displayed of the objectors' point of view.

About 60,000 men and 1,000 women applied for registration

as conscientious objectors: roughly eight million were enrolled in the armed services. Of the applicants for C.O. status the local tribunals registered 4.7 percent unconditionally and 37.9 percent on condition that they did civilian alternative service; 27.7 percent were directed to noncombatant duties in the army and 29.7 percent were removed from the register altogether. About a third of these decisions were appealed; appellate tribunals then varied the terms of registration in about half the cases that came before them. Some tribunals were liberal in granting unconditional exemption; others gave it only infrequently. Agricultural work or forestry was the condition most favored by tribunals, followed closely by hospital work, civil defense and, towards the end of the war, coal mining. "Some Tribunals made frequent use of the condition of 'present occupation,' while others made a point of putting men to other work as a rough and ready means of preserving equality of sacrifice." [7]

Conscience v. the Law

The clash between conscience and the law was less dramatic, and less painful, than in World War I. This stemmed from two main factors; on the one hand, the declining impulse toward an absolutist stand on the part of the objectors themselves and their greater willingness to accept some form of service as an acceptable witness and, on the other hand, the increased toleration and understanding of conscientious objection shown both by the authorities and the community at large. Nevertheless, despite the efforts of parliament to prevent the harrying of conscientious objectors that had taken place in World War I, and the genuine attempt made by most tribunals to reach a fair decision in the cases which appeared before them, some 5,500 objectors (of whom nearly 500 were women) were sentenced to terms in civil prison. In addition over 1,000 conscientious objectors were court-martialed and sentenced to detention in military prisons.

Not all the imprisoned objectors found themselves in jail for refusing to abide by their tribunal's judgment. A few were libertarian nonregistrants who objected to voluntary cooperation with the machinery of conscription; but in such instances the authorities usually registered the objector willy-nilly and his case was heard by a tribunal *in absentia*. There were objectors to service in the

Home Guard, a part-time militia in which compulsory service was required in January 1942 for able-bodied males up to the age of 51. Conscientious objectors were automatically exempt—so long as they were registered as such either temporarily or permanently. However, objectors whose applications had been dismissed, or older pacifists whose age group had not yet been registered for military conscription, were sometimes prosecuted for refusing to serve in the Home Guard. There were objectors, too, to compulsion for various forms of civil defense, in particular for fire-watching in the cities which became obligatory in 1941 after Britain had experienced the *blitz,* as well as to industrial conscription introduced in April of the same year. In neither case was the character of the duties demanded usually regarded by pacifists as in itself objectionable; exception was taken to their ultimately military purpose and to the element of governmental compulsion.

Immediately prior to the war some pacifists had opposed Air Raid Precautions as part of the machinery of war preparation. After raids had begun, however, pacifists along with the rest of the population shared in the measures taken to save life, care for the homeless, and prevent the destruction of property resulting from air bombardment. As the Minister of Labour, Ernest Bevin, told the House of Commons in December 1943: "There are thousands of cases in which conscientious objectors, although they have refused to take up arms, have shown as much courage as anyone else in Civil Defence" [8]—either in a part-time capacity or in the performance of their alternative service. Some pacifists, however, continued to regard civil defense as an integral part of the war effort and therefore objectionable for that reason. And absolutists, although some of them readily performed such duties voluntarily, were not prepared to accept civil defense or indeed any other condition in exchange for exemption. There were some 575 cases where men were prosecuted (one of them nine times!) for refusing compulsory fire-watching or other part-time civil defense duties; about 90 women were convicted for the same offense, the best known of whom was the Quaker scientist, Dr. (now Dame) Kathleen Lonsdale. A short term of imprisonment, usually of three months' duration, was the normal penalty imposed.

Those pacifists refusing directions imposed under industrial conscription, writes the historian of conscientious objection in World

War II Britain, "were handled with circumspection and re-straint." [9] The labor and trade movement, as in World War I, was itself disquieted by the possible implications of conscription of labor in regard to its own freedom of organization, for wartime regulations controlled in practice almost the whole industrial field: both wages and conditions of employment were frozen. The Min-istry of Labour made no attempt to force an objector to go into munitions or other work directly connected with the prosecution of the war, but it did refuse to allow the same right to seek un-conditional exemption as was permitted objectors to military service. Since most able-bodied male objectors were covered by the machinery of military conscription, and since conditions of alternative service prescribed by tribunals were not ordinarily sub-ject to alteration by industrial direction (though this was legally permissible), those prosecuted were usually either young women, sometimes as young as 18 years of age, or respectable older citizens. Courts, therefore, were reluctant to convict in such cases. Some "industrial" objectors, however, were sentenced to short terms of imprisonment. A total of 610 men and 333 women were convicted for resisting industrial conscription.

The main body of objectors who clashed with the law were not the comparatively small number of nonregistrants and Home Guard, civil defense and "industrial" objectors, discussed just above, but those whose conscientious scruples had not been ade-quately dealt with at their tribunal hearings. Over 3,600 men were sent to prison for resisting induction into the army to which their tribunals had assigned them for either combatant or noncombatant services, and a further 355 persons (59 of them women) were jailed for noncompliance with their conditions of alternative ci-vilian service, an offense which carried a maximum of twelve months' imprisonment if committed without "reasonable excuse." The latter were almost entirely of the absolutist persuasion; the former group included men who would willingly undertake some form of alternative service under civilian auspices but were pre-pared to go to jail rather than enter the army.

After an objector had had his application rejected successively by local and appellate tribunals, he was faced, if he wished to persevere in his stand, with two alternatives. One alternative was to submit to medical examination and subsequent induction into the army and thereafter refuse to obey military orders or in some other way make clear his objection to army service. Later, he might occasionally be the object of some sporadic, unorganized ill treatment of a none too serious nature if he declined to don an army uniform or was otherwise uncooperative. "The only organized savagery directed expressly at C.O.'s during the war took place at two army training centres . . . at Liverpool, during September and October, 1940." [10] This incident—usually known as the Dingle Vale case from the name of one of the two centers involved—became the subject of public protest and official enquiry. The maltreatment of objectors was then stopped and no further affairs of this kind occurred.

If the objector were sentenced by court-martial to a term of three or more months in a civil prison, he was entitled to apply for a review tribunal, which could then order his release. On the other hand, if the sentence, though a civil one, amounted to less than three months or if the court-martial decided that it should be served in a military detention barracks, the law did not permit the objector to renew his application to a tribunal. Despite recommendations from the War Office to the contrary, until the middle of 1941, nearly 50 percent of court-martial sentences were of the inadequate kind. In most instances this policy resulted not from ignorance of the law but from deliberate intention. For it permitted a species of "cat-and-mouse" treatment, to which objectors had been subjected in World War I. Repeated sentences could be inflicted on the objector in an effort to break down his resistance. One objector was court-martialed and sentenced as many as six times; two or three trials were quite usual. Sentences in detention barracks, where the regimen was extremely tough for all prisoners, might run up to two years (they were normally very much less). Eventually the worst abuses in regard to misplaced objectors in the army ceased, but the position still remained unsatisfactory.

A related problem that should be mentioned here was that of the "soldier C.O.'s," men who had joined the army as volunteers or conscripts and later developed an objection to fighting. At first they were not eligible to apply for a tribunal after sentencing. The army authorities were apprehensive that, once the right to opt out of service was granted to serving soldiers, this concession might undermine discipline and cause a rush of the unconscientious to gain release in this way. In fact, though, these fears proved quite unfounded. In May 1940, soldiers who became objectors were permitted, under the same terms as other conscientious objectors under army control, to apply to an "Advisory Tribunal" for exemption and subsequent release from service according to the conditions laid down by the tribunal. Yet by the end of 1946 only 415 men had taken advantage of this provision.

The second alternative open to the civilian objector whose application had been dismissed by his tribunal was to refuse to undergo the prescribed medical examination. If he did this, there was no legal way of actually forcing him into the army. However, he could be—indeed he almost invariably was—haled before a civil court and sentenced to imprisonment for nonattendance at the statutory "medical." At the beginning, a small fine or a short prison term in lieu of a fine was all that the courts could impose. But, by the new National Service Act of April 1941, prison sentences of up to two years, or a fine of one hundred pounds, became the legal penalty for this offense. In fact, although there was considerable variation from place to place, courts usually sentenced objectors to terms of between six and twelve months. Only one objector, a Jehovah's Witness, received the maximum penalty of two years' imprisonment with hard labor.

At first it looked as if the same species of "cat-and-mouse" treatment as we have discussed above in connection with objectors in the army would come into operation in regard to the larger number of objectors who refused medical examination. But in December 1941 parliament permitted objectors in this last category, if their sentence amounted to a minimum of three months, to apply once again to an Appellate Tribunal for reconsideration of their case and for release from prison even before the expiry of their term. The concession was a wise one. There was indeed no sense, especially as most objectors were engaged outside in some kind of productive activity, in crowding the understaffed jails with prisoners whose reformation was extremely unlikely.

There were, it is true, still cases of re-imprisonment for what was, in fact, essentially the same offense. Some objectors had received sentences too short to qualify them for a rehearing; others had their applications rejected again on appeal; yet others were unwilling to appear at all before a tribunal. But the Ministry of

Labour soon adopted a policy of usually leaving such men alone (as well as those convicted for not observing their conditions of exemption), though use was sometimes made of the Ministry's powers of direction within the framework of industrial conscription. A second prosecution then became fairly rare, a third exceptional.

The Conscientious Objector

From what sections of the population were objectors in the Great Britain of World War II drawn? What kind of reasons impelled them to take a minority and unpopular stand in a country that eventually became united behind its government to a degree that had scarcely been reached during World War I? What differences may be detected between the community of objectors in the First World War and that which took shape in the course of the second conflict?

"No class," writes Hayes, "had anything approaching a monopoly of 'conscience'. . . . C.O.'s [before their call-up] could be found performing the hundred and one tasks that go to make up the wealth of the nation." [11] But we do see a preponderance among them of "white-collar" workers and a relative scarcity of manual laborers. Objectors from the lower income groups included a high proportion of members of the fundamentalist sects: Jehovah's Witnesses, Plymouth Brethren, Seventh-Day Adventists, Christadelphians, etc. The Quakers, on the other hand, contributed a high percentage of professional men: university students and graduates played an important part in their Friends' Ambulance Unit. The number of creative artists—painters, composers and musicians —who took the conscientious objector position is worth noting. although naturally they formed a quantitatively insignificant element. The ugliness of modern war, its anarchic destructiveness, appeared to many of these men a denial of the values they stood for.

The majority of objectors were church members, if not churchgoers. Hayes is probably right in his view that statistics in this case are misleading, since the objector's religious affiliation, as with the rest of the population, might be nominal or his pacifism drawn primarily from nonreligious sources. "A good proportion of the applicants labelled 'religious' might properly have been included as 'general objectors,' typified by what one might call 'the Peace Pledge Union C.O.' " [12] Of the churches, the Methodists provided the highest percentage of conscientious objectors, followed by Anglicans (we find even as conservative a member of the established church as Dean Inge asserting: "As Christians we are bound to be pacifists" [13]), Baptists and Congregationalists. The British Society of Friends was a small body, numbering about 20,000 members. Though some of its young men, as in World War I, did combatant service, the majority of those who remained close to Quakerism became conscientious objectors.

Religious or religio-ethical motivation provided, then, the impulse for the overwhelming number of objectors. But there was, too, a small minority of political objectors who did not claim to be complete pacifists. A few of them were libertarians who objected to conscription and not to war (several men in this group even volunteered for the Home Guard—a stand that does indeed seem curious but was in fact not illogical). There were also nationalist objectors: Welsh, Scottish, Irish and a handful of Indians, who were quite prepared to fight for their own country's independence and protection but not in a war they felt to be an alien cause. Some Mosleyites claimed objector status as did a few persons of Italian origin who were unwilling to take up arms against their kin. Most political objectors, however, were drawn from the socialist "sects," from the Independent Labour Party, by now a mere shadow of its former self, and various smaller Marxist splinter bodies, as well as from anarchist groups of various kinds. There were, of course, objectors belonging to the Labour Party, but they were almost all thorough pacifists. Certainly not political, but also not strictly pacifist, were the objectors belonging to such denominations as the Jehovah's Witnesses, who declared their willingness to fight at God's behest at Armegeddon but who were until then unwilling to take part in the wars of this world. Whereas the Witnesses, as we have seen earlier, carried on a militant propaganda for their beliefs and mostly claimed (and were usually denied) unconditional exemption, other groups of this kind lived withdrawn from the world and readily accepted noncombatant service in the army.[14]

Nonpacifist objectors—today we would call them "selective objectors"—were most often removed from the register by local tribunals. But the Appellate Tribunals adopted a much more liberal stand. They were prepared to accept the validity of such objection if convinced of the sincerity of the applicant. Though some appellants were still unsuccessful and went to jail, the veteran antimilitarist, Fenner Brockway, was right in claiming the Appellate Tribunal's stand as a "notable victory for liberty." The Appellate Tribunals, in their search to give every sincerely held view its just due, were even ready to recognize that employment on work connected with the manufacture of war materials did not in itself exclude the genuineness of an objection to fighting. This decision arose from the application for C.O. status of four Christadelphians, whose church based its noncombatancy on a literalist interpretation of the Biblical injunction: "Thou shalt not kill."

In comparing the pattern of conscientious objection in Britain in the two world wars of this century, several observations may be made. In the first place, there was general recognition among pacifists that the present liberal regulations concerning conscientious objection and the more understanding attitude adopted both by the authorities and a considerable section of public opinion were largely the result of the steadfast resistance to persecution put up by the objectors, and in particular the absolutists, of World War I. The rights now accorded to conscience were gratefully acknowledged, and many nonpacifists, too, welcomed them as a significant achievement in the struggle for preserving individual liberty, even in wartime, against the increasingly powerful modern state. At the same time—and this is the second point that needs to be made here—the conscientious objectors of World War II were less militantly crusading in spirit, less certain of being completely in the right than their predecessors. A dilemma similar to that presented in having to make a choice between the evil of war and the evil of Hitlerism had been absent in the earlier struggle. The objectors of World War II were also in some ways less politically involved. In addition, in World War II the straight political objector was no longer an important factor in the pattern of conscientious objection. Though the average objector might not be particularly religious in the usual meaning of the word, his stand resulted from an ethical decision rather than a political choice.

Thirdly, in World War II it was no longer the absolutists—"the logicians of conscience, the extremists of peace," as Hayes has

aptly called them—who made the most vital contribution to the
wartime pacifist movement. For one thing the earlier absolutists
by the uncompromising character of their war resistance had effectively made their point, had won a fairly general, if sometimes
grudging, recognition of conscientious objection. This did not
really need to be done over again. In addition, the complex organization of mid-twentieth-century war, at least in a country so involved as Britain was, embraced the whole community, including
its conscientious objectors. To attempt to withdraw from society
to the extent the absolutist position required appeared now to
many pacifists unrealistic. A desire to give a more positive content
to their witness against war seemed to them a more appropriate
response in the existing situation.

An academic philosopher with experience on a World War II
tribunal, who was especially critical of the absolutist variety of
objection, once asserted that it was "chiefly to be found among
the more extreme members of the Society of Friends." [15] This
judgment may well have been correct, for a libertarian streak
developed very early in the history of the Quaker peace testimony.
It found some confirmation at any rate in the recollections of an
objector jailed in the Second World War, who wrote of the visiting
Quaker chaplain, a member of the Quaker absolutist group of
1914–18 period: "I remember a kind of shy fervour with which
he referred to the absolutist position; he would . . . have been
capable of staying in prison *indefinitely* for a reason of conscience
—and that is a very rare quality—and I think he looked a little
disappointedly for signs of a similar quality in the C.O.'s of a
generation later." [16]

Indeed it is probably true that in World War II one should not
turn to its absolutists to find the representative type of objector.
One must look rather to those who worked on the land as farm
laborers or in forestry units or as market gardeners, to those who
served in the understaffed hospitals as porters, orderlies or ambulance drivers, to those who chose civil defense or the Auxiliary
Fire Service as the field of their alternative service, or to those
engaged in social work of the kind carried on, for instance, by
privately organized Pacifist Service Units among the depressed
sections of the populations in large industrial cities like London, Liverpool, Manchester or Cardiff.

In most cases the work done by objectors was undramatic; often it was unskilled as well as monotonous. It rarely possessed any peculiarly pacifist flavor. Whereas objectors on the land frequently felt isolated and ineffective in their witness, those employed in the cities integrated more easily with the community. "The C.O. in the hospital," one of them wrote, "is in no way cut off from the world but rather constantly in touch with the fact of war. He works side by side with men who support the war, yet his views are rarely held against him. . . . It is by the way he does his job that he is judged." [17] Occasionally the nature of the objectors' employment succeeded in attracting public attention: the human "guinea-pigs," for instance, who assisted Dr. Kenneth Mellanby in his researches on scabies at the Sorby Institute (University of Sheffield), or the volunteers from the Non-Combatant Corps who acted as medical orderlies with British paratroopers at the battle of Arnhem, or the Anglican pacifists who ran the Hungerford Club for vermin-ridden London tramps.

Though only a small percentage of the total number of objectors served with the Friends' Ambulance Unit, this body—like its predecessor in World War I—deserves brief notice. The FAU was not officially sponsored by the Quakers but its association with the Society of Friends was now closer than in the earlier war.[18] Part of its work was devoted to civilian relief in the blitzed cities of Britain and the devastated areas of western Europe as well as in India, China and the Near East. But it also continued its tradition of ambulance work with the Allied armies. The Unit remained a strange, though not disheartening, anomaly: a voluntary association of pacifists maintaining its identity and basic philosophy despite close integration into the army system. On a British troop ship, for instance, a Unit member *en route* to China once found himself asked to lecture on the work of the FAU. "I doubt," he has written with astonishment, "whether there are other armies in the world that would invite a man who refused to undergo military service to talk about other 'conchies' to a group of soldiers going overseas!" [19]

Finally, in comparing the situation of British pacifism in the two world conflicts, we may note the absence in the Second World War of any organization comparable to the No-Conscription Fellowship. The PPU continued to function, of course, but it lacked the aggressive antimilitarism of the NCF. Moreover, the PPU included only the "pure" pacifists whereas the NCF, had, in fact, embraced the political opponents of war and the selective objectors as well. Its nearest equivalent in World War II was perhaps the Central Board for Conscientious Objectors, set up in 1939, soon after the re-introduction of conscription, with representation from some seventeen organizations sympathizing with the objectors' stand. The Board acted as a coordinating body to protect the interests of objectors of every variety (including, for instance, members of the Non-Combatant Corps refusing to do what they considered military work) and to make the objectors' case known to the public. It advised them concerning their legal rights and the consequences of the stand they had decided to take; despite occasional allegations in the press that the Board was attempting to coach conscience, it aimed not at manufacturing objectors but at clarifying their minds. Like the NCF in World War I, the Board lobbied parliament and supplied sympathetic M.P.'s with information which would be helpful to them in debate. It published periodically an information bulletin which included details of all legislative and executive rulings of concern to objectors, and it kept an accurate record of the wartime careers of almost all conscientious objectors. The Board performed its varied tasks with efficiency and zest. The establishment of a network of regional branches and local advisory panels helped, too, to make it effective in the provinces.

Associated with the Board, though an independent body, was the Pacifist Service Bureau, which acted as an employment exchange for objectors doing alternative service—with a license from the London County Council issued for this purpose! Calls to place objectors on the same pay as army privates had been strongly opposed by the powerful Trade Union Congress as a threat to the rights of labor; in any case there were serious practical difficulties in the way of implementing any such proposals. Especially at first, some discrimination existed as a result of private employers or local authorities refusing to employ objectors, but it was of limited occurrence.

Britain's wartime objectors were gradually released from their obligations under conscription in 1946 and the first half of 1947, along with their contemporaries who had been serving in the armed forces. Some objectors continued in their wartime employment; in social service, in particular, there were those who found a lasting vocation. A few went on to take part for a time in postwar relief in war-torn Europe. Others, especially in the youngest age groups, started to train for a future career in a university, teachers' training college or technical school. Most objectors, however, returned to their prewar jobs. In returning to peacetime conditions objectors met with little victimization and only infrequently with hostility. This had not been expected, for the intensity of the recent struggle, the losses in battle, and the destruction of the cities tested Britain perhaps as no other war had done. The tolerance shown toward a dissident minority, both during the struggle and after it was over, had its source not only in a long-standing respect for nonconformity, to which attention has already been drawn, but also to a growing feeling that in mid-twentieth-century war the traditional distinction between civilian and combatant had lost much of its meaning. This indeed posed a challenge, too, to pacifists. In this situation where, if at all, could pacifism make a significant contribution? The question was given renewed urgency by the explosion of the first atomic bombs in August 1945.

AMERICAN OBJECTORS: CAMP *v.* PRISON

The Legislative Framework and Its Interpretation

As in Great Britain conscription in the United States was reintroduced before the country actually became involved in war. The Selective Training and Service Act of 16 September 1940, which called for the drafting of able-bodied males between the ages of 19 and 44, contained a section—5(g)—outlining procedure for obtaining exemption as a conscientious objector. Exemption was allowed in the case of men who "by reason of religious training and belief" objected to participation in all warfare. It might cover only combatant service (1-A-O classification), or it might include noncombatant service as well (4-E classification). For those exempted from the latter, "work of national importance under civilian direction" was to be provided; the exact nature of such work, however, was not specified in the legislation. The task of assessing whether an application for exemption was genuine, a task which in practice also included that of deciding whether the objection was conscientious according to the definition laid down in the act, fell not as in Great Britain to specially constituted tribunals but to the local draft boards. If this Selective Service board decided positively on an application, it then had the obligation to assign the objector either to noncombatant duties in the armed forces or to civilian service, as it judged fitting. Appeal could be lodged against a local board decision through the Department of Justice, which would then refer the matter to a regional Board of Appeal.

If we compare these provisions with the legislation concerning conscientious objection passed by Congress in 1917, several improvements will be noticed. In the first place there was no requirement that the applicant belong to a pacifist denomination before his objection could fall within the meaning of the act. Secondly, alternative service outside the army was specifically provided for. Indeed, as we have seen, World War I experience had forced the administration in practice both to extend the categories of those entitled to exemption and to furlough men unwilling to accept noncombatant service for work in agriculture. The legislators in 1940 were wise to embody this experience in their conscription act. Yet there were serious deficiencies, too, in the new legislation. For one thing the sincere nonreligious objector, even when he was a complete pacifist, was left with no alternative except to submit or go to prison. And, of course, the same choice faced the selective objector. Again, the position of the absolutist received no consideration: no provision was made for unconditional exemption. A final shortcoming in the section of the act relating to conscientious objection may be mentioned: its failure to ensure that the work of national importance required of objectors as their alternative service would be not merely, as laid down, under civilian direction but would also, so far as possible, be unconnected with the war. Much, of course, would depend on the spirit in which this legislation was administered, whether it was interpreted formalistically or with a broader vision.

A registrant under the act who wished to apply for the status of conscientious objector was required to fill in a special form (D.S.S. Form 47) giving details about his background and the reasons why he objected to participation in the war. His application was then considered by the local Selective Service board. These boards, each consisting of some three or four members including one government-appointed lawyer, were made up largely of middle-class citizens: businessmen, members of the professions, substantial farmers in rural areas. There was rarely working class representation. Ex-servicemen and officers of the American Legion were numerous; this was not unnatural in view of the boards' main function in administering military conscription but scarcely conducive to an impartial consideration of conscientious objection to war.

Decisions were usually handed down without a hearing: only about 25 percent of objectors actually appeared before a board in person. However, if the applicant received a classification for which he did not ask, he had the right not only to lodge an appeal but also to demand a hearing first from the local board. Some boards treated objectors with courtesy and fairness; a few were clearly hostile (at Washita County, Oklahoma, for instance, the board referred to objectors as "un-American yellow dogs"). On the whole they tended, like the British tribunals, to put greatest reliance in reaching a decision on exterior criteria: membership in a church (especially in one of the peace sects) or in a pacifist society, or the length of time an applicant had been a pacifist. In some instances, especially in the rural Midwest where antipacifist feeling ran high and where communities of German-speaking Mennonites, Amish and Brethren aroused patriotic fears, boards, either through ignorance or prejudice—and certainly in contradiction both to the letter and the spirit of the law—refused altogether to grant IV-E (civilian service) classification. There were not infrequent cases, too, where local boards refused objectors the deferment to which they were legally entitled on grounds of hardship, age or character of employment. Misclassification, as we shall see, was of course often rectified on appeal.

A special problem was presented by the group of men, who may for convenience sake be called "humanitarian objectors." They did not belong to any church, though occasionally they might be members of an ethical society or secularist league. Many of them were affiliated to the War Resisters' League; some, though, had not participated in any organized pacifist activity. Their objection certainly did not stem from any religious training or belief. Yet these men opposed all war as contrary to their ethical code; they claimed a sanction for their stand as absolute as that of the religious ob-

jector. The local boards, understandably, were confused as to what
to do. They could follow the letter of the law and reject applications automatically; some boards did this. Or they might stretch its
meaning a little and identify an ethical code with a religious belief.
To add to the confusion—at least of those boards ready to take
heed of government directions in the matter—the Selective Service
administration was evidently itself perplexed how to proceed. Its
first director, Clarence A. Dykstra, in December 1940 adopted an
extremely liberal view. Membership in a religious body was not an
essential qualification for classifying a man as a conscientious objector, he said. Any genuine conviction as to the ultimate purpose
and value of life, which led a man to refuse participation in war,
should be considered the outcome of "religious training and belief." Fifteen months later, in March 1942, General Lewis B.
Hershey, who had succeeded Dykstra as director, considerably nar-
rowed his predecessor's definition of religious belief. General
Hershey now demanded "recognition of some source of all existence, which, whatever the type of conception, is Divine because
it is the Source of all things." Thus belief is a transcendent deity
now appeared essential. But the next year, 1943, the Second
Circuit Court of Appeals in the case of Matthias Kanten provided
a third interpretation. "A conscientious objection to participation
in war under any circumstances," said the Court, "may justly be
regarded as a response of the individual mentor, call it conscience
or God, that is for many persons at the present time the equivalent
of what has always been thought a religious impulse." [20] This
almost Gandhian identification of God with truth was the farthest
point reached in liberalizing the law on the subject until the decision in the Seeger case in 1965, referred to in the next chapter.

In regard to the selective objectors, the boards most often
(though by no means invariably) rejected their applications. These
men were usually, as in Great Britain, socialist or anarchist "sectarians," professedly antireligious men, who refused to fight in imperialist wars carried on by capitalist powers like Britain or U.S.A.
or by renegades from socialism like Stalinist Russia. But there
were borderline groups where a decision was extremely difficult.
The objections to fighting of the Jehovah's Witnesses, for instance,
were incontestably the result of religious training and belief. But
should the Witnesses not still be considered ineligible for exemp-

tion since their refusal to participate in war was not absolute? They had no theoretical compunction against taking human life; a few Witnesses did not object to defending themselves or their families by arms or to employment in munitions or other war industry. They all approved the wars waged by the Jews in the Old Testament as a fulfillment of God's commandments (an approval incidentally that had always been shared by fundamentalist pacifists of the old school). They looked forward to fighting against Satan's forces in the battle of Armageddon at some unspecified, but imminent date in the future. Like Alice faced by the White Queen through the looking-glass, members of the Selective Service boards were frequently puzzled how to interpret the Witnesses' program of war tomorrow, war yesterday, but never war today. Impressed by the patent sincerity of most Witnesses and their devotion to their church, some boards gave them exemption in one form or another. On the other hand, there were boards who were offended by the Witnesses' unyielding stance, which neither Hitler's concentration camps nor the *lagry* of Stalinist Russia were to succeed in breaking down, and dismissed their applications.

A further complication ensued from most Witnesses claiming unconditional exemption under Section 5(d) of the 1940 act, which gave this status (4-D classification) to all theological students and accredited ministers of religion (a concession that had resulted, ironically, from pressure from the Roman Catholic hierarchy). Many Witnesses on being refused 4-D classification —where given the choice—preferred to go to prison rather than accept either noncombatant duties in the army or civilian public service. In 1942, however, General Hershey ruled that Witnesses putting in over 80 hours a month on work of a ministerial character had a justifiable claim for 4-D classification. Again, whether from ignorance or through prejudice against the Witnesses, boards in many instances continued to deny their claims for ministerial status.[21]

A second group whose unwillingness to fight straddled the borderline between pacifist and selective objection was formed by the Roman Catholic opponents of war. American Catholics who took, or supported, the conscientious objector position constituted only a very tiny fraction of the total active membership of the church (and there were even fewer of them on other continents). Yet the group, which in World War I had been almost nonexistent, was slowly growing and would continue to expand in size and influence in the decades following 1945. Some Catholic objectors were of the "evangelical" type arguing against war from its total incompatibility with the Christian spirit. A second group, drawn largely from among readers of that lively organ of radical religious dissent *The Catholic Worker,* have been well defined as "perfectionists," who believed that Christians have an obligation to follow exactly the counsels of the Sermon on the Mount. And there were also, of course, Catholic objectors who, without claiming to be unconditionally pacifist, refused to fight in modern wars because they considered the conditions under which such wars would be waged as inevitably contravening traditional Catholic teaching concerning a just war. Since there were priests and even bishops who stated publicly—though quite uncanonically—that a good Catholic could not be a conscientious objector, Selective Service boards were sometimes inclined to reject Catholic applicants without more ado.[22]

Appeals by conscientious objectors against decisions of the local boards were in fact successful in over 50 percent of cases. Recourse could be had from the judgment of the regional Board of Appeal, provided this were not given unanimously, to a panel appointed by the Director of Selective Service at the President's request. Such panels were made up mainly of army officers, despite the protests of pacifist organizations. Sibley and Jacob in their invaluable study of American conscientious objection in World War II (to which, on almost every page, my account is greatly indebted) wrote of "military domination of the appellate system, particularly with respect to the presidential appeals committee." [23] This situation was indeed symptomatic of the control exercised by the army over the whole administration of conscientious objection, an authority which resulted in turn from the powerful influence in such matters then exerted on Congress by the military.

No completely accurate figures exist of the number of men who became conscientious objectors to military service in World War II. The official Selective Service System estimate for the period 1940–47 totalled 72,354. But this is certainly too low. For one thing the record systems of the local boards were not infrequently defective. Again, this figure does not include most of the Jehovah's

Witnesses since they applied for IV-D classification. Also, the official number of noncombatants in the army (1-A-O), which Selective Service reckoned as 25,000, may in actual fact have been as high as 50,000. The Selective Service System's figure of 11,950 for IV-E assignments to alternative service (which in practice was to mean work in Civilian Public Service camps) is roughly accurate, for it is known that 11,868 men actually reported at camp. The System also listed an additional 1,624 men who were convicted for failure to report at all: this may be taken to represent the core of consistent absolutists among the objectors. A further 13,780 described as "reclassified from 1-A-O or 4-E as not available" and 20,000 "claimants never classified in 1-A-O or 4-E," this last figure admittedly a guess, make up the Selective Service System's grand total. On the other hand, Sibley and Jacob believe that the total number of conscientious objectors should probably be as high as 100,000, i.e., 0.30 percent of the 34 million registrants for military service, though they admit that this is merely an approximation.

The Noncombatants

Of the men who accepted 1-A-O classification and served as noncombatants in the armed forces, somewhere between a quarter and a half were drawn from the Seventh-Day Adventist Church. In July 1940 their leader had stated: "We are not pacifists nor militarists nor conscientious objectors, but noncombatants . . . as to the noncombatant [Adventist] he merely believes that he should not take human life. But he is willing to cooperate with his Government in any capacity that he can without having to violate his conscience in regard to taking a life." [24] Well before the outbreak of war Seventh-Day Adventists had begun to train their young men as medical cadets in preparation for "man-made disaster." [25] They felt no hesitation, therefore, in entering upon noncombatant duties when called upon for service.

Apart from members of religious sects like the Adventists, whose collective testimony against war stemmed from a literalist ban on taking life, noncombatant service appealed primarily to objectors who sought in it an opportunity to relieve suffering humanity and to share the hardships of the soldier. Such service, even if closely linked with the war machine, appeared more directly useful than any alternative civilian service. There were indeed members of most religious denominations among the noncombatants (be it noted, however, American Christadelphians disowned members accepting noncombatant duties as they had done in World War I). Some men, especially those with heavy family commitments, accepted 1-A-O status rather than 4-E because they felt they could not shoulder the economic burdens entailed by the latter. "In Civilian Public Service one had to pay one's own way or rely upon what one might regard as the charitable contributions of others";[26] the authorities' steady refusal to approve government pay for civilian service assignees stemmed in part from a desire to push as many of them as possible to accept 1-A-O. There were also objectors who, though they would have preferred civilian work, did not turn down noncombatant service when assigned it, since to do so would have entailed prosecution and imprisonment and they did not feel strongly enough in the matter to face these consequences.

Although American noncombatants, unlike members of the British army's Non-Combatant Corps, did not wear a distinctive badge, they could not be required to carry arms or to train in their use. They might nevertheless have to bear a club on guard duty, since the War Department did not define this as a weapon; they could, too, be given such quasi-armed duties as setting up targets for use in a rifle range (for refusal to do which one objector was in fact court-martialed). From the beginning of 1943 objectors were assigned only to the Medical Corps. Even so, problems arose here too, for in 1944 in the Pacific theater of war medical units were armed. "The pressure on objectors to bear all types of 'arms' was great, and some 1-A-O's undoubtedly succumbed . . . often a whole Medical Corps unit would be armed with the exception of the few objectors serving in it. It is not difficult to imagine how isolated and curious the objectors must have seemed, both to themselves and to the nonobjector members of their unit. But men like the [Adventist] Desmond Doss, who won the Congressional Medal of Honor, remained unarmed throughout the severe Pacific fighting, even though medical corpsmen were frequently fired upon." [27]

The army authorities in World War II were not confronted with the question, which had faced them in World War I, of what to do with large numbers of objectors unwilling to accept non-combatant status. A similar problem, however, did exist, though of much smaller proportions. There were, for instance, the misclassified objectors who, after induction, refused to take the military oath or to don uniform or obey military orders; they might have been classified as 1-A-O but object to army noncombatancy; or they might have been given straight combatant service (1-A classification) instead of the desired 1-A-O or 4-E, as the case might be. Such men, write Sibley and Jacob, "constituted in many instances the most difficult disciplinary problems from the viewpoint of the military and naval authorities." [28] Among them were men who, through inexperience or lack of education, did not properly understand the official procedure for registering conscientious objection and thus could easily find themselves in the army with 1-A status. Secondly, there were soldiers who, while they had not claimed objector status either on registering or after induction, nevertheless developed a conscientious objection after having served for a short or long period.

At first these misclassified objectors along with the soldier objectors received short terms of up to six months' detention in guardhouses or camp stockades. If they persevered in their resistance, a court-martial normally followed with long prison terms usually ranging between five and ten years. One man, a socialist objector named Henry Weber, was condemned to death: the only sentence of its kind in World War II America, which was, however, on account of public protest, eventually whittled down in stages to five years' imprisonment.

After a while the army authorities devised procedures to try to eliminate its refractory objectors. In the first place, they became ready to assign a man, when willing to accept, to noncombatant duties even though he was not officially in possession of the 1-A-O status, which only the local or various appellate boards were entitled to grant. But, of course, this sensible decision might be reversed arbitrarily at some later date and the man transferred back to a combatant unit. If this happened, court-martial and imprisonment followed automatically on refusal of a military order. A second way out of the impasse resulted from a decision handed down by the Supreme Court in 1944 in the Billings case. This made it possible for men who had not actually taken the military oath (many of course had done so) to obtain a writ of *habeas corpus* and receive trial and sentence in a civil court. A third possibility, though one that was open only if a court-martial had not yet taken place, lay in the objector obtaining his discharge through the army's own general administrative procedure. In this case, however, the initiative lay solely with the man's commanding officer; thus everything depended here on the latter's attitude, on whether he wished to get rid of the objector either because he found him a nuisance or because he was convinced of his genuineness. However, sincerity by itself was not grounds for a discharge. The officer had to urge it as a convenience to the army, or because of the man's inadaptability to life in the services, or on account of what were considered undesirable traits in his character. After discharge, the objector was reclassified by his Selective Service board.

For those misclassified objectors in the army's grip, who were neither prepared to accept unofficial noncombatancy nor eligible to apply for a writ of *habeas corpus* nor fortunate in having a commanding officer sympathetic enough—or irritated enough, as the case might be—to initiate the discharge procedure, court-martial and imprisonment continued to be the routine. Sentences were normally served in disciplinary barracks, though sometimes an objector was assigned to an army "rehabilitation center" (the sources are silent as to any cases where the treatment was successful). "It is fairly certain," write Sibley and Jacob, "that there was more actual physical brutality in military than in civil prisons—beatings of Jehovah's Witnesses, for example, and long periods in 'solitary' on bread and water." Such brutalities, however, were inflicted usually without the approval of higher authorities and were not comparable in either extent or intensity to those suffered in this sort of institution by objectors in World War I. Almost at the end of the war, in June 1945, an Advisory Board on Clemency, manned by civilians and not by military officers, was set up to review court-martial sentences imposed on conscientious objectors, something that religious and pacifist organizations had long been urging. "But . . . its performance was disappointing to civil-liberties and objector groups. . . . In general, it seemed to give great weight to the opinion of Selective Service." [29] For instance, contrary to some official pronouncements cited above, the Advisory

Board refused to recognize the objections of men like the socialist Henry Weber, however genuine, as being "conscientious" within the meaning of the act, and it therefore rejected their claims.

Civilian Public Service: The Sponsoring Agencies

In the 1930s all the major Protestant churches had been influenced to a considerable degree by pacifist ideas. Yet, when war came, while the fierce hostility shown by most clergy to their pacifist minority in World War I was now almost entirely absent, the pacifists still remained a minority, and a comparatively small one. The feeling that war was basically unchristian was general in the Protestant churches and was embraced by those supporting the war ("agonized participants," to adapt Edward LeRoy Long, Jr.'s telling phrase) as well as pacifist churchmen. Christian pacifists, from their side, admitted to "a mood of depression and frustration." Each party, therefore, felt a certain bond of unity in acknowledging their common inadequacy when faced by the challenge of war, despite the diversity of their responses to this challenge. The nonpacifist churches expressed sympathy and respect for the pacifist position and they called on legislators to give conscientious objectors from their midst the same rights as objectors from traditionally pacifist denominations would enjoy.[30]

Shortly after the passing of the Selective Training and Service Act the three historic peace churches—Quakers, Mennonites and Brethren—joined in October 1940 with other churches and groups interested in the plight of conscientious objectors to form a National Service Board for Religious Objectors, which would both coordinate activities on behalf of the objectors and undertake combined negotiations with the government. A Quaker, Paul Comly French, was appointed secretary. Because of their long-standing concern for peace and the comparatively high percentage of objectors among their young men of military age, these three peace churches played the dominant role both in contacts with the administration and in shaping the policies that would govern the community of objectors.

In fact, the three churches had been active in the matter as early as January 1940 when they presented personally to President Roosevelt a memorandum proposing, in view of the likelihood of conscription being introduced shortly, a scheme of alternative

civilian service for objectors willing to accept it as well as provision for complete exemption for the absolutists. These efforts,
which were backed by the pacifist movement in general, were only
partially successful. The sponsors were able to broaden the original
intention of the legislators to follow closely the pattern of World
War I and give exemption only to members of pacifist sects, and
then only from combatant service, so as to eventually get them to
include all religious objection to war and to add the possibility of
civilian alternative service. But, as we have seen, the September
1940 act, unlike its earlier British counterpart which was taken as
a model by the pacifist lobbyists, gave no satisfaction either to
the unconditionalist or to the nonreligious humanitarian pacifist
(not to mention the selective objector). Although a few Congressmen were sympathetic, American pacifists lacked the support
enjoyed by their British confreres at Westminster among the pacifist
and ex-conscientious objector M.P.'s, who included several former
absolutists in their ranks. Many Congressmen feared that if exemption were permitted in the case of nonreligious objectors, the door
would be opened to Communist infiltration; there was little understanding, either, of the unconditional stand.

From the position of the historic peace churches and their
pacifist colleagues (and from the vantage point of hindsight) it
would probably have been ultimately better if they had turned down
government proposals for their collaboration, however well meant,
in view of the exclusion of part of the community of objectors from
the benefit of the act and the privileged position this gave to the
religious pacifist. Yet there were also cogent reasons for accepting
the hand proffered them, despite the admitted shortcomings of the
legislation. Some of the disadvantages of such cooperation were
indeed difficult to foresee at the outset.

What the administration then proposed appeared to be a decided
step forward from the position its predecessor had taken in 1917.
It offered to the three historic peace churches—or rather to their
service committees—representing, as it were, the community of
religious objectors, the running of alternative civilian service. Thus,
though prime responsibility for the scheme would still rest with the
government, its day-to-day organization was to be in the hands of
independent bodies staffed by pacifists. Assignees to Civilian Public
Service (CPS) would be employed on soil conservation and in

forestry, occupations clearly unconnected with the war and at the same time of obvious national importance; the model for this kind of project being drawn from the New Deal's Civilian Conservation Corps for the able-bodied unemployed of the depression period. The Selective Service System promised to provide camp sites and camp equipment with the technical supervision and work equipment coming from the Departments of Agriculture and the Interior. On the other hand, the administration of the camps and the men's maintenance were to be the responsibility of the historic peace churches; if, however, they became financially unable to carry out their obligations in this respect, the government promised to continue the program on its own. In any case Selective Service reserved to itself the right to exercise overall supervision of the camps and to lay down general lines of policy.

Records of the negotiations leading up to the final acceptance by the three peace churches of the government's conditions are unfortunately defective. There is some disparity, too, between the versions presented by the two sides to the bargain. It appears certain that the peace churches, while ready all along to shoulder full responsibility for their own objectors, urged the administration to open—for those not wishing to participate in the church units—a series of government-sponsored camps and to pay objectors for work done there. It seems, too, that Selective Service was inclined to accept these proposals, when they were vetoed by the personal intervention of President Roosevelt, who felt they provided objectors with too soft an option to military service. The peace churches were then faced with the alternative of either rejecting collaboration altogether or accepting the government terms, which involved them in sole responsibility (that is, within the framework of Selective Service direction) for all conscientious objectors assigned to CPS. In December 1940 the three historic peace churches and their allies capitulated, agreeing to sponsor and finance the camps—at first, however, for a trial period of six months. The CPS program was officially inaugurated in February 1941 and the first camp opened on the following May 15.

Objectors given 4-E classification and prepared, as at first most of them were, to accept its conditions, had no choice but to serve without pay in a church-organized camp; the sponsoring churches in their turn were obliged to receive all such men. This restricted freedom of action appeared the main drawback at first. However, as was later revealed, the full extent of the control exercised by Selective Service had also not been properly defined and serious misunderstanding and friction arose on this account.

Yet, "although the program fell short of the full desires of those concerned with the conscientious objector, Civilian Public Service was generally accepted as the best alternative which could be secured." [31] Even radicals like A. J. Muste approved the arrangement at the beginning; opposition voices like that of Dr. Evan Thomas, the socialist leader's brother and an ex-absolutist of World War I, who was then chairman of the War Resisters' League, were rare even if many pacifists did indeed have considerable misgivings. So far as one can judge, at first the rank-and-file objector also welcomed in outline a scheme that allowed him to perform his alternative service under pacifist auspices and in a sympathetic milieu. As for Selective Service, its leaders, and especially General Hershey, were enthusiastic. For them it appeared an experiment in vital democracy. They extolled it for promoting collaboration btween the state and a nonconformist minority, even in a period of national emergency.

Before we move on to describe how the CPS experiment worked out in practice we should briefly discuss the wartime stands of the three sponsoring agencies, which helped to initiate CPS, and later shared the major responsibility for administering it—as well as the blame for its shortcomings and failures.

Of the three historic peace churches the Quakers were probably the best known to the American public. "The Friends," wrote Sibley and Jacob (themselves members of the Society), "were deeply divided in their attitudes toward the war. Only a minority in most meetings were pacifists, and many actually denounced the C.O.'s and opposed any action on their behalf." [32] This situation was especially true of the evangelical and, in places, fundamentalist Quaker meetings of the mid-West and Pacific coast (the Quakerism that has produced a President Nixon). But even in the liberal meetings of the East, by World War II conscientious objection had become "a minority position." "75% is a conservative estimate of the members of the Society of military age who were in the armed forces." [33] Of course, some of these men were only nominally Quakers but the majority were members in good

standing in their Society. The pacifist impulse in American Quakerism was centered in the American Friends Service Committee,
with its headquarters in Philadelphia—a body that was suspect with
some Quakers on account of alleged theological liberalism and
political radicalism. Tradition in the Society of Friends, however,
was opposed to war and the antipacifist position was rarely given
considered expression.[34] Many Quakers, especially among the
older generation, eschewed any political implications to their
renunciation of war and nurtured a purely vocational pacifism,
which they claimed, not without reason, as "the classic Quaker
position." [35] But there were also Quaker peace radicals and
Quaker absolutists; at least one respected Friend resigned on
joining the army because he believed the Society should maintain
an uncompromising pacifist witness. The hallmark of wartime
American Quakerism was thus one of very considerable diversity
in regard to its peace testimony.

The Mennonites were more fragmented than the Quakers but
the various bodies into which their church had separated in the
course of the nineteenth century were more united than the Society
of Friends in maintaining their traditional pacifist testimony. The
majority of the sixteen branches of Mennonitism still disfellowshipped members who accepted military service; some did this
even in the case of members who served as noncombatants. Where
the barriers between the isolated sect and the world had largely
broken down, there the enforcement of the discipline in regard to
war service as in other aspects of life relaxed. The Mennonite
Service Committee collaborated with Quakers and Brethren and
other pacifist bodies in promoting the scheme of alternative service
for objectors;[36] but Mennonites kept a little aloof, for they feared
the influence which liberal pacifism of the FOR variety could
exercise on their young men and the degree to which its proponents
might undermine the Bible-centered nonresistance of Mennonite
tradition. Since, however, they believed in rendering Caesar what
in conscience they felt was his due, Mennonites welcomed the
opportunity offered by CPS for amicable collaboration between
their church and the state. CPS had had its prototype in their
historical experience; from 1881 until 1918 Mennonites in Tsarist
Russia had performed alternative service in forestry camps under
not dissimilar conditions from those now proposed by the govern-

ment of the United States. In 1940–41, therefore, they once again entertained hopes of a harmonious relationship with the authorities, mixed with some apprehension concerning the impact of worldly ideas and values on the Mennonite conscripts.[37]

The Church of the Brethren at this date stood halfway between Quakers and Mennonites. Like the latter, emerging, though more rapidly, from its rural isolation and sharing the same German background and a similar traditional Biblical nonresistance, the church reflected, on the other hand, something of the Quaker outreach on the subject of peace. During the interwar years the Brethren, or at least the church's most intellectually and spiritually aware members, had become increasingly concerned with the social and economic implications of pacifism. Disarmament, international reconciliation and violence in labor relations were subjects which exercised their thought and attracted their study. But, as the war was to show, this social concern, this renovated witness for peace, was the demesne of a relatively small section of the total membership. There had been a failure to communicate the message so that, as the Brethren communities became integrated into the mainstream of American life, their members often shed their pacifism along with the traditional peculiarities of speech, dress and way of life (which many of the Mennonite denominations still retained intact): a process that had been enacted a half century or more earlier in the case of the Quakers, though with less immediately alarming results. In World War II the overwhelming majority of Brethren, it was discovered, accepted combatant service. Of 24,228 men from the church drafted up to March 1945, 21,481 accepted full military service, whereas only 1,382 entered noncombatant duties and slightly less—1,365—chose CPS.[38] This retreat from a clear pacifist witness came about despite the fact that Brethren leaders officially urged members of military age, who wished to follow the teachings of their church, against noncombatant as much as against combatant service.

The history of CPS reflects the interplay of a number of different human factors. Selective Service officials, from General Hershey down, were optimistic as to the outcome, viewing the program as a remarkable positive achievement for a country about to become involved in a gigantic war. The three peace churches and the groups associated with them shared something of these feelings, modified however by their disappointment at not actualizing a still more liberal plan and their regret at the restrictions now set to their freedom of action in the program's administration. But they were anxious at any rate to make a success of the scheme. The third factor, on which the ultimate fate of CPS depended, were the men themselves, those conscientious objectors who over the next half decade or so were to receive 4-E classification from the Selective Service System.

Civilian Public Service: Assignees or Inmates?

CPS, when compared with the pragmatic method of dealing with conscientious objectors in Great Britain, was a more grandiose, and at the same time a less elastic design. Its promoters among the pacifists hoped it would become, as it were, "a religious order whose members, though under legal compulsion, were moved primarily by their personal ideals to perform a sacrificial service." [39] It would reproduce, they hoped, the enthusiastic atmosphere and the devoted service of the voluntary work camps, which Quakers and other pacifists had been sponsoring before the war as twentieth-century youth's moral equivalent to fighting. It did not provide an easy option; the men received bare maintenance (and some even covered this themselves), did hard manual work and lived usually under conditions similar to those of an army camp. True, they were not subjected to the risks to life and limb that servicemen were but it would scarcely have been possible to devise a scheme of alternative civilian service where this would have been so.

The root cause of CPS's subsequent *malaise* lay, it would appear, in the fact that it is impossible to create a quasi-religious order of the kind envisaged by compulsion (as the whole experience, for example, of the Roman Catholic Church has shown). It was just this element of compulsion in CPS that finally eroded its idealism to a vanishing point.

Sibley and Jacob have summarized the work performed by CPS men, including the "detached service" units permitted from March 1942 onward, and have evaluated its significance in the following words:

They served in conservation and forestry camps, in hospitals and state training schools, at university laboratories and agricultural experiment stations, on individual farms and government survey crews. They made roads, cleared truck and foot trails, fought forest fires, dug irrigation ditches, constructed dams, built fences, planted trees, pulled weeds, conducted soil-conservation experiments, acted as "guinea-pigs" for medical and scientific research, tended dairy cattle, tilled the soil, built sanitary facilities for hookworm-ridden communities, cared for the mentally ill, the feeble-minded, and the juvenile delinquent. . . . The conscientious objectors' records of service must also be measured in less tangible terms [than the millions of dollars saved by the government as a result of the objectors' unpaid labor]: the long-range values of the medical and scientific discoveries stemming from experiments performed with conscientious objectors; the demonstration of nonviolent techniques of treatment in the care of mental patients; a new care for the fate of the deranged as C.O.'s brought the appalling conditions in state institutions forcefully to public attention; the continuity of conservation experiments and programs which would have been broken by the war had it not been possible to staff them with C.O.'s.[40]

Yet, granted that both in camp and, even more, in the special projects much useful and creative work was done, there was a reverse side to the picture, too. "Much of Civilian Public Service was unworthy either of the calibre of men and convictions placed at its disposal or of the sacrifices of freedom and security which were imposed." [41] Much of the labor seemed to be just "made" work or lacking in any special urgency or importance. Selective Service was responsible for work assignment: it unaccountably (so it seemed at least to CPS men) rejected many requests for permission to take up special projects in hospitals or social welfare, which urgently needed personnel. Often little notice was taken in job assignment of a man's specialist skills. An outstanding botanist consigned to maintenance work in a mental hospital; an electrical engineer pulling weeds in a market garden; a leading research physicist clearing a swamp; a penicillin researcher sent to a wildlife reserve: such cases were by no means exceptional. A serious blow to CPS hopes come at the end of June 1943 when Congress by an amendment to the Army Appropriation Act refused permission for conscientious objectors to go overseas in relief work (a group of men seconded by AFSC for work with the British FAU in China had to turn back in mid-ocean) or even to train in colleges for this purpose. The motive underlying such restrictions was fear that these activities might help to glamorize the conscientious objector.

If the content of civilian public service often left the individual conscientious objector with a sense of unfulfilment and sometimes of concrete grievance, a lack of homogeneity among the campers often made it hard to create a feeling of group responsibility. Both these difficulties indeed stemmed from the fact that neither the sponsoring church bodies nor the men themselves were free agents. By the terms of their contract, as it were, they had delivered their freedom of action over into the hands of the Selective Service System.

Uniformity in background and belief was most apparent in the camps run by the Mennonite Central Committee. Mennonite objectors, who constituted almost 40 percent of the total number of CPS men, came mainly from farming communities; in CPS, therefore, their work did not greatly differ from their peacetime calling and they suffered, on the whole, from less frustration than city-bred CPS men. The strictly Bible-centered tone prevailing in the MCC camps did not attract outsiders to make them their choice, unless an objector shared a similar religious outlook; nor did the MCC seek recruits from elements whose way of thinking was markedly different from their own. The Mennonite leaders exercised, too, firm control over the intellectual life of their camps. They carefully vetted visiting speakers, not infrequently refusing permission to pacifists suspected of theological liberalism, political radicalism or a *penchant* towards the absolutist position. They also controlled the reception of literature from the outside, excluding those papers and books which they feared might cause unrest among their assignees. As a result, in cleaving to traditional ways of thought despite the potentially upsetting experience of CPS, Mennonite young men remained "remarkably steadfast" (to use the words of a sociologist in her study of the Amish branch).[42]

A similar harmony (or should one perhaps say a parallel intellectual aridity?) did not exist in either the Brethren or the Quaker camps. For one thing Brethren represented here only about 11 percent and Quakers as little as 7 percent of the total number of campers. It would thus have been difficult for these two groups to achieve the uniform composition of some Mennonite camps, where up to 90 percent of the assignees belonged to the Mennonite faith. Secondly, the fact that the three peace churches had agreed to administer CPS on behalf of any conscientious objectors whom

Selective Service chose to assign to alternative civilian service meant that all CPS assignees had to find a place in a church-run camp. As explained above, comparatively few nonmembers selected a Mennonite camp. A large number chose the Brethren. But most objectors, who did not belong to the historic peace churches (and assignees of this kind amounted to as much as 40 percent of the CPS total), chose to join the Quakers. This was especially true of the religious liberals and the ethical objectors. Indeed, at least at first, they had really no alternative in most cases (as the Quakers had no alternative but to accept them). True, several camps or detached service units were started by other bodies—e.g., Catholic objectors, the NSBRO or certain agencies attached to nonpacifist Protestant denominations—but these were either short-lived on account of lack of funds or very limited in numbers.

"Conscientious objection on a personal basis . . . was found in most of the religious organizations of the United States," writes Colonel Wherry.[43] Most objectors who entered CPS belonged to Protestant churches. But in addition there were humanists and spiritualists as well as Roman Catholics and practicing Jews,[44] Moslems and Buddhists and Hopi Indians. The camps also contained a sprinkling of nonreligious socialist and anarchist objectors, whose claims to exemption their Selective Service boards—more generous than the legislators—had been ready to acknowledge. Many of the religious sects represented were small; they were often obscure and occasionally eccentric. However, some denominations, like the Methodists or the Baptists, were present in considerable numbers. The educational background of CPS men varied considerably, ranging from occasional illiteracy to the university professor level; however, the average of intelligence, especially in the Quaker camps which contained a much higher proportion of students and professional men as well as of urban dwellers than those run by Mennonites or Brethren, was considerably higher than among the CPS men's contemporaries who had been conscripted into the army.[45]

The proportion of Quakers in a Friends' camp or project was rarely more than a third; often it did not amount to more than a quarter. The diversity of belief and social background mirrored in the community of objectors at large was thus reflected in the

Quaker camps to a greater degree than among the assignees under the care of the other two peace churches. Diversity can serve as a creative agent. There was no reason in theory why lack of homogeneity should necessarily act as an agent of disintegration. There was indeed every reason to hope that men united by a shared pacifist faith and dedicated to the resolution of conflict by loving means would be able to solve their problems to their mutual satisfaction. But this was, in fact, only partially the case. Tension, strain and friction were soon generated, due primarily (that is, in so far as the internal composition of the Quaker camps was concerned) to the presence of two potentially explosive elements: a group with an intense concern for the furtherance of social justice and (often overlapping) a group which was opposed on principle to the presuppositions on which the whole CPS experiment was built. Let us call these two groups the "social actionists" and the "crypto-absolutists."

Mennonite nonresistance, like that of the smaller fundamentalist sects represented in CPS, was still largely an inward-looking witness, an attempt to withdraw from contact with a warmaking world. The Quaker peace testimony in the twentieth century reached out to men in an attempt to transform domestic and international relations. "Because of the widespread peace program of AFSC," its secretary has written, "we tended to draw into our camps those CPS men who were more aggressively concerned with social measures that might prevent war and make for creative living. When such men found themselves in a camp far removed from the mainstream of life, this social impulse often seemed completely thwarted." [46] Objectors of this kind, like the left wing C.O.'s of World War I, derived their pacifism from a strong belief in human brotherhood, a belief they might express in either religious or ethical or political terms. Most of these men had been involved in social action of some sort before entering CPS. But there were those, too, whose social conscience and drive to action were first aroused only as a result of experience in CPS; by witnessing perhaps the harsh treatment of patients in mental institutions, or through the first contact with racial discrimination in communities where they now worked, or from sympathy with fellow objectors imprisoned for their more radical stand. Especially in view of the presence in many camps of a small group of convinced social actionists, the very isolation of camp life could bring CPS men greater opportunity to ponder social problems than the rush of city life had provided. Even Mennonite men, as their directors feared, might not always be immune to such an awakening.

In constant camp discussions, as well as in mimeographed weekly newssheets, the social actionists pressed their views. Their demands for fargoing reforms in mental care were not likely to arouse hostility either among the church administrators of CPS or in the Selective Service direction; indeed they could expect to find sympathy in these quarters. But they also broached other and more controversial issues. They called for a more democratic organization of CPS and for increased autonomy *vis-à-vis* Selective Service. They criticized in particular the unpaid character of CPS work, as well as the failure of the government to provide the normal dependents' allowances and workmen's compensation, as an infringement of the rights of labor and the dignity of man. (General Hershey adamantly opposed CPS pay as likely to damage relations with the public and as an unmerited concession to men who were not being required to risk their lives on active service.) The social actionists protested vehemently, too, against Selective Service's refusal on occasion to assign Negro objectors for work in localities where segregationist feeling was strong. Selective Service claimed that it did this to avoid trouble and not from any racial discrimination. The sponsoring agencies, while stating their support for racial equality, refused to give a general undertaking that they would withdraw from sponsorship of any unit where such a practice had occurred. In the end AFSC went so far as to promise that it would not start any new project unless its interracial character were guaranteed. In the arguments in favor of caution put forward by the church agencies, whether in regard to internal camp organization or to the race question, the social actionists scented apostasy. They agitated in the camps; they organized inter-camp conferences to plan a strategy of social activism. These conferences were frowned on both by the sponsoring agencies and by General Hershey, who attempted to ban them.

The question of camp democracy was a complicated one. Camp councils chosen from the men existed in every unit alongside the camp directors appointed by the sponsoring agency. The degree of responsibility in running the camp allotted to these councils varied. In Mennonite camps, where the councils were nominated by the directors, they were largely advisory; in Brethren, and still more in Quaker camps, where the councils were elected, they exercised a considerable degree of authority. Quakers and Brethren also gave the men in CPS some representation on their service committees in an effort to disperse the resentment building up against them among the assignees. But camp administration was not simply a problem to be worked out between the men and their sponsoring church agency. Overall control lay in the hands of General Hershey and the Selective Service System, which claimed the right of inspection to see that its regulations were being observed and of taking disciplinary action in case of nonobservance. The System had its representative on the spot in the person of the project superintendent responsible for the work performed by the CPS men. Selective Service disliked the Quakers' way of running their camps (indeed this did have its disadvantages with sometimes too much talk and too little decision-making). The Service indeed seemed to regard the historic peace churches as its agents whose task it was to see that the men carried out the policies of Selective Service. Camp directors were answerable not only to their service committee (and in practice often to the men in camp, too) but also to Selective Service, which demanded an array of reports showing how its orders had been fulfilled.

The stand of Selective Service—which in fact it was far from being able to enforce, as we shall soon see—is reflected in the following passage from a report drawn up by one of its officials, Colonel Franklin A. McLean:

From the time an assignee reports to camp until he is finally released he is under the control of the Director of Selective Service. He ceases to be a free agent and is accountable for all of his time, in camp and out, 24 hours a day. His movements, actions and conduct are subject to control and regulation. He ceases to have certain rights and is granted privileges instead. These privileges can be restricted or withdrawn without his consent as punishment, during emergency or as a matter of policy. He may be told when and how to work, what to wear and where to sleep. . . . He may be moved from place to place and from job to job, even to foreign countries, for the convenience of the government regardless of his personal feelings or desires.[47]

One did not need to be in basic disagreement with the concept of civilian public service to reject with indignation the view of CPS's role outlined here by Colonel McLean. And there were men in CPS who went much further than the majority of their colleagues in opposition to the system of conscription. For these "misplaced absolutists" (to use Sibley and Jacob's apt description) CPS was no better than a system of "slave labor." We may agree that there was much to criticize in the shape imposed on CPS by Congress and, equally, in the attitude subsequently adopted by Selective Service. In particular, the failure to provide sufficient outlet for the impulse towards community service was a serious shortcoming in the administration of CPS. But to speak of slavery, surely, was an exaggeration—if the word is to retain any significant content; indeed it manifested a certain lack of balanced judgment on the part of those who used it.

Slow-downs on the job or work strikes as well as demonstrative fasts were employed not merely to register protest against what the participants considered abuses in the system, but also to protest against conscription itself and the whole CPS system. What these men were in effect demanding as a minimum was a complete transformation of the pattern of administering conscientious objection so as to provide for unconditional exemption and a purely voluntary camp set-up freed from its connection via Selective Service with the military machine. There was really only one legitimate, though illegal, method of expressing such total protest: that was to walk out of camp altogether. Some men did this; the consequences for them of their action will be dealt with *inter alia* in the next section of this chapter. But to remain in camp and deliberately pursue there a policy of passive resistance and work sabotage, as others did, lacked straightforwardness.

As discontent grew, spreading from the social actionists and crypto-absolutists to embrace many who only partly shared their outlook but nurtured genuine grievances—mixed with some less conscientious, but not unnatural "gripes"—against the working of the civilian service system, camp administrators (especially in Quaker units) were faced with a dilemma. "Must they discipline men for taking conscientious action to express their disapproval of war and conscription?" [48] Selective Service regarded such action as a minor crime. The religious agencies strove to establish "redemptive discipline," i.e., the remedying of any legitimate complaints (so far, of course, as this lay within their power) along with an acknowledgment of fault on the part of any camper guilty of a real delinquency. This appeal to the sensitized consciences of the men often worked but, as Sibley and Jacob admit, "some C.O.'s scorned redemption." [49] This was especially the case where church administration and assignees were divided by opposing views of what was right.

Apart from minor infractions of discipline, punishable by loss of privileges, problems which camp directors dealt with on the spot, the latter were required by law to report to Selective Service any assignee refusing to work ("R.T.W.") or absent from camp without leave for more than ten days ("A.W.O.L."). For these offenses CPS men were liable to prosecution in the civil courts. But courts were not always willing to sentence offenders; for example, in the case of work strikes there were federal courts which displayed considerable sympathy with the strikers and their struggle for more equitable conditions of labor. Selective Service also attempted reclassification, which would deprive delinquents of their 4-E status; but this was a lengthy and complicated procedure, which the Service found more effective as a threat than as an actual punishment. Reclassification was, moreover, strongly opposed by the religious agencies. They entertained qualms at taking any part, even a passive one, in a process which might end in depriving a man of his status as a conscientious objector and they were quite ready on such occasions to stand up, "sometimes quite vigorously," to Selective Service in defense of what they considered the Service's arbitrary treatment of the objector. Finally, in its search for a realistic deterrent to employ against dissident CPS elements, Selective Service compiled a "black list" of men it considered trouble-makers, which it used in order to refuse them assignment to the more interesting and creative special projects. But none of these means of coercion, which represented the utmost Selective Service could do "within the constitutional limits of American democracy," [50] proved particularly successful.

Whereas Selective Service and the Department of Justice advocated increasing the compulsory powers of the government to deal with infractions of CPS discipline, the three sponsoring church agencies, instead, urged as their remedy for the growing demoralization and rising discontent a relaxation of coercion together with a broadening of the outlets for more creative and useful service. In this way they hoped that the initial spiritual dynamism could be revived. They finally converted Attorney-General Francis Biddle to their standpoint; but in the meanwhile, as a result of their experiences in running the camps, they had subjected their own views on CPS to radical revision.

One last attempt was made to rescue CPS from the *impasse* in which it found itself when in July 1943 the first of several government-sponsored camps was opened: a step which the historic peace churches had urged on the administration from the beginning. Indeed, if at the outset the administration had heeded their advice, government camps might have helped to assuage the discontent of the nonreligious at being forced to serve under religious auspices and thus have removed at least one source of unrest. In fact, their inauguration now proved a disaster. They became, in the words of Sibley and Jacob, "the ultimate penal colonies of Civilian Public Service." [51]

The venture was ill-starred almost from the very beginning. Three major errors were committed by those who planned it. In the first place, a good proportion of those who were transferred from church-run camps—though, of course, by no means all, for campers who did not expressly opt for a church camp were so transferred—were noncooperators, extremists who were out to fight conscription by destroying CPS as a system of state slavery. Secondly, this mistake was compounded by the Selective Service System's habit of punishing men from church camps found guilty of indiscipline by banishing them to the government camps, thereby increasing the number of misfits there and underlining the penal character of such institutions. In the third place, the government's policy of stubbornly refusing to assignees in the camps directly under its control any say in their administration, which rested solely with outside officials, had the effect of turning even those inclined to collaborate into rebels against authority, for it appeared as a direct challenge to the often not unjustified demands of CPS men for greater internal democracy. The results of this policy soon showed themselves in the obstructionist tactics pursued by a majority of government campers: work slow-downs, inflated sick-lists and even failure to cooperate in keeping the camps clean and tidy. Thus, largely through the administration's ineptitude, and in part, of course, through the actions of the campers themselves, assignees to the building of a cooperative society had indeed become inmates of a quasi-penal system.

But was not the general decline of CPS due at bottom neither to the attitude of Selective Service, for its leaders were only acting according to their light, nor to the CPS men, whose position was not altogether one of their own choosing, but to the stand of the three sponsoring churches and the pacifist organizations which had supported them? Had they not perhaps betrayed their mission, with however good intentions? If this were the case, was it not now their duty to acknowledge their mistake and free themselves, and thereby the men under their care, from the incubus of voluntary servitude to the military machine? Questions of this kind were being asked not only by the men in the camps but also fairly generally in pacifist and peace church circles. Several smaller groups eventually withdrew from collaboration with the coordinating National Service Board for Religious Objectors. Finally, in March 1946, the Quaker AFSC itself withdrew from CPS administration, handing over its camps to the government. The Mennonites and Brethren continued their cooperation with Selective Service until the government's decision in March 1947 to bring CPS to an end in view of the near completion of demobilization, which had been proceeding since October 1945, i.e., from a month after the surrender of Japan.

After CPS was over, those who had participated in it, whether as assignees or overseers, began the postmortem. No consensus of opinion emerged; no agreement was reached concerning the relative success or failure of the experiment. Both the government and the pacifists acknowledged that they had made mistakes, but they differed as to what these were and as to the remedies that should have been applied. On the whole, the Mennonites and those objectors who believed in going the second mile agreed with the government viewpoint that CPS had provided an opportunity for constructive service unconnected in any direct way with the prosecution of the war and performed in a relatively free and congenial environment. They regarded it not merely as the best possible alternative in view of the wartime state of public opinion and of Congress's attitude, they also believed it expressed American democracy's capacity for tolerating an unpopular minority opinion. At the same time they were at one with the many Quaker pacifists and other objectors, who came, on the other hand, to doubt the wisdom of pacifist involvement in the administration of conscription, in criticizing certain aspects of the CPS program: its failure to recognize the nonreligious objector or to provide unconditional exemption for absolutists, its direct dependence on the military and denial of real autonomy to the sponsoring civilian agencies, and its semi-penal labor conditions.

Sibley (differing on this occasion in his assessment from his colleague Jacob, who believes that the historic peace churches were right to undertake the administration of CPS) has summed up the case against the churches' involvement as follows: "The pacifist churches, by their mere presence as administrators for a military agency, lent an air of religious sanction to a quasi-military treatment of conscientious objection." "While gaining incidental benefits for objectors in the process," he goes on, "they allowed themselves to be manipulated by the state for its own ends." Whereas the principle of alternative service for a wide variety of objectors was a definite advance on the position in World War I, the collaboration of pacifist bodies in running it was a retrograde step. In exchange for the privilege of administering the CPS camps, an agreement for which the churches did not even insist on receiving, a written contract defining their rights *vis-à-vis* Selective Service, thus leaving them dependent on the goodwill of the military men who ran the Service, these churches had ended up by acting as (unpaid) policemen for enforcing the Selective Service discipline on conscientious objectors. In this way, through the churches' collaboration with Selective Service, their men themselves eventually became partly alienated, while by their periodic and commendable resistance to the demands of Selective Service they failed to appease the military men who ran the Service. The large sums expended on their camps by all three churches would, in Sibley's view, have been better spent on their postwar relief programs.[52]

CPS appears today (at least to the present writer) as a classic example of what Lewis Mumford in another connection has described as "baroque planning": a style especially beloved by the military mind. Its principle was uniformity, regularity. Individual peculiarities must yield before the demands of the plan. Thus all objectors unwilling to accept noncombatant service were to be treated according to the same pattern. (Were not their contemporaries in the armed forces subjected to the same procedure?) But it was this planned freedom that proved CPS's undoing, for what would satisfy the conscience and vocational sense of a rural Mennonite nonresistant would not necessarily prove acceptable to the city-born Quaker or a war resister of the Social Gospel type. In the pacifist community, too, there were conditionalists of every sort as well as a number of absolutist objectors. Unlike the British legislation, the American attempt at providing for conscientious objection—although in many respects well-intentioned and certainly generous in comparison with World War I or with most other belligerent countries in World War II—suffered from a proclivity to press conscience into a uniform mold.

Conscientious Objectors in Prison

We have seen that some objectors attempted to actively protest against conscription from within CPS—though often with rather unfortunate results. There were others who chose to become law violators and go to prison because they disagreed with the principle of CPS. There were also, it should be added, men who were sent to prison not on account of any objection to CPS but because they were refused 4-E classification.

In World War II America, nine times as many conscientious objectors were in jail as in World War I (or between two and three times as many if we take into consideration the greater number of objectors drafted in the later conflict). In all, some 6,000 objectors were given civilian prison sentences down to the end of March 1947, when the Selective Training and Service Act of 1940 expired. This, however, represented only a little over a third of the total number of prosecutions under the Act for draft evasion. Some at least of the remaining draft-dodgers should undoubtedly be considered also as conscientious, for "sometimes the so-called evader had genuine objections but was not articulate about them." [53]

Over three quarters of the imprisoned objectors were Jehovah's Witnesses, whose Selective Service boards had rejected their claims for complete exemption as ministers of religion. In contrast, although Mennonites represented by far the largest group in CPS, very few—in fact less than fifty of them in all—were jailed. Their church's generally known pacifism and their own readiness in almost all cases to do alternative service led to their seldom being refused 4-E status by their draft boards. The average sentence for a Jehovah's Witness was four years; for other objectors the average was around three years (a much higher average, incidentally, than occurred with violators of narcotics or white-slave laws and much higher, too, than was the case with objectors in Great Britain, where prison sentences tended on the whole to be considerably shorter). The maximum sentence that could be imposed was five years and a $10,000 fine. Under 500 sentences ran to a year or less. The heaviest sentencing took place, as might be expected, in the period between Pearl Harbor and the surrender of Japan.

There were roughly 100 cases of "cat-and-mouse," i.e., repeated sentencing of an objector for what was in fact, if not in law, the same offense. There was a tendency, too, in some courts, as the number of cases began to accumulate, to hold mass trials of thirty to forty objectors at once. On the other hand, courts were often sympathetic to objectors and did their best, within the framework of the law they were duty-bound to administer, to respect conscience; one magistrate in Philadelphia, who was a Friend, expressed his dilemma at having to sentence young Quakers for doing what they believed the Inner Light told them to do. Some federal judges, especially those in the Los Angeles area, showed intelligence and understanding by imposing probation instead of prison on objectors appearing before them. The number of probationary sentences, however, remained small. For this situation three factors were responsible. First, the practice was discouraged by the Selective Service System. The System disliked, in particular, the fact that probationers worked for pay, even when directed to CPS, whereas (largely at the insistence of Selective Service) objectors assigned to CPS by reason of their 4-E classification labored without remuneration. In the second place, public pressure was often mobilized against the probationing of conscientious objectors, especially by groups like the American Legion. Thirdly, many sentenced objectors themselves felt unable to comply with the legal prerequisite for a probation order: a general promise to abide by the law. Yet, particularly for the misclassified objector anxious to perform alternative service if given the chance, probation, if more generally applied, would have provided a reasonable solution.

The prison community of objectors was quite a varied one. Apart from the Jehovah's Witnesses (unsuccessful candidates for ministerial status) who predominated, the misclassified alternativists, and the CPS delinquents prosecuted either on account of walks-out or work strikes, most of the remaining objectors in prison may broadly be described as convinced absolutists. Some refused to collaborate with the conscription system at all and became nonregistrants in respect to the draft. Others registered but at some later stage made clear their opposition to alternative civilian service, at least of the kind that was offered by the existing legislation or as an enforced change from what they regarded as their vocation. They might balk at filling in their draft questionnaire, or they might refuse to go for induction into army or CPS as directed by a Selective Service board.

Among the nonregistrants (who did not total more than 300) were nonpacifist Black Muslims and Black Jews, whose conscience forbade them to fight in a struggle that they believed was not a holy war. The group also included young Quakers as well as Christian pacifists like the eight students from Union Theological Seminary in New York then living in voluntary poverty in Harlem, who refused to register for the first draft in mid-October 1940. In a published declaration of *Why We Refused to Register,* the Union students stated:

It is impossible for us to think of the conscription law without at the same time thinking of the whole war system, because it is clear to us that conscription is definitely a part of the institution of war. . . . To us the war system is an evil part of our social order, and we declare that we cannot cooperate with it in any way. War is an evil because it is in violation of the Way of Love as seen in God through Christ. It is a concentration and accentuation of all the evils of our society. . . . If we register under the act, even as conscientious objectors, we are becoming part of the act. . . . We do not expect to stem the war forces today; but we are helping to build the movement that will conquer in the future.[54]

This manifesto, clothed in the language of the Social Gospel, expresses admirably the core of the unconditionalists' argument against conscription.

A number of older pacifists above the current draft age, including such veterans as A. J. Muste, Evan Thomas and Richard B. Gregg, also refused to register. Though they made a public declaration of their law violation—as indeed most nonregistrants did, for usually their position had to some extent the character of a public protest—the Department of Justice wisely decided not to prosecute. Indeed it slyly turned the tables by declaring that it accepted the men's statements as an effective registration! It did prosecute in 28 cases of "counseling and aiding evasion" of national service. But this number was small, especially when compared with the situation during and immediately after World War I. It illustrates both the Department of Justice's commendable caution in such matters and the fact now "that there was relatively little 'political' opposition to the war." [55]

Sentences imposed on conscientious objectors were served in federal prisons, except for a small number of men with terms of less than a year who went to county jails. These institutions, so the latter reported, were "for the most part dirty, badly managed and dominated by graft and corruption." [56] Concerning the various types of federal prison—penitentiaries, correctional institutions, reformatories, prison camps and prison farms—in which some objectors were now to spend three or four or even more years, reports were on the whole rather more favorable. They were usually very clean and sometimes not unattractive in appearance. Yet the atmosphere was cold and repressive. The unchanging routine, combined with petty restrictions and irritating punishments for their infringement, produced an oppressive monotony and a feeling of intense constriction: conditions, of course, that were as much the lot of the ordinary convict as of the prisoner of conscience. At the same time longer sentences allowed for a more creative use of labor than in British prisons. There was provision for sports as well as for recreational and educational activities, entirely absent in the jails of wartime Britain. In American prisons, objectors were employed *inter alia* on farm work, truck driving, craftwork and the teaching of illiterate or undereducated prisoners. [57]

Most jailed objectors served out their terms without coming into conflict with the prison authorities. The Jehovah's Witnesses, for instance, who "possessed a high sense of group solidarity" and "tended in each prison to act as a group under the direction of a chosen leader," were cooperative. For the most part they kept to themselves, practicing work slow-downs or such only where prison authorities placed restrictions on their meetings or the reception of Witness literature from the outside.[58] On the other hand, many pacifists, Christian or secularist, with a strong social commitment (sometimes, be it noted, such commitment was generated as a result of contact with the problems of prison society) found reason to oppose the prison system. In protest at injustices in the system they organized jail strikes or undertook individual work or hunger strikes. Racial segregation at meal tables or during recreation time, arbitrary censorship of literature and correspondence, employment on work connected with war industry were among the matters at issue.

Refusal to work, which was punishable by solitary confinement (sometimes in so-called "dark holes," officially abolished but in fact still retained in some prisons) as well as by dietary restrictions, was also practiced by libertarian objectors, who wished to register a total disengagement from conscription. Among work strikers of this kind were members of a sect of Russian origin, the Molokans, whose fathers had suffered severe manhandling in World War I for a similar stand. One of the most stubborn resisters was Corbett Bishop, who went on a hunger strike throughout the whole time of his incarceration. He was forcibly fed by the prison authorities as were two other absolutists, Stanley Murphy and Louis Taylor, whose case became something of a *cause célèbre*. They had walked out of CPS in October 1942 when they realized that they disagreed basically with the system it represented. Convicted and imprisoned, they embarked on a hunger strike in protest against conscription, which they kept up for 82 days. Despite incarceration in an institution for the criminally insane and attempts to get them certified as themselves insane, which were thwarted by the refusal to agree of the outside doctor required by law to confirm the verdict of the prison medical service, the two men continued to smuggle out reports of serious abuses in the treatment of other inmates, accusations that were eventually backed by the testimony of members of the prison staff. Many pacifists and socially concerned nonpacifists felt that "in dramatizing these facts . . . Murphy and Taylor rendered the same kind of service to the community as those objectors who, with different tactics, exposed the conditions surrounding patients in mental hospitals." [59]

Conscientious objectors, like other prisoners, were eligible for various types of parole, if they had been cooperative in the course of their incarceration and were prepared to abide by certain restrictions on their activities after release (for instance, Jehovah's Witnesses had to promise not to preach!). Failure to observe these conditions, which were quite unacceptable to many absolutists, could lead to a man's return to prison for completion of sentence. After the war was over the jails were gradually emptied of their wartime conscientious objectors either through paroling or by expiration of the latter's sentences. However, the widespread campaign organized by pacifist groups to obtain a blanket amnesty for all imprisoned objectors, which would remove the legal disqualifications incurred by persons convicted of federal crimes, was unsuccessful. The government granted amnesty on a purely individual basis, excluding thereby the overwhelming majority of objectors from its scope.

"Absolutism," wrote Sibley and Jacob of the group which provided the backbone, if not the numerical preponderance, of the prison C.O. community, "became something of a sect within the ranks of pacifists and conscientious objectors." [60] It had its own professional association, as it were, and its own press organ, with the War Resisters' League acting as its spokesman in regard to the wider public. Some friction existed between absolutists and alternativists. While the latter sometimes regarded the absolutists as fanatical and cranky, the absolutists tended to view pacifists in CPS (not to speak of noncombatant objectors) as compromisers and half-measure men. In many cases the absolutists were strong individualists, for whom protest was almost a vocation. Their actions were often controversial, sometimes colorful, and occasionally a trifle bizarre. By their challenge to accepted norms, even while in prison, by their confrontation of pacifist orthodoxy as much as the presuppositions of militarism, by their refusal to cooperate where prudence indicated compromise, they contributed something of value to a society whose already existing tendency to conformism had been accentuated by the pressures of wartime. That they were able to make a protest of this kind at all, shows, however, that the libertarian impulse in American political life, if already long on the wane, still retained sufficient strength to absorb the shock of radical dissent.

CONSCIENTIOUS OBJECTION OUTSIDE GREAT BRITAIN
AND THE UNITED STATES

In the three British dominions where wartime conscription was introduced—Australia, New Zealand and Canada—the legislative pattern approximated in some respects more closely to the American than to the British one. In none of these countries was there provision for unconditional exemption. However, in all three countries nonreligious claims, if based on pacifist grounds, were recognized in practice, if not always in law. Canada and New Zealand instituted schemes of civilian alternative service, somewhat similar to the American CPS. But they were government-run and unconnected with the military draft organization. In New Zealand some 800 absolutists were detained for the duration of the war in so-called "defaulters' camps" under semi-penal conditions.[61] In Canada, on the other hand, few objectors were jailed, at least for long, even if their applications had been rejected by the "Mobilization Boards," which were the equivalent of the Selective Service local boards. Individual work assignments on soldiers' pay became frequent, especially from 1943 on. In Canada, too, blanket exemption deriving from earlier legislative guarantees was granted to two religious groups: the Mennonites who had emigrated from Russia and a sect of Russian ethnic origin, the Dukhobors. One small section of these Dukhobors, the Sons of Freedom in British Columbia, whose spiritual anarchism has led them on occasion to symbolic nudity and a certainly reprehensible display of arson, refused to register but remained untouched by the authorities, who may have feared the consequences of strong measures in stirring up an ethnic hornets' nest.

In New Zealand there were barely 3,000 objectors, with an approximately similar figure recorded for the much larger population of Australia. Canada produced nearly 11,000 conscientious objectors, of whom almost three quarters were drawn from Mennonite sects.[62] As in World War I, the sparseness of conscientious objection in these countries reflected the previous weakness of their pacifist movements. In Canada, though pacifism there had its political representative in the veteran parliamentary leader of the socialist Cooperative Commonwealth Federation (CCF), James S. Woodsworth,[63] he was no more able than George Lansbury had been a few years earlier with the British Labour Party to carry his party along with him in his ethical opposition to war. Though pacifist pockets existed in Canada's Protestant churches, a product to some extent of the same Social Gospel as motivated contemporary religious pacifism across the border, Canadian conscientious objection was largely a matter of the sects.

In Germany, as in Soviet Russia, the pacifist movement had been ruthlessly suppressed by the ruling dictatorship long before the outbreak of war. As we have seen in the last chapter, the German movement's leaders who were unable to flee the country were mostly imprisoned by the Nazis. Their followers melted away. Apart from Jehovah's Witnesses, whom Hitler put into his concentration camps, or a few individuals who, when called up, managed to get assignment to the army medical corps, conscientious objection to war scarcely existed in Germany. We do know, however, of one man, Dr. Hermann Stöhr, former secretary of the dissolved German branch of the Fellowship of Reconciliation, who adamantly refused induction into the army and was executed for this crime on June 21, 1940.[64] Stöhr was a Protestant, as was another German FOR member executed by Hitler for her antiwar activities, Elisabeth von Thadden (a sister, ironically, of the leader of West Germany's extreme nationalist party today, Adolf von Thadden). An American Catholic sociologist recently carried out an extensive investigation to discover whether any of his co-religionists refused military service in Hitler's armies. He could find only seven who had done so, despite the fact that before its suppression in 1933 Father Stratmann's antimilitarist Peace Association of German Catholics had numbered over 40,000 members and had, moreover, functioned with the approval of influential members of the church hierarchy. In their refusal to fight for Hitler in a war that surely might be classed as "unjust" if ever this definition were to have any meaning, these seven objectors, among whom were several priests and lay brothers, got at best a cold, if not an actually hostile, response from their clerical superiors. Six of the men were executed; one of them had his death sentence commuted to confinement in an army mental hospital and thus survived the war. Most of these men were from the intelligentsia, but one was an Austrian peasant, Franz Jagërstätter.[65]

In German-occupied Europe only Denmark, Norway and Holland had effective pacifist groups, however small, before invasion. A Danish war resister has spoken of the dilemma facing pacifists under occupation as follows:

> We could work on the illegal press, and some did so. But it was a very militaristic press and it often made quite unreasonable attacks on Danish officials, most of whom did good work in extremely difficult circumstances. Some took part in sabotage against such things as railway lines, etc., but most found that this was not the right way for them. When the Germans started to take hostages and kill them, and to blow up over-crowded trains as revenge for railway sabotage, nearly all found that they could not take responsibility for the consequences of sabotage. We came to know that our opponent used methods so inhuman that we did not want to give him any excuse to use them. And we saw how the fight produced hatred and the spirit of revenge, and in that way poisoned Danish minds with the Nazi outlook.[66]

Denmark, where the reaction of government and populace approximated most closely to passive resistance of the Gandhian variety (where, too, Nazi methods were rather less barbaric than elsewhere), the small pacifist movement continued to function openly, publishing regularly its monthly paper *Aldrig Mere Krig* (No More War) with articles protesting both against the Nazis' treatment of the Jews and their persecution of religion and culture in neighboring Norway. In the latter country pacifists, steering clear—like their Danish colleagues—of the more violent manifestations of sabotage, participated in the largely nonviolent resistance of the civil population against attempts to nazify cultural life; some of them were arrested and imprisoned by the Germans for such activities. But they were too small a group either to initiate or to guide this resistance. In regard to such efforts, a Norwegian pacifist leader admitted: "It . . . proved . . . more difficult . . . than our propaganda had led us to believe such resistance would be." From his wartime experience he drew the same conclusion as Gandhi had done from his campaigns against the British, namely, "that the open uncompromising resistance was the best and produced the most effective results." [67]

Whether driven underground in Nazi-occupied Europe, or able

to function openly as in Great Britain and the Commonwealth or in the United States or in certain neutral countries, pacifism in World War II appeared a small and seemingly ineffective sect. A war of hitherto unexampled destruction was raging throughout large parts of the globe. Under Nazi rule, atrocities that had not been seen since the days of Tamerlane were being committed daily. On the allied side, Stalin's Russia enforced a system as despotic as that of the Pharoahs' Egypt and the Anglo-American democracies carried out the incineration of tens of thousands of civilians, because they lived in enemy cities. One might well ask whether, in the peace that would eventually succeed the turmoil of war, pacifism could ever regain political relevance or become anything more than a purely personal ethic or a counsel of withdrawal.

NOTES

1. Quoted in Richenda C. Scott, *Herbert G. Wood: A Memoir of His Life and Thought* (London: Friends Home Service Committee, 1967), p. 125.

2. Sybil Morrison, *I Renounce War: The Story of the Peace Pledge Union* (London: Sheppard Press, 1962), p. 45. Cf. the pamphlet by Alexander Miller, *The Irrelevance of Pure Pacifism* (London: A Group of Pacifist Socialists, n.d.), pp. 6–9, for severe criticism of the campaign from a left wing pacifist viewpoint.

3. For public recantations of pacifism, see the two Macmillan War Pamphlets, London, 1940: C. E. M. Joad, *For Civilization,* and A. A. Milne, *War with Honour.* See also *The Autobiography of Bertrand Russell,* Vol. II (London: George Allen and Unwin Ltd., 1968), pp. 191, 192, 233.

4. See F. A. Lea, *The Life of John Middleton Murry* (London: Methuen & Co. Ltd., 1959), esp. Chap. XXIII. Best of all, consult the files of *Peace News* during Murry's editorship, which lasted until October 1946.

5. Beverley Nichols, *"In the Next War I Shall be a Conscientious Objector"* (London: Friends Peace Committee, 1932, reprinted from *Good Housekeeping*), p. 4. Nichols had ceased to be a pacifist by about 1938.

6. Quoted in Denis Hayes, *Challenge of Conscience* (London: George Allen and Unwin Limited, 1949), p. 4.

7. *Ibid.,* p. 37.

8. Quoted in *ibid.,* p. 182.

9. *Ibid.,* p. 266.

10. *Ibid.,* p. 91.

11. *Ibid.,* p. 202.

12. *Ibid.,* p. 28.

13. William Ralph Inge, *A Pacifist in Trouble* (London: Putnam, 1939), p. 23.

14. Roman Catholics and Anglo-Catholics, who have refused to participate in twentieth-century war on the ground that it did not fulfill the traditional conditions of a "just war" laid down by the church's moral theologians, probably belong in this category too. Classic statements of this position are to be found in Franziskus Stratmann, *The Church and War: A Catholic Study,* translated from the German (London: Sheed and Ward, 1928) and *Les Catholiques en face de la guerre* (Enfield, Middlesex: War Resisters' International, 1929). See Robert Speaight, *The Life of Eric Gill* (London: Methuen & Co. Ltd., 1966), pp. 303–307, and Hugh Ross Williamson, *The Walled Garden: An Autobiography* (London: Michael Joseph, 1956), Chap. XII, for Catholic antimilitarism of this kind in World War II Britain, where it was organized in a Pax Association. Gill was a sponsor of the Peace Pledge Union; Ross Williamson, on the other hand, did not consider himself a pacifist.

15. G. C. Field, *Pacifism and Conscientious Objection* (Cambridge: The University Press, 1945), p. 93. For a critique of Field's book, see E. L. Allen, Francis E. Pollard, G. A. Sutherland, *The Case for Pacifism and Conscientious Objection: A Reply to Professor G. C. Field* (London: Central Board for Conscientious Objectors, 1946).

16. Stuart Smith, in Clifford Simmons, ed., *The Objectors* (London: Gibbs and Phillips, 1965), p. 65.

17. Quoted in Hayes, *op. cit.,* p. 218.

18. See A. Tegla Davies, *Friends Ambulance Unit: The Story of the F.A.U. in the Second World War* (London: George Allen and Unwin Limited, 1947), and—for the activities of the official Quaker relief organization—Roger C. Wilson, *Quaker Relief: An Account of the Relief Work of the Society of Friends 1940–1948* (London: George Allen & Unwin Ltd., 1952).

19. David Morris, *China Changed My Mind* (London: Cassell & Company Limited, 1948), p. 42. Morris's book tells how the questions raised by working in a country like China, where the framework of law and order was only tenuously maintained and where religious pacifism was only very rarely comprehended, led eventually to the author's abandoning pacifism and joining the army. See esp. pp. 177–179, 191.

20. Quoted in Mulford Q. Sibley and Philip E. Jacob, *Conscription and Conscience* (Ithaca, N.Y.: Cornell University Press, 1952), pp. 68, 69.

21. See Nathan T. Elliff, "Jehovah's Witnesses and the Selective Service Act," *Virginia Law Review,* vol. 31, no. 4 (September, 1945), pp. 811–834.

22. Gordon C. Zahn, *War, Conscience and Dissent* (New York: Hawthorn Books, Inc., 1967), pp. 153, 154. Two chapters in this book ("Catholic Conscientious Objection in the United States" and "The Social Thought of the Catholic Conscientious Objector") are especially useful.

23. Sibley and Jacob, *op. cit.,* p. 81.

24. Quoted in Neal M. Wherry, *Conscientious Objection,* 2 vols. (Washington, D.C.: Selective Service System Special Monograph, no. 11, 1950), Vol. I, p. 72.

25. David Mitchell, *Seventh-day Adventists: Faith in Action* (New York: Vantage Press, 1958), pp. 49–52, 65, 115–117.

26. Sibley and Jacob, *op. cit.,* p. 89.

27. *Ibid.,* p. 97.

28. *Ibid.,* p. 87.

29. *Ibid.,* pp. 109 and 108.

30. See, for example, Kirby Page, *20,870 Clergymen on War and Economic Injustice* (New York: "The World Tomorrow," 1934); F. Ernest Johnson, "The Impact of the War on Religion in America," *The American Journal of Sociology,* vol. 48, no. 3 (November, 1942), pp. 354–356; Ray H. Abrams, "The Churches and the Clergy in World War II," *The Annals of the American Academy of Political and Social Science,* vol. 256 (1948), pp. 110–119.

31. Sibley and Jacob, *op. cit.,* p. 120.

32. *Ibid.,* p. 328.

33. Quoted in Bertram and Irene Pickard, *The Quaker Peace Testimony Today* (Philadelphia: Friends World Committee for Consultation, 1946), pp. 23, 26.

34. An exception here is the Quaker philosopher Brand Blanshard's forthright article "Non-Pacifist Quakerism," *Friends Intelligencer* (Philadelphia), vol. 99, no. 25 (June 20, 1942), pp. 393, 394; no. 26 (June 27, 1942), pp. 409, 410.

35. See, for example, D. Elton Trueblood, "The Quaker Way," *The Atlantic Monthly,* vol. 166, no. 6 (December, 1940), pp. 740–746. Trueblood's counterpart in England was Herbert G. Wood, referred to above in footnote 1.

36. See Melvin Gingerich, *Service for Peace: A History of the Mennonite Civilian Public Service* (Akron, Pa.: The Mennonite Central Committee, 1949).

37. Guy Franklin Hershberger, *The Mennonite Church in the Second World War* (Scottdale, Pa.: Mennonite Publishing House, 1951) tells the story for the more conservative of the two main branches of American Mennonitism.

38. Wherry, *op. cit.,* Vol. I, p. 322. The figures which, it must be remembered, include the unbaptized sons of Brethren as well as full members were supplied by the Brethren Service Committee. For the BSC's work for CPS, see Leslie Eisan, *Pathways of Peace: A History of the Civilian Public Service Program Administered by the Brethren Service Committee* (Elgin, Ill.: Brethren Publishing House, 1948).

39. Sibley and Jacob, *op. cit.,* p. 111.

40. *Ibid.,* pp. 124, 126.

41. *Ibid.,* p. 224.

42. A. G. E. Huntington, "Dove at the Window: A Study of an Old Order Amish Community in Ohio" (Ph.D. diss., Yale University, 1956), p. 557.

43. Wherry, *op. cit.,* Vol. I, p. 27. On pp. 24–27 the author lists 345 religious bodies with members claiming registration as conscientious objectors between 1940 and 1947, and on pp. 318–320 he provides details concerning church membership of CPS men during the same period.

44. A Jewish Peace Fellowship was founded in 1942 with the support of several pacifist rabbis. The position of Jewish objectors was peculiarly difficult. In their own community they were frequently regarded as traitors because of their scruples concerning an armed struggle against their people's Nazi persecutors; patriots with antisemitic proclivities tended to view their stand as treason to their country. Catholic and Jewish objectors, unlike objectors coming from nonpacifist Protestant denominations, had this in

common that their spiritual leaders for the most part were actively hostile
to their position.

    45. Sibley and Jacob, *op. cit.*, pp. 170, 171, 529. See also G. C. Zahn, *A Descriptive Study of the Social Backgrounds of Conscientious Objectors in Civilian Public Service during World War II* (Washington, D.C:. Studies in Sociology—Abstract Series, No. 7, Catholic University of America, 1953).
    46. Clarence E. Pickett, *For More Than Bread* (Boston: Little, Brown and Company, 1953), p. 330.
    47. Quoted in Sibley and Jacob, *op. cit.*, p. 202.
    48. Pickett, *op. cit.*, p. 331.
    49. Sibley and Jacob, *op. cit.*, p. 216.
    50. *Ibid.*, p. 478.
    51. *Ibid.*, p. 242.
    52. *Ibid.*, pp. 471–475. Despite prolonged efforts by the historic peace churches, the government adamantly refused to release for postwar relief the "Frozen Fund," which had been formed out of the impounded wages paid for objectors' labor in off-camp assignments.
    53. *Ibid.*, p. 334.
    54. Staughton Lynd, ed., *Nonviolence in America* (Indianapolis: Bobbs-Merrill Co., Inc., 1966), pp. 297–299. Lynd in his anthology has reprinted the whole statement.
    55. Sibley and Jacob, *op. cit.*, p. 339.
    56. *Ibid.*, p. 352.
    57. Among several accounts of prison life written by World War II objectors two may be mentioned here: Alfred Hassler, *Diary of a Self-Made Convict* (Chicago: Henry Regnery Company, 1954) and Jim Peck, *We Who Would Not Kill* (New York: Lyle Stuart, 1958).
    58. Sibley and Jacob, *op. cit.*, p. 356.
    59. *Ibid.*, p. 416.
    60. *Ibid.*, p. 400.
    61. See Lincoln Efford, *Penalties on Conscience: An Examination of the Defaulters' Detention System in New Zealand* (Christchurch, N.Z.: The Caxton Press, 1945).
    62. *Reconciliation* (Toronto), vol. 2, no. 4 (June, 1945), pp. 3, 4, 12, 13. See also J. A. Toews, *Alternative Service in Canada during World War II* (Winnipeg: Publication Committee of the Canadian Conference of the Mennonite Brethren Church, 1959). The Mennonite author does not deal exclusively with his own denomination.
    63. Kenneth McNaught, *A Prophet in Politics* (Toronto: University of Toronto Press, 1959), pp. 309–312, also 298–300.
    64. *Ein Christ verweigert den Kriegsdienst: Hermann Stöhr zum Gedächtnis* (Zwiefalten, Württemberg: Sonderheft der "Versöhnung," 1951).
    65. G. C. Zahn, *German Catholics and Hitler's Wars* (New York: Sheed and Ward, 1962), p. 55. Zahn has devoted a whole book to Jägerstätter's case, *In Solitary Witness: The Life and Death of Franz Jägerstätter* (New York, Chicago, San Francisco: Holt, Rinehart and Winston, 1964). Jägerstätter objected to fighting in what he was convinced was an unjust war; he was, therefore, a selective objector rather than a complete pacifist. Of course, there was also a handful of pacifists in Hitler's wartime Greater Germany who, because of age or occupation, were not called upon for military service. Let me cite just two examples: the

scholarly Jesuit fathers, Hermann Hoffman of Breslau and Johannes Ude of Graz.

66. Hagbard Jonassen, *Resistance in Denmark* (Enfield, Middlesex: War Resisters' International, 1945), p. 7.

67. Diderich Lund, *Resistance in Norway*, translated from the Norwegian (Enfield, Middlesex: War Resisters' International, 1954), p. 6.

VI. Pacifism in the Nuclear Age

THE PACIFIST MOVEMENT AND THE CAUSE OF CONSCIENTIOUS objection emerged at the end of World War I still intact in its strongholds of Great Britain and North America but decidedly shaken. It was, curiously enough, the coming of the atomic bomb, first exploded over Hiroshima on August 6, 1945, and the subsequent threatened proliferation of nuclear weapons that eventually brought renewed relevance to the problem of pacifism.

This fresh impetus derived from two considerations. First, the destructive powers of nuclear warfare, enlarged so tremendously that the ultimate annihilation of man thereby seemed not incredible to realistic minds, have raised in more intensive form than ever before the moral problem of war. Is the use of such weapons consistent with a civilized ethic, not to speak of an advanced religious code? As a leading American newspaperman wrote: "For perhaps the first time in history reflective men have had to grapple with the pacifists' question: Can national interests and human values really be served by waging a war with atomic and hydrogen weapons?" [1] Further, can the war-game in fact be played at all if resort to nuclear armaments be renounced? In the second place, men began with increasing urgency to search if there did not exist some alternative method of resolving the conflicts, which appear to be an inevitable concomitant of man's functioning as a social animal. Was there possibly a nonviolent alternative in international relations to nuclear deterrence with its danger of spilling over into mutual destruction? Even the author of that futuristic nightmare *1984* could remark: "It seems doubtful whether civilization can stand another major war, and it is at least thinkable that the way out lies through nonviolence." [2]

The search for freedom from war, together with the parallel search for freedom from want, presented the mid-twentieth-century world with its greatest challenge. The story of the (so far unsuccessful) efforts conducted over the last two and a half decades to bring about an agreed elimination of nuclear, and a planned re-

duction of conventional, weapons in the hands of national states
does not lie within the framework of this book. My purpose is to
discuss attempts, by no means necessarily conflicting with institutional and internationalist channels of conflict resolution, to develop a pacifist alternative to violence in the nuclear age.

For more than a decade after the conclusion of World War II
the pacifist movement in both Great Britain and on the North
American continent suffered from declining vigor. Adjustment to
the new conditions of warfare came no more easily to most
pacifists than to the bulk of military men. In the pacifist movement there was for some time little creative thinking on the problems of peace and war and generally a lack of dynamic action.
There was much repetition of old slogans and shibboleths and a
tendency to walk in the well-worn paths trodden already by two
generations of war resisters. The older pacifist societies like the
British Peace Pledge Union, the American War Resisters' League
and the religiously oriented Fellowship of Reconciliation continued
to function, but with diminished membership.

With the coming of peace the wartime conscientious objectors
in Britain and the United States had returned to their prewar jobs
or entered on a new career. In most cases, as has been already
noted, they suffered now—in contrast to the position after World
War I—from little discrimination on account of their refusal to
fight. Some objectors remained active in the pacifist movement or
in the peace programs of their churches; others ceased to take
much interest in any positive way. Conscription continued in both
countries; the number of conscientious objectors among young
men reaching military age, however, was extremely small. To
members of the Anglo-American postwar generation, who had
grown to manhood during the war years, compulsory military
service appeared a normal part of life, unless they happened to
have been reared in a pacifist church or home. On the European
continent, which has contributed several outstanding figures to
the postwar pacifist and nonviolent movement (e.g., Danilo Dolci
the spokesman of the Sicilian poor or Pastor Martin Niemöller,
one of Hitler's staunchest opponents), compulsory military service
continued as the dominant pattern. Although several additional
governments, including the French and the East German (*D.D.R.*),
eventually permitted some form of alternative service for conscien-

tious objectors, repeated imprisonment of war resisters has persisted in Europe and elsewhere. In the United States, efforts to assert the unconstitutional character of peacetime conscription (backed in particular by a Quaker law professor, Harrop Freeman) proved unsuccessful.

Above all, the cold-war atmosphere of the time, which climaxed in the Korean War and in McCarthyism in America, proved uncongenial to the expansion of pacifist ideas, even in their Anglo-American homeland. In Britain we find men like Bertrand Russell and the ex-pacifist, ex-editor of *Peace News,* John Middleton Murry, advocating threat of war, even nuclear war, as a means of pressuring Stalin's Russia to accept cooperation with the West; while in the United States, for instance, a wartime convert to complete pacifism, like the able journalist Dwight Macdonald, soon abandoned it as inadequate in face of Soviet totalitarianism and expansionism. Indeed most pacifists remained suspicious of the Communist-sponsored world peace movement, feeling it functioned essentially as a cloak for furthering the foreign policy of the Soviet Union, although a few participated in its activities.

Thus widespread belief in armed preparedness and in negotiation from strength as the sole means of continuing the Communist bloc's will to aggression, combined with an absence of nonconformity and of political radicalism among the young, caused a general neglect of pacifism. To the new *Realpolitik* the idea of nonviolence appeared to be lacking either moral strength or political validity.

"The revival of pacifism as a significant social movement," writes one of its most recent historians, "awaited the maturing of a generation with less emotional investment in the tragic world crisis, [one] that did not perceive this particular war as the prototype." [3] The rebirth occurred in the second half of the fifties, though it had its roots of course in the previous decade. The present account of this renewed pacifism must necessarily be selective. Four aspects only, those in fact which the writer considers of greatest significance, will be treated in detail here, namely; 1) fresh developments in nonviolent theory and organization taking place in India since Gandhi's death; 2) the adaptation of Gandhian nonviolence for use in the struggle of American Negroes for civil equality; 3) the emergence of so-called nuclear pacifism

in Great Britain and its relationship to the older pacifist movement; 4) recent trends in the peace movement in the United States,
which have included both the practice of nonviolent direct action
against war preparation and the appearance of a largely new type
of selective objection in the course of the Vietnam War.

NONVIOLENCE IN INDIA AFTER GANDHI

"Contemporary India," it has been observed, "bears, unmis-
takably, the Gandhian stigmata." [4] Yet even if independent India's
policy of nonalignment in regard to the two great power blocs
into which the post-1945 world has been divided draws part of
its inspiration from Gandhi's teachings, India's failure to adopt
nonviolence and the military measures taken by the government
to round off its territories in Hyderabad or Goa have shown that
its principles are far different from those which underlay Gandhi's
campaigns. Gandhi's followers, however, have not remained in-
active. The Mahatma's quest for a peaceable world has been taken
up and developed by one of his leading disciples, Vinoba Bhave.[5]

Gandhi's use of nonviolence was directed primarily (though not
exclusively) toward the achievement of national independence.
Since his death the Gandhians have explored, in particular, two
new dimensions of the philosophy of nonviolence. First, under
Vinoba's leadership they have evolved a practical program aimed
at creating a nonviolent social order. In the second place, they
have tentatively brought into being a nonviolent peace corps, as
it were—a "Peace Army" (*Shanti Sena*), the avowed object of
whose members is to find a nonviolent solution to conflict situations in so far as they involve India. Both in relating nonviolence
to society and in stressing the urgency in the nuclear age of
thinking out a strategy of nonviolent conflict resolution, Gandhians
have found common ground with Western pacifists. That there
still remain serious differences in the approaches of the two groups
will emerge in the pages that follow.

Toward a Nonviolent Society

The Gandhians' positive program has centered in the Indian
village, just as Gandhi's own thoughts on nonviolence always
returned to the idea of village reconstruction. Like Gandhi's, their
"political doctrine is mildly anarchist." [6] It is an attempt to create

—or to recreate, the Gandhians would say—a lively grass-roots democracy based on the village community, largely self-sufficient, simple in its needs and practicing cooperation in all its undertakings. To achieve such a society, land reform was essential. Thus, in April 1951, the hard core of convinced Gandhians rallied to Vinoba's call to establish "a land-gifts mission" (*Bhoodan Yajna*), which would work nonviolently towards this end.[7] The first objective of Vinoba's mission was to persuade the country's well-to-do landowners to donate one sixth of their cultivable land for distribution among landless peasants. Vinoba and his disciples, walking from village to village and talking to landlords in an effort to persuade them to relinquish their sixth of the land, have achieved a number of remarkable successes since the movement was inaugurated nearly two decades ago. They have likewise made converts to the crusade among old and young: the most outstanding recruit to the movement to date being the ex-Marxist Jayaprakash Narayan, who in 1954 abandoned his leadership of India's democratic socialist party to follow Vinoba. Yet the problem of India's expanding population and of landlessness has continued, threatening a violent social upheaval in the future if some solution is not found in time.

Vinoba, on one occasion, described his land reform efforts as "nonviolent assistance" (in contrast to the resistance offered by Gandhi to British rule before independence). "I desire," he wrote, "to stave off a violent revolution and bring about a non-violent one." [8] He warned recalcitrant landowners that if they remained stubbornly attached to their possessions, they and the whole society which supported them would be swept away in the not too distant future. His aim was to transform society at its foundations.

Vinoba has been criticized, e.g., by the independent socialist Ram Manohar Lohia, for not using *satyagraha* as an aggressive technique for achieving social justice and for combating political tyranny and economic exploitation, as Gandhi had used it in his civil disobedience campaigns. To such arguments Vinoba has replied that in a democracy *satyagraha* is a last resort; it should come only after every constitutional channel, every avenue of peaceful persuasion, has been explored and found to yield no result. It cannot, in his view, be regarded as a nonviolent substitute for the class war.[9]

A Peace Army[10]

In Vinoba's concept *Bhoodan*, the landlords' voluntary gift of land to the landless, must be followed by *Gramdan* whereby the villagers are themselves persuaded to renounce private property in land and to institute communal ownership—rather in the style of the pre-revolutionary Russian *mir* beloved by the nineteenth-century *narodniki* (populists). And *Gramdan*, in Vinoba's view, "will not be able to bring about a revolution by peaceful methods, unless the people also feel at the same time that our ideas offer them a powerful means of self-defence even in the present state of affairs (that is, even while unjust differences remain)." Thus, the nonviolent character of the quiet revolution envisaged by Vinoba and the Gandhians, the quest for a nonviolent social order, must have a secure base in the masses. It should not remain a middle-class movement passively imposed on the people but should put down roots in the countryside among the peasants.

This kind of approach appears sound. Yet in practice the nonviolent movement, under Vinoba's leadership, has never reached the mass dimensions that Gandhi succeeded in achieving on occasion. The Peace Army, which Vinoba set up in August 1957, was indeed foreshadowed in Gandhi's thinking. But its purposes and its organization do not exactly correspond to those of his *satyagraha* campaigns. And, unlike the proposal by English pacifists in the early 1930s for a nonviolent army discussed in an earlier chapter, Vinoba's *Shanti Sena* was designed from the beginning primarily for employment within the state. It was intended as a means to promote *sarvodaya*, "the welfare of all." In promoting a Peace Army, Vinoba wrote:

The goal which we have set before us is a society free from external government. When this "anarchist" society comes into being, it will need no *Shanti Sena*. . . . Everywhere, and in every house, there will be people ready to take upon themselves the task of withstanding wrong-doing. If a father does something wrong, the son will be prepared to withstand him. A father will feel responsible for his son and the son for his father. A neighbour will feel responsible for his neighbour, and one village for the next. In some way or other the matter will be dealt with on the spot and there will be no need for anyone to go from a distance to make peace. That is the state of affairs which we ultimately want to bring about.

Until a system of "village states" was set up, however, there would be need for peace-makers "from a distance." It was to fill this role that Vinoba created his Peace Army. Its members, in his view, should form a body of dedicated, disciplined men and women ready to go at a moment's notice to any part of the country where violence threatened. In the intervals between calls to active service of this kind they were to engage, either part-time or full-time, in the constructive work recommended by Gandhi for his *satyagrahis*.

Vinoba, like Gandhi, demanded strict discipline from his "peace volunteers" (*Shanti Sainiks*). He did not regard unquestioning submission to the orders of a commanding officer, if this were necessary, as inconsistent with his goal of an anarchist society or with freedom of thought, and he readily accepted the title of "Supreme Commander for the *Shanti Sena* for the whole of India." *"Ahimsa,"* he wrote, "is not going to grow beyond its infancy until the two thousand *Shanti Sainiks* on our register report for duty at any given point as soon as the need is proclaimed." Volunteers should regard themselves as nonviolent soldiers (indeed we might well compare them to members of a rigorous religious order). They must drill regularly to keep themselves fit and capable of acting in unison and with effect in a situation of tension. They should train, too, "in the techniques of various kinds of useful work," taking care to keep in close touch with the people whom they strove to serve as social workers. But in regard to politics the Peace Army should be strictly neutral; Vinoba frequently stressed the need for his volunteers to stand aloof from party politics if they were to fulfill their function of reconcilers and act as true servants of the people.

Three concluding points may be made in regard to the Peace Army. First, although popular support is envisaged ("a hank of yarn" monthly from "every family of five persons")—as well as a form of associate membership drawing in "hundreds of thousands" whose aid could be called upon in an emergency—the organization remains a professional body of "picked people," a nonviolent elite corps. From the hoped-for total of 70,000, however, not many more than 12,000 have so far been recruited. The Peace Army, in the second place, is viewed by Vinoba and the Gandhians not as an alternative to the regular Indian army and police force—at least for the time being. "We do not refuse to co-operate with the present government," he has declared. "On the contrary we have got its full sympathy in this work. The great leaders of the nation have welcomed the concept of *Shanti Sena.*" Thus its main function to date appears to have been to act as an auxiliary to unofficial efforts at agrarian reform, such as his own "Land-Gifts Mission," rather than to serve as an embryo organ of nonviolent national defense. Thirdly, Vinoba does not seem to contemplate his organization being directly serviceable as an international peace brigade, which *inter alia* could interpose itself between the sides in situations of conflict (though in 1961 Narayan did propose this idea, with the support of some Western pacifists as well as of nonpacifist internationalists like Salvador de Madariaga). Vinoba believes, however, that it should serve as witness to the possibility of a nonviolent solution to world conflict. "If," he writes, "we can demonstrate that there is no need of the army to keep the peace within our own borders, the force of peace in India will be strengthened and the world will be shown a new path. . . . First . . . let us try to cleanse the atmosphere which prevails within India itself—everything will follow from that." Successful employment of "non-violent power" at home thus leads the way toward using it with effect internationally.

The Gandhians and the Sino-Indian Conflict of 1962

The border dispute between India and Communist China, which in the summer and autumn of 1962 led to armed clashes between the troops of the two states and presented Indians with the possibility of a Chinese invasion, aroused a wave of patriotic feeling throughout the country. The Gandhians themselves did not prove immune to its infection. The incident showed that, while Vinoba and his followers might aim at building an anarchist society in the future, they were first and foremost, as Gandhi had been, nationalists in the present. They identified themselves wholeheartedly with the stand of their government. "We believe," stated the Sarva Seva Sangh, the "People's Service Organisation" which represented the Gandhian movement, "that this conflict has been forced upon India, for India has been working consistently for a peaceful solution of the border question." Their declaration, after branding China as the aggressor, expressed "our full sympathy . . . with India." [11] Only as to the means of resistance did they differ from the administration, for they continued to press for nonviolent defense as the most efficacious response to aggression and to advocate "the idea of the co-operative society" [12] as the positive answer to the challenge of communism.

After the outbreak of hostilities the statement in the Peace Army's pledge denouncing war as a crime had even been softened so as not to cause offense. Some Gandhians felt that to retain the original wording would signify accusing their government of committing a crime in organizing armed resistance to the Chinese. "I cannot call Nehru a criminal," one of them explained.[13]

To many Western pacifists, especially those in the United States, the readiness with which the Gandhians had rallied to their government, their unwillingness to contemplate the possibility of their own side being to some extent at fault and their placing blame for the quarrel, even as to its remoter origins, exclusively on the other party, were puzzling and even distressing phenomena. In the history of American pacifism there was indeed a close parallel in the last century: the nonresistance movement led by the abolitionist, William Lloyd Garrison, had given fervent support to the Lincoln administration in the Civil War (that is, while reserving, like the Gandhians, a personal conscientious objection to fighting). But in the twentieth century Western pacifists have usually been highly critical of their government's policies and suspicious of the motives behind patriotic slogans. Nonviolence in India, on the other hand, owed its origins to the nationalist struggle against the British: it was former colleagues of the Mahatma, in many cases the Gandhians' friends, who now occupied the top posts in independent India's administration.

In this moment of crisis there was considerable uncertainty as to the proper role of Vinoba's Peace Army, which had hitherto concentrated on the domestic situation; all his followers were united, at any rate, in opposing attempts now to hinder the nation's war effort. Unprovoked aggression, in their view, could only be met with some form of resistance; though, it is true, the Gandhians —like the Mahatma himself in conflict situations of this kind— urged the need to find a negotiated solution to the dispute, if this were at all possible.

There was no military conscription operative in the country at that time: the Gandhians, however, stressed their personal alle-

giance to nonviolence and unwillingness to render combatant service. Two years earlier a leading Gandhian of the older generation,
Kaka Kalelkar, had stated his belief that, in circumstances similar
to the present crisis, a supporter of nonviolence should allow
himself to be inducted into the army, if conscripted, since he paid
taxes used in part for military purposes and also took advantage of
what the government provided for his welfare. Once in the army
he should inform the military authorities of his unwillingness to
kill and of his readiness at the same time to undertake, as a demonstration of the power of nonviolence, some dangerous unarmed
mission at the front or other perilous noncombatant service. Most
Gandhians, however, felt such a stand was unrealistic and that it
would most likely be misunderstood. They advocated the rejection
of noncombatant duties in the army, should compulsory military
service be introduced.[14]

The confusion was greatest in regard to what positive action, if
any, should be taken in the existing emergency. An American
observer recorded:

Some felt that a *Shanti Sena* (Peace Army) should proceed to the
border to offer non-violent resistance to the Chinese. The question
arose then as to whether they should fight beside the Indian Army,
though nonviolently, and the additional question as to whether the
Indian Army would ever let them reach the border. Doubts were also
voiced as to how such a Peace Army would conduct itself in order
to be effective. For example, if they were to stand quietly in the
middle of a road down which the Chinese wished to proceed, placing
their bodies in the path of the on-coming army, and then if the
Chinese simply went off into the woods and later came back to the
road, what would they do? How could non-violent resistance be effective in such a situation? There was also a realization that perhaps a
Shanti Sena could function effectively only by placing itself in the
territory between the two armies, thus not opposing one army more
than another, but trying to bring an end to the operations of both
military bodies. These questions, however, remained academic since
no action was taken.[15]

The Gandhians were hampered by the comparative smallness
of their numbers. They did not see any way of winning over their
fellow countrymen to their belief in a nonviolent solution to conflict, except by slow propaganda. They nursed a keen sense of
disappointment that the latter had turned aside from the methods
of resistance employed earlier by Gandhi against the British. Above

all, the Gandhians' effectiveness in acting as an agent of conciliation
was restricted by their strong commitment to their own nation's
position. Many Gandhians were blind (or so at least they appeared
to outsiders) to the element of power in India's policies, while
remaining acutely aware of the aggressive factors in the policies of
the Western world or of the Soviet bloc or of Communist China.
For them Indian nationalism retained a special quality. "I have
no fear," wrote Vinoba at this time, "that India will lose her
soul and that war fever will take over . . . because the whole
spiritual background of a thousand saints will not allow India to
go the violent way whole-hog." [16] Here we may detect the same
Messianic note as Gandhi struck in some of his nationalistic utterances. Nonviolence, so both Gandhi and Vinoba have believed,
was India's gift to the world. For the Gandhians in the 1960s,
even an India that was obviously as yet unwilling to adopt nonviolence as national policy seemed to be peaceloving in comparison to its neighbors and rivals on the international scene.

In the application of nonviolent theory to relations between
states, the post-Gandhians have not been particularly successful.
Their chief contribution has lain in exploring the interconnections
between nonviolence and domestic society. They have tried to
create a cooperative base for the successful adoption of nonviolence not merely as a personal philosophy but as a social technique for achieving justice. Their experiment was set in a
predominantly agrarian country. The village, therefore, became
the center of their concern. The search for a nonviolent society,
however, need not be thus restricted. Indeed it is likely to prove
abortive if it is found to be incapable of undergoing adaptation
when applied to other environments.

NONVIOLENCE AND THE CIVIL RIGHTS MOVEMENT
IN THE UNITED STATES

The influence of Gandhian nonviolence was not in fact confined to the Indian subcontinent. It affected, for instance, some
of the African nationalist leaders responsible for leading their
countries into independence after 1945. Take the case of Kwame
Nkrumah of Ghana, for instance. At first, as a Marxist, sceptical of
any talk of nonviolent action and placing reliance on armed
revolution, he later began to study the history of Gandhi's cam-

paigns against the British. "I began to see," he wrote, "that, when backed by a strong political organization, it could be the solution to the colonial problem." [17]

But Nkrumah's support for a nonviolent political strategy, as Nehru's had been in India, was based on expediency. As Howard Horsburgh has remarked, "the non-violence of mere expediency is itself inexpedient," [18] at least in so far as any long-term policy based on nonviolent techniques is concerned. What attracted Nkrumah and several of the later African nationalist leaders, like Kenneth Kaunda of Zambia, to Gandhian techniques of conflict for a time was the successful use of such techniques against the British; they did not experience any theoretical or temperamental affinity to the philosophical and religious concepts underlying Gandhi's cultivation of *satyagraha*. And they abandoned interest in such methods after their countries had gained independence. In the still unliberated areas of southern Africa confidence in nonviolent methods declined rapidly during the early 1960s after the ruthless massacre of Africans at Sharpeville in March 1960, perpetuated by the white government's police. After Sharpeville, African nationalists, with very few exceptions (the late Chief Albert Lutuli was one of these exceptions), now thrust aside the idea of nonviolence even as an expedient technique for achieving political freedom. "Sharpeville," wrote an American Quaker pacifist, "convinced the Africans that the forces they confronted would not yield to campaigns of nonviolent resistance, whatever Gandhi may have achieved in India and South Africa or Martin Luther King in America. The white regimes in southern Africa [in the African view] are inhuman and impervious to appeal to a degree so different from the British in India and the whites in Mississippi as to constitute a difference in kind." [19]

Whatever the verdict concerning the humanity of whites in Mississippi, Gandhian nonviolence certainly succeeded in making more headway among the Negro population of the United States than in the emergent nations of Africa. Let us first look briefly at the origins of the nonviolent movement for racial equality in the United States.

The Precursors

The Congress of Racial Equality (CORE), for long the main

institutional center of the movement, "came into being in 1942," [20] when a small group of concerned people carried out the first sit-in against segregation in a Chicago restaurant. Next year a national organization—at first somewhat makeshift—was set up; it was not until 1944 that it received its present name.

The founders of CORE and its earliest members were drawn mainly from radical FOR members and other social activists among the country's conscientious objectors. For instance, in June 1941 we find George M. Houser, one of the student nonregistrants from Union Theological Seminary whose stand was discussed in the last chapter, writing from Danbury Correctional Institution: "We must raise up a movement based on non-violence as a method." Houser was shortly to become a co-founder of CORE. For pacifists like Houser, who was white, or James Farmer, also a student of theology and a Negro, or Bayard Rustin, a Negro FOR worker and convert to Quakerism who spent considerable periods in jail in World War II, race relations and international relations were part of one problem. "Beneath the formal differences," as Rustin remarked, "these issues are really inseparable." [21] Pacifism, if it were to have any relevance for the contemporary world, must measure up to the problems of society as fully as it sought to find a solution to the question of war. Thus these young men were following the dominant trend within the interwar American FOR with its concern for the resolution of domestic conflict and its sympathy for a revolutionary, albeit nonviolent, approach to social justice. Nevertheless they were somewhat impatient with many traditional pacifist approaches. In particular, they regretted the absence in pacifist programs of nonviolent techniques for achieving a just social order; the older generation of FOR leaders, with the exception of A. J. Muste, cleaved to democratic processes and remained suspicious of extra-parliamentary methods of rectifying abuses or resolving social conflict. The young FOR radicals, however, avidly read the interpretations of Gandhian nonviolence by Richard B. Gregg and Krishnalal Shridharani. They thirsted to be able to apply what they had read to the problems of their own country. Having girded themselves with the weapons of non-violence, they wished to do battle for their ideas. They saw in the unequal status accorded within American democracy to its Negro citizens not merely a shameful injustice, a denial of Christianity and a gross contradiction of the country's declared ideals, but a direct challenge to pacifists. Their pacifist faith could only prove itself if it dared to face this problem squarely and find a solution. Gandhi's message to American Negroes had been: "With right which is on their side and . . . non-violence as their only weapon, if they will make it such, a bright future is assured." [22]

Some of the founding members of CORE, especially if they were themselves Negroes, may have been impressed by the fact that pacifism had made scarcely any impact on America's racial minorities; these minorities had contributed very few conscientious objectors. CORE also drew support from young white pacifists who had been brought face to face with racial inequality when in prison or while working in CPS camps. The concern of most of the early nonviolent leaders for racial injustice, however, was already developed before they became conscientious objectors. Some had participated, too, in Gandhian-style *ashrams,* usually short-lived ventures, and in training-centers in nonviolence.

"The leading staff members of the early CORE were . . . on the payroll of the Fellowship [of Reconciliation]. Until 1957, indeed, the office of CORE was at the FOR headquarters and the two organizations co-operated closely." [23] But long before this, CORE had expanded in membership and support far beyond FOR circles. Soon it had succeeded in interesting such veteran campaigners for civil rights as the president of the Brotherhood of Sleeping-Car Porters, A. Philip Randolph, a nonpacifist, in the idea of non-violent civil disobedience. In 1947 CORE sponsored a "Journey of Reconciliation" to the Deep South, led by two secretaries of the FOR, George Houser and Bayard Rustin, with pairs of mixed black and white challenging the long established rule of segregation in this area.[24] Here indeed was an attempt to directly confront injustice, forcing its upholders either to yield to change or to face the consequences of enforcing the old conditions despite the mounting resistance to them.

The application of nonviolent techniques to race relations within the United States, we have just seen, had its origins among the radical social actionists of the conscientious objector community. This was undoubtedly the most promising development in World War II pacifism. "Although the historic pacifist impulse withered during the most destructive war in history," to quote the words of a young American historian, "it harbored within itself the seeds of its own regeneration." [25]

The Emergence of Martin Luther King

Yet the nonviolent civil rights movement did not really gain momentum or mass support until the appearance of Martin Luther King, Jr. King was a southern Negro by birth and domicile. His leadership marks the transition from a northern-based movement carried along largely by the efforts of middle-class white sympathizers, which was typified in the activities of the early CORE, to one which, both in leadership and rank-and-file, was firmly centered in the South, where the main struggle was now located.

The event symbolizing this transition was the bus boycott organized by the Negro community of Montgomery (Alabama), in which King, while he did not initiate it, played a leading part. The boycott commenced in December 1955 and lasted about a year. Its immediate occasion was the arrest, trial and jailing of a Negro seamstress Mrs. Rosa Parks who, returning home after a long and tiring day, had refused to give up her seat to a white passenger when ordered to do so by the conductor. The incident aroused great indignation among the town's 50,000 Negroes, who had long been subjected to similar treatment of an arbitrary nature. Negro leaders, among them two young Baptist ministers Martin Luther King and Ralph D. Abernathy, decided to call a one-day bus boycott which was almost a hundred percent effective, and then to extend its duration for an indefinite period, when a similarly high participation was still reached. The boycott was nonviolent throughout, an act of passive resistance but not one of civil disobedience, for no law was broken. It was rather noncooperation of the type practiced by Gandhi in some of his campaigns.

Seventy percent of the passengers on Montgomery's municipal buses were Negroes: a boycott of this kind, therefore, caused much disquiet among city officials. Yet it was not the bus boycott that in fact brought desegregation of the city's transport system (which became the boycott's objective) but the decision of the U.S. Supreme Court on December 1, 1956. The Court on appeal being made to it by the boycotters' organization, the Montgomery Improvement Association, had ruled that segregation on buses was indeed unconstitutional. Thus an element was introduced into the situation that was absent from Gandhi's India under British rule. In the United States the nonviolent movement for racial equality worked within a constitutional framework, with appeal made by the passive resisters not solely to a higher righteousness than man-made law but also to the highest court of appeal in the land, from which support for civil rights might be expected.[26]

Soon after the boycott began, a sympathetic white librarian, Juliette Morgan, had written a letter which was published in the segregationist *Montgomery Advertiser,* comparing the boycott to Gandhi's famous Salt *Satyagraha* of 1930 (although in fact in the latter case the breaking of an unjust law was involved). In this way Gandhi's name became familiar for the first time to large numbers of the city's Negro inhabitants. And it was not long before a couple of staff members of the FOR, both of whom had been active in their organization's nonviolent quest for racial equality, arrived on the scene. In Montgomery the two men were able, as a result of their previous thought and experience in regard to nonviolence, to play an important role behind the scenes in directing the boycott movement into nonviolent channels. Yet the seminal influence lay elsewhere. It was the attachment to the idea of nonviolence of Dr. Martin Luther King, with his almost charismatic gift for leadership and his devotion to the cause of his Negro people, that, above all, gave the movement its nonviolent direction.

Whence did King derive his belief in nonviolence? [27] As a student in college he had read Thoreau's essay on civil disobedience several times; when the boycott began, he now pondered once again on the implications of Thoreau's message, with its appeal to refuse obedience to the demands of society, if unjust, in the name of a higher law. After graduating from college and entering divinity school he became interested in Gandhi's nonviolent campaigns and read widely on the subject. He was impressed by what Gandhi had to offer to other oppressed peoples; yet at the same time, under the influence of Reinhold Niebuhr's critique, he rejected theoretical pacifism along with the optimistic liberal theology with which it was often associated in the West. When he moved on to Boston University, where he studied for his doctorate, he came under the influence of two pacifist professors then teaching in the School of Theology: Dean Walter Muelder and Allen

Knight Chalmers. Both men were members of the FOR. Therefore, when he arrived in Montgomery in 1954 to take up a pas-
torate in the city, he was by now extremely sympathetic to the
pacifist idea as well as open to the potentialities of Gandhian nonviolence as a technique for achieving political justice on the part
of an oppressed segment of the population. For King, while gradually emancipating himself from the influence of Niebuhr's stric-
tures on pacifism, had retained the latter's intensely social Christianity.

When I went to Montgomery as a pastor [he wrote], I had not the
slightest idea that I would later become involved in a crisis in which
nonviolent resistance would be applicable. I neither started the
protest nor suggested it. I simply responded to the call of the people
for a spokesman. When the protest began, my mind, consciously or
unconsciously, was driven back to the Sermon on the Mount, with
its sublime teachings on love, and the Gandhian method of nonviolent
resistance. As the days unfolded, I came to see the power of nonviolence more and more. Living through the actual experience of the
protest, nonviolence became more than a method to which I gave
intellectual assent; it became a commitment to a way of life. Many
of the things that I had not cleared up intellectually concerning nonviolence were now solved in the sphere of practical action.[28]

After the boycott started, King got rid of the gun he had kept
for an emergency (in this respect more consistent than some of his
colleagues in the movement, who did not repudiate the use of fire-
arms where the law became inoperative and could not afford protection to citizens). "Through nonviolent resistance," King now
told his people, "the Negro will be able to rise to the noble height
of opposing the unjust system while loving the perpetrators of the
system." He thus points to an essential in the nonviolent technique
of struggle: the appeal to the conscience of the opponent, the effort
to win over sympathetic members of the opposing side. "Nonviolent resistance is not aimed against oppressors, but against oppression. Under its banner consciences, not racial groups, are enlisted." The struggle, said King, is "between justice and injustice." [29] Like Gandhi, he believed, too, that a nonviolent movement might recruit supporters among those who did not accept
nonviolence as a principle of life, provided they were ready to
stay nonviolent for as long as the campaign lasted. To the Negroes

of Montgomery, King and his fellow ministers presented non-violence "as a simple expression of Christianity in action." [30]

Although their followers had no previous experience in the use of nonviolent techniques, these leaders were able to prevent the outbreak of violence, despite attempts at intimidation and at provocation by the segregationists. A newspaperman from Minneapolis reported their achievement of "the almost unbelievable by pulling the hoodlums out of the crap games and honky-tonks into the churches, where they sang hymns, gave money, shouted amen and wept over the powerful speeches." [31] The packed evening services in the churches, where King and his associates expounded the idea of nonviolence and its relation to the Christian ideal of love and instructed their followers not to hate or humiliate their white oppressors but instead to oppose only their oppressive acts, served the same purpose as the prayer meetings and sing-songs in Gandhian campaigns in sustaining the morale of the passive resisters. Workshops in Gandhian ideas and techniques were also held throughout the period of the boycott. And as an equivalent of Gandhi's constructive program, which the Mahatma always stressed was an essential component of successful *satyagraha,* King began to stress the role of such positive activities as the raising of educational and cultural standards of southern Negroes, the fight against adult illiteracy and juvenile delinquency and (later) the campaign for voter registration.

In the Montgomery bus boycott nonviolent resistance emerged for the first time in the United States as a mass movement. Henceforward the campaign for racial equality, for so long—and in so far—as it remained under the leadership of Martin Luther King, was to be one (to quote his own words) where "Christ furnished the spirit and motivation, while Gandhi furnished the method." [32]

Montgomery soon became a symbol. It helped to create a new self-image among southern Negroes and to destroy their traditional submissiveness dating back to the days of slavery. It started a chain reaction with similar nonviolent assertions of civil rights by the Negro communities of other southern cities; bus boycotts took place in Birmingham, Tallahassee and elsewhere. Many city authorities now took steps to desegregate their bus systems, often not waiting on a court order to do so. A Southern Christian Leadership Conference was set up under King's leadership to coordinate activities on a national scale; the nonviolent movement for civil equality ceased to be a merely local affair. It appeared, moreover, to most people that the desegregation which was now being accomplished was the result of a successful nonviolent boycott, although, as we have seen, this was in fact only partly true. "Here was a powerful legend that would inspire others to authentic victories based wholly or largely on nonviolence." [33]

James Farmer has described the civil rights movement during the decade after Montgomery as "a kind of wedding of two forces." Both went back to the war years: "the means-oriented idealists of a pacifistic turn of mind [like himself], for whom non-violence was a total philosophy, a way of life—we had founded CORE [he notes]; and the ends-oriented militants, the New Jacobins, disillusioned with America's rhetoric of equality, who saw in direct action a useful weapon and viewed non-violence only as a tactic." [34] Solely by a fusion of these two forces, as Farmer points out, did the creation of a "revolutionary mass movement" become possible; just as, one may add, in India earlier only an alliance between Gandhian idealists, devoted to the principle of *ahimsa,* and the nationalists prepared to adopt nonviolence as an expedient for winning their country's independence, made possible the creation of a really broad independence movement. In both cases the binding link was the charismatic leader endowed with the gift of harnessing the energies of the masses. That in both cases this leadership emerged from the side of the devotees of nonviolence was surely no coincidence. Only idealism of this kind was likely to generate the spiritual dynamism needed for such a task.

In the early years of the civil rights movement the Gandhian influence was strongly marked in most of its undertakings. Beginning in May 1961 CORE organized a series of "Freedom Rides" to test the state of desegregation—or, rather, lack of it— in the amenities on interstate bus routes; the project was modelled on the "Journey of Reconciliation" CORE had sponsored in 1947 with the testing done as before by mixed teams of Negroes and whites. In some places on their route, mob violence was displayed against the demonstrators; in a number of instances Freedom Riders were arrested and jailed. A Negro student from Howard University, who participated, reported: "The name of Gandhi was constantly on the minds and lips of most of the imprisoned Riders.

Anything Gandhi had said or done was interpreted and reinter-
preted to be applied to the [present] situation." Different views
often arose as to what was required of a consistent Gandhian by
the existing circumstances. Some Riders felt called upon to embark
on individual protest fasts; others argued that the Mahatma would
have approved such a step only if it were more clearly a meaningful sacrifice.[35]

The *satyagraha* of the Freedom Riders was directed against a
federal authority and not against a southern segregationist authority as had been the case in Montgomery. This fact may have
contributed to the fairly rapid success of the movement; on November 1, the Interstate Commerce Commission issued new regulations guaranteeing integration on interstate bus routes. On the
other hand, unlike Montgomery where the protesting community
could exercise considerable economic pressure by its boycott, the
Freedom Riders possessed very little economic leverage to back
their demonstration. It was mainly one of nonviolent witness to
principle. The Riders' steady refusal to retaliate with counter-
violence, despite repeated provocation and harassment on the part
of segregationist mobs and police, made a big impression not only
on wide sections of the American public but also abroad. A number of prominent white citizens took part in the Rides (including
the chaplain of Yale University and a son-in-law of Governor
Nelson A. Rockefeller).

In its clear presentation of the truth at the center of protest, in
its fidelity to nonviolent means of struggle and in its ability to
win outside sympathy and support, the American Negroes' movement for civil equality had achieved by the early sixties a considerable measure of success. An expansion of nonviolent protest took
place in the Deep South during these years. Martin Luther King
insisted on its maintaining a nonviolent stance; he was indeed prepared, like Gandhi, to call off action where violence threatened
to break out from the side of the demonstrators (violence, of
course, was endemic on the part of the segregationists).

SNCC: From Nonviolence to Black Nationalism

Meanwhile, important developments were taking place among
Negro college students in the South. The Fellowship of Reconciliation had recently published and distributed on the campuses of a

number of southern Negro colleges a picture-strip account of the Montgomery bus boycott under the title *Martin Luther King and the Montgomery Story*. A freshman at Shaw University in Greensboro (N.C.) getting hold of a copy was inspired to follow the example of what had happened in Montgomery; he and three other students entered a cafe in the town and sat down at a lunchcounter segregated for the use of whites. On being refused service, they continued to sit at the counter. This incident occurred on February 1, 1960. The four students went on with their protest day after day and were joined by other Negro students, as well as a sprinkling of white sympathizers. As news of the Greensboro "sit-in" spread, the pattern was repeated in dozens of other college and university towns in the South; the movement eventually extended, too, to the Negro high schools. There were occasional disorders, for the demonstrators were young, and therefore highspirited, and utterly inexperienced in the practice of nonviolence, and in addition subjected to abuse and severe physical and psychological harassment by sections of the white community who opposed their action. Yet on the whole the protestors did not succumb to the temptation to retaliate violently.

"Here and there the growing movement centered around groups that had attended seminars and workshops conducted [by FOR organizers]. Copies of Richard Gregg's *The Power of Nonviolence* were sought out and studied. Dozens of these had been given to Negro college libraries. . . . Thousands of copies of the FOR leaflet, *How to Practice Nonviolence,* and the leaflet *CORE Rules for Action,* found their way into the students' hands. Many of the students were not primed at all, however, and knew about nonviolence only by word of mouth." [36] The FOR sent a three-man team into the area to instruct students in nonviolent techniques and to prevent, if possible, the outbreak of violence among the uninitiated. Local leadership, however, soon developed. This crystallized around the many CORE groups which had sprung up in the South and, above all, around a new organization which emerged from among the students themselves, with some help from the Southern Christian Leadership Conference as well as from pacifist bodies in the North.

This new body, the Students Nonviolent Coordinating Committee (SNCC), was set up in April 1960 at a conference in

Raleigh (N.C.), attended mainly by Nergo students who had taken part in the recent sit-ins. It concluded by adopting a platform affirming "the philosophical or religious ideal of nonviolence as the foundation of our purpose, the presupposition of our faith, and the manner of our action." Practitioners of nonviolence, the conference statement continued, should be able to forgive "even in the midst of hostility." "By appealing to conscience and standing on the moral nature of human existence, nonviolence nurtures the atmosphere in which reconciliation and justice become actual possibilities." In the following month SNCC's executive committee, assisted by King himself as well as by representatives of the Quaker AFSC, reiterated these principles, stressing their derivation from the Judaeo-Christian tradition and positing as the organization's final goal "a social order of justice permeated by love." [37] Thus we can see clearly that SNCC's roots lie equally in FOR pacifism and its preaching of the Social Gospel as in the Gandhian ethic of nonviolence.

As the sit-in movement widened over the next year or two to include not only restaurants and lunch-counters but also the picketing or boycott of the stores which supplied them, and as clergy—both Negro and White—and other sympathizers from the older generation began to express support for the students' action, the white communities showed increasing nervousness at the consequences of a prolongation of the movement. Concerning its outcome, W. R. Miller in his study of nonviolence makes two points. In the first place, "settlement almost invariably occurred through direct negotiations rather than court rulings." Secondly, "opponents were seldom if ever won over to the side of justice as a result of voluntary suffering or Christian love on the part of the demonstrators." The decisive element in extracting concessions in this case was the fear of economic loss.[38]

The sit-ins, followed by the Freedom Rides, gave considerable impetus to the civil rights movement and an added prestige to King's nonviolent leadership. These protests highlighted the courage and determination of Negro demonstrators. They were able to show, too, a number of successes in extending the range of civil rights enjoyed by the Negro population in the South.

At the same time a note of uncertainty emerged concerning the direction in which the movement should travel in the future. Voices were raised demanding not piecemeal concessions, not just tinkering with the existing structure of southern society, but a thoroughgoing restructuring of this society: the achievement by nonviolent means of black power in the area where Negroes were in a majority. For instance, in 1961 at the Southern Christian Leadership Conference's annual congress we find the FOR delegate, James M. Lawson, Jr., proposing the formation and training of a nonviolent "army" of up to 8,000 members. "Let us prepare these people," he said, "for mass nonviolent action in the Deep South. Let us recruit people who will be willing to go at a given moment and stay in jail indefinitely." [39] Community programs, voter registration and slum renovation would form, as with Vinoba Bhave's movement in contemporary India, the positive, constructive aspect of the nonviolent revolution. As the legal status of Negroes improved in the course of the decade, through action taken by Federal courts to uphold their civil equality, some—but by no means all—Negro activists (e.g., Bayard Rustin), while still maintaining their adherence to nonviolence, came to feel that the movement should concentrate henceforward not so much on civil rights, the battle for which they considered virtually won, but on the struggle for economic and cultural equality by means of political pressure. For the economically retarded and the culturally backward Negro masses, even if they were to be endowed with full civil rights, would remain in practice outcasts in American society. Therefore, those who supported this way of thinking called now for a march of the poor toward economic and cultural prosperity in place of the old campaign for civil equality.

The most serious challenge to the leadership of Martin Luther King and to the nonviolent character of the Negro movement came from the gradual development within it in the course of the sixties of a militant Black Power faction. This group attracted support from Negro intellectuals of the younger generation; it drew off the interest of many who had adhered to nonviolence rather from expediency than from any belief in its inherent superiority to violent methods of social or national liberation. Black nationalism represented to some extent, too, a return of the center of agitation to the North—but not to the predominantly white liberal and pacifist intellectuals, among whom the nonviolent movement had originated. Black nationalism began to make headway in the overcrowded and poverty-stricken ghettos of the great northern industrial cities. Their inhabitants, more alienated and more isolated within a potentially hostile environment than their southern brethren, were also less susceptible to the traditional Christian ethos, which had provided an effective background to the spread of nonviolence in the South. The messianic sects that flourished in the Negro quarters of cities like New York or Philadelphia provided a religious equivalent to the secular national separatism that now rejected nonviolence as both ineffective and actually destructive of the Negro's will to resist.

King was always aware of the difficulties he would encounter in keeping his people nonviolent. "The method of nonviolence," he wrote, "will not work miracles overnight." [40] There was little likelihood of an immediate and largescale change of heart on the part of white segregationists. Reconciliation and the way of love would be slow and fraught with suffering and travail for those who entered upon it. In his *Letter from Birmingham City Jail* [41] of April 16, 1963, in the course of the long, drawn out civil rights struggle in that city, King was to express his keen disappointment at the attitude of those white moderates who disapproved the employment of civil disobedience to fight segregation (though, of course, civil disobedience, it may be added, is essentially nonviolent[42]). King had indeed been under fire recently from Negro radicals for his alleged subservience to white opinion. In his letter now he endeavored to explain why Negroes could not wait for the slow and uncertain working of the legal machine. "We know through painful experience," he said, "that freedom is never voluntarily given by the oppressor; it must be demanded by the oppressed." The awakening Negro will demand his rights ever more insistently. "If his oppressed emotions do not come out in . . . nonviolent ways, they will come out in ominous expressions of violence. This is not a threat," King wrote, "it is a fact of history." If he were unsuccessful in his attempt to channel "this normal and healthy discontent . . . through the creative outlet of nonviolent direct action," then violence would necessarily follow. Like Gandhi, King clearly believed a man should react to injustice, even by violence if he were unable to rise to a higher level of resistance, rather than meekly submit.

The nonviolent movement for desegregation in the South aimed primarily at assimilation of the Negroes into American society. It strove to win the support, either active or passive, of the country's white majority for its assertion of the civil equality of the Negro. If it should seem to have failed to achieve what its supporters regarded as sufficient progress toward this objective, it was extremely probable that a reversion would take place toward a policy of violent action.[43] Martin Luther King's assassination in April 1968 deprived the disciples of nonviolence within the Negro civil rights movement of their most effective and dedicated leader. Black nationalism aims—at least in theory—at separation from American society, even at the price of permanently antagonizing its white majority, and at a voluntarily accepted segregation in preparation for the coming of a vaguely conceived independence. In principle it would not be impossible for the proponents of Black Power to return to nonviolent techniques to pursue their nationalist aims. (Gandhi pursued purely nationalist goals in some of his later *satyagraha* campaigns, with the support of all but the most extreme nonpacifist Indian nationalists.) At the moment of writing, however, this eventuality does not seem likely. Both SNCC and CORE in the course of the last few years appear to have firmly repudiated their nonviolent roots and to have transferred their allegiance—at least for some time to come—to the ideology of militant Black Power. Yet, whatever the future holds, the contribution of Gandhian nonviolence to one of the most vital stages in the American Negro's struggle for freedom is undeniable; it is securely anchored in the historical record.

PACIFISM AND NUCLEAR DISARMAMENT: GREAT BRITAIN

It is not the task of this volume to provide, even in outline, a history of the British campaign for unilateral nuclear disarmament. Discussion must necessarily be limited (as in the account above of the nonviolent struggle for civil rights in the United States). Something needs, however, to be said concerning the relationship of pacifism to this new development in the peace movement.

For more than a decade after 1945 the pacifist movement in Great Britain displayed, we have seen, little vitality or original thought. It stood as before for complete disarmament, unilaterally if that were necessary. It opposed German rearmament and was highly critical of American foreign policy. It continued the fight against conscription and campaigned against the utterly inadequate measures of civil defense attempted in face of atomic warfare. It toyed with the idea of a "third camp" of nations disengaged from, and standing between, the two opposing blocs. Renewed interest did indeed emerge in this period among some pacifists in Gandhian techniques of conflict resolution; this development will be dealt with in the next section of this chapter. It was, however, the explosion of Britain's first hydrogen bomb in November 1957 that galvanized British pacifism into life.

A leader of the new nuclear pacifism, the Anglican Canon John Collins, has criticized the older pacifist organizations for failing to realize the need for fresh techniques and approaches as follows:

They saw the nuclear bomb, not so much a challenge to old pacifist ways of thinking, as simply a further and more pressing reason for going on with them. . . . They were slow to realize that the old debate between pacifists and non-pacifists was now an academic one and had been raised to a new level, a level at which pacifists would be able to carry along with them countless others who are not, and would not wish to be, pacifists in the pre-nuclear use of that word.[44]

The Campaign for Nuclear Disarmament (CND), which now emerged in Britain, represented a fusion of the moral individualistic urge of the old-school pacifists with the new impetus imparted by mass protest against the use of nuclear weapons. The most striking fact about CND, something that came as a surprise at first to its initiators, was its ability to mobilize the younger generation, men and women in their twenties and early thirties as well as boys and girls in their late teens, behind the movement and to bring them out into the streets in large numbers in protest marches and demonstrations.

CND was officially founded at the end of January 1958. From the beginning it called for nuclear disarmament on the part of Great Britain and other nuclear powers, with Britain leading the way: a program that was summed up in the slogan "Ban the Bomb." The campaign crystallized out of the protest which had been mounting in Great Britain throughout the summer and autumn of 1957 as a result of the recent British nuclear testing.[45] Pacifists were active here as were socialist intellectuals, like J. B. Priestley and Kingsley Martin of the *New Statesman,* and reform-minded clergy of both the established church and the nonconformist denominations. The protest found support, too, in the Labour Party among its left wing M.P.'s and trade-unionists as well as among many nonpolitical scientists appalled at the destructive ends to which scientific discovery was being applied. Communists participated in the protest movement only with some hesitation and after CND had already commenced activity (the Campaign indeed had some awkward implications *vis-à-vis* the Soviet Union and its nuclear armament program); their influence on the direction taken by CND thereafter was in fact very limited. Other small leftist splinter groups also took part but again their contribution was minimal.

At the outset it was the pacifists who provided much of the moral fervor and many of those most active in the local branches set up by CND; leftist intellectuals also helped to shape the movement's ideology. The idea of an Easter-time protest march to the Atomic Weapons Research Establishment at Aldermaston, first undertaken in 1958, originated with a group of pacifist direct actionists, though civil disobedience did not become part of the marchers' program. These annual Aldermaston marches, in which tens of thousands of persons participated, marked the end of apathy in Britain on the peace question.

At first CND concentrated on an educational and propaganda campaign to influence public opinion. One writer speaks of the organization's "anti-political tone" at the beginning.[46] It represented to a large degree a feeling of alienation from the bureaucratic parties, which had hitherto monopolized the political scene and thereby prevented politically relevant debate on the implications of current war preparation. Campaigners, old and young, tended to be critics of existing society as well as merely opponents of the bomb. CND in fact represented a contemporary variant of English radical political dissent. (With its quasi-religious tone and strong moral enthusiasm, its mass techniques combined with a predominantly "respectable" middle-class composition and leadership, and its extraparliamentary structure, CND has been aptly compared to the Anti-Corn Law League of the early 1840's.[47]) It was, above all, "a form of witness against the values of the wider society." [48]

CND's attempt to capture the Labour Party for nuclear unilateralism in 1960, when the annual party conference in October passed a resolution calling on Britain to abandon its nuclear deterrent, was ultimately unsuccessful, for in the following year the decision was reversed. Indeed the passing of a unilateralist resolution was more the product of a temporary upsurge of opposition within the party and trade unions to the leadership of Hugh Gaitskell, a firm opponent of unilateralism, than of any genuine conversion of the British labor movement as a whole to the ideology of CND. As a political pressure group CND proved a failure.

Critics have accused CND of lacking an ideology. And it is true that even on the one issue which provided a focal point for the campaign, Britain's unilateral renunciation of nuclear weapons, there was considerable diversity of view. There were campaigners who did not disapprove of American retention of nuclear armaments; there were others who looked favorably on the Soviet Union's nuclear arms program.

From the pacifist point of view serious reservations were possible in regard to the Campaign, and in fact pacifist organizations like the Peace Pledge Union or the Fellowship of Reconciliation gave CND rather a cold welcome. The PPU finally disaffiliated its weekly organ, *Peace News,* which had become an ardent supporter of CND. Pacifist "purists" felt that it was a betrayal of mission to single out one particular group of weapons, as CND was doing with nuclear armaments, instead of agitating as hitherto against all forms of weaponry. Howard Horsburgh has expressed this view as follows: "To enter a war is to ensure that it will take place. Consequently, any prospective combatant who fails to come to moral terms with it, for example . . . by continuing to justify wars in a way that demands moral discrimination in the choice of means, is radically dishonest." [49]

To many pacifists, however, the situation did not appear in this light. They argued that the menace of nuclear warfare was so overwhelming that any movement organized to oppose nuclear weapons should command the pacifist movement's support. As a PPU worker, active also in CND, wrote: "Prior to propagating pacifism we have a duty towards human life." [50] Moreover, CND might help to arouse outside interest in pacifism, especially among the younger generation whom the traditional type of pacifism had failed to attract. Concern for nuclear disarmament could be the first step toward a total repudiation of war. As Canon Collins com-

mented: "CND has speeded up and prospered the dialogue between pacifists and non-pacifists." [51] The task of pacifists within
CND, it was argued, was to keep the campaign to a policy of
unilateralism, and away from the compromises which would result
if the movement converted itself into a merely political pressure
group.

By the middle of the sixties the impulse behind CND had already
begun to wane without its having reached its goal of Britain's unilateral disarmament. The nuclear deterrent remains today to
threaten mankind's destruction as well as the enemy's, and nuclear
proliferation continues. In practical terms CND achieved little.
What may be put to its credit is something that is not at all easy to
define. First, we may say that the Campaign succeeded in bringing
the moral implications of nuclear warfare out into the open and in
making them a live issue in British political life (something that
the pacifist movement had attempted to do during the interwar
years with war in general, though with rather less effect). Like
the Anglo-American reform movements of the nineteenth century,
CND presented basically a simple message. Nuclear war is sin,
it said in effect, as those earlier movements had denounced drink
or slavery as 'sin'. Perhaps just because of its somewhat simplified
appeal CND, in the second place, was able to inject an awareness
of the practical dangers inherent in the nuclear threat into the
general public, which had previously displayed apathy and ignorance concerning the issue. This happened not only in Britain but
also to some extent in Western Europe and in North America
where the movement was transplanted, though in less vigorous
form.

One of the shortcomings of the case for nuclear disarmament
lay in the probability that resort to nuclear weapons would eventually be made if war ever broke out. The retention of conventional
weapons, which CND did not concern itself with directly, contains
a potential nuclear threat. Some supporters of the movement,
therefore, began to turn their attention increasingly toward the
possibilities of "civilian defence," as they came to call their proposed policy, a policy implying total and unilateral disarmament
based primarily, however, on expediency rather than on pacifist
principle.

Among its most energetic proponents was Commander Stephen

King-Hall, a political commentator and retired naval officer. "I am not a pacifist in the accepted sense of that word," wrote King-Hall. "But I see no reason why opinions held by pacifists for moral causes are therefore necessarily to be ignored by non-pacifists if such opinions are useful for defence purposes." [52] In face of the threat posed by the unleashing of nuclear war, even if one side were employing the bomb for defensive purposes, he urged his countrymen to disarm and develop a nonviolent strategy for defending Britain physically in case of enemy occupation and for upholding the democratic values inherent in the British political tradition. "A radical change in the basis of [Britain's] defence policy would not alter the fundamental nature of the 'war' between Communism and Democracy, but it would profoundly change its character by transferring the centre of gravity of the difference between the two ways of life from the sphere of violence to that of ideas." [53] If Britain were to give a lead of this kind, other countries would gradually move over from violent to nonviolent defense, a shift in strategic outlook which King-Hall considered essential if mankind was to avoid nuclear destruction.

King-Hall made three practical suggestions concerning the implementation of such a policy: the appointment at once by the government or the Imperial Defence College of a committee to study the potentialities of a nonviolent defense policy; the setting up within half a decade of a "non-violent resistance Defence Service"; the training in nonviolent resistance at the same time, and alongside this professional nonviolent Defence Service, of part-time volunteers from the civilian population.

King-Hall in his writings drew heavily on historical and other data provided by earlier pacifist literature dealing with nonviolent resistance. And it was among members of the more radical wing of the pacifist movement that his ideas found the readiest response rather than in government circles or among his former colleagues in the armed services where he had hoped to evoke interest, if hardly immediate assent. Pacifist radicals, influenced by Gandhian ideas, wished to advance beyond the hitherto essentially negative slogans of the peace movement: "Thou shalt not kill," or "No More War," or "Ban the Bomb." [54] They sought to confront the new nuclear situation with a positive technique of conflict resolution that could gain widespread support because it promised the preservation of a given society's values by means that did not threaten to destroy in the process of defense both the values themselves and the men and women who upheld them. But first, so it seemed to these pacifist radicals, the trend toward nuclear war must be reversed by direct action rather than by the more conventional methods of agitation pursued by CND, which were proving ineffective.

NONVIOLENT DIRECT ACTION FOR PEACE

Nonviolent direct action has been defined as "a special form of . . . resistance, in which the dissenter uses his own body as the lever with which to pry loose the government's policy." [55] In previous sections of the book we have discussed attempts to employ direct action of this kind for various purposes: to rectify economic or social abuses or to gain political concessions, as in some of Gandhi's earlier *satyagraha* campaigns; to win national independence and effect the withdrawal of a colonial power, as Gandhi tried to do in the 1930s and early 1940s and certain African nationalist leaders after World War II; or to achieve full civil equality for a politically depressed section of the population, as in the United States under Martin Luther King.

We have seen, too, that nonviolent direct action has usually, though by no means always, entailed civil disobedience. Civil disobedience can be direct and consist in refusing an objectionable law or, where a direct confrontation with wrong is impossible, it can be indirect and consist in the violation of laws that are in themselves unobjectionable. In the latter case, in particular, disobedience may act either as "a symbolic gesture," a form of witness, calling attention to an injustice and attempting in this way to mobilize opinion against it. Or, on the other hand, it may have almost revolutionary implications and be aimed at creating disruption so as to force an immediate change in official policy or even to overthrow the government altogether.

Great Britain

Within the PPU a small group had crystallized towards the end of the forties with an interest in exploring the possibilities of nonviolent action and its implications for the peace movement. At the beginning this interest was purely theoretical; it consisted entirely of study and discussion. A resolution passed at the PPU's annual conference in 1947 calling for the organization of a campaign of noncooperation with peacetime conscription had evoked such a furor among part of the membership that it was reversed shortly afterwards at a specially convened meeting.

A Non-Violence Commission was, however, set up by the PPU in 1949. Some of its members eventually grew restive at what they considered a too academic approach. In 1951 they organized a "sit-down" in front of the War Office; next year they demonstrated outside the Atomic Weapons Research Establishment at Aldermaston. At first they used the name "Operation Gandhi" for their work, but in 1953 they adopted the title "Non-Violent Resistance Group," changing it in 1957 to "Direct Action Committee against Nuclear War." During this period they staged a number of civil disobedience protests against nuclear armament; these demonstrations attracted little attention or support, even within pacifist circles. Though most of the participants were members of the PPU, the PPU itself cleaved to its old policy of acting as an umbrella organization embracing all varieties of pacifism and was therefore unwilling to sponsor activities which met with the disapproval of many members.

When news appeared in the spring of 1957 of Britain's projected explosion of its first hydrogen bomb, two Quakers—Harold and Sheila Steele—with a group of pacifist direct actionists attempted to enter the area off Christmas Island in the Pacific Ocean where the test was to be conducted. The attempt proved abortive. But the publicity given to the venture in the press and the fears now rapidly emerging among the general public concerning the consequences of nuclear warfare, together provided the initial impetus in the formation of CND.[56]

Among the diverse elements which went into the making of CND none proved more devoted and energetic than the direct action group—or at times more trying to the Campaign's less radically inclined leadership. In June 1958 we find Canon Collins writing: "I'm still struggling with direct action enthusiasts and enthusiastic groups of extremists of all types! But I think we're slowing down dissidence and gradually getting things on an even keel." [57] The direct actionist leaders were all young, mostly in their twenties. They were more interested in the successful demonstration of nonviolent techniques than in a propaganda campaign for the banning of the bomb (or so it seemed to Canon Collins[58]). The loose organization of CND in its early days permitted the existence within it of a direct action group, which engaged in work-obstruction at nuclear rocket bases and attempted to persuade workers on these sites to strike or leave their jobs. Eventually the original nucleus of pacifist direct actionists expanded by drawing into its orbit some of the CND's young recruits as well as older supporters of the campaign, of whom the octogenarian Bertrand Russell was among the most illustrious, and one of the most vigorous, examples. These new converts to direct action did not, for the most part, completely share their pacifist predecessors' devotion to nonviolence as a matter of principle. Yet many of them now felt, as one of them wrote, that "in the twentieth century Gandhi is in fact a more relevant political thinker than Marx." [59]

A series of international incidents during the summer of 1960 raised the temperature of antinuclear feeling in Britain as elsewhere. Russell was now persuaded by a young graduate student at the London School of Economics, Ralph Schoenman, to inaugurate what both men hoped would become a mass antinuclear civil disobedience campaign. In the early autumn of 1960 a "Committee of 100" was formed; its one hundred sponsors being drawn from sympathizers prominent in the political or cultural life of the country. "Russell and Schoenman . . . set out to combine the mass support of the CND with the capacity for sensational civil disobedience of the Direct Action Committee." [60]

The setting up of the Committee of 100 was accompanied by much publicity in the newspapers; the conservative press accused its sponsors of planning subversion and sabotage. The leadership of CND was perturbed too, for men like Canon Collins, who did not share the sanguine hopes of the direct actionists, feared the effect which adverse publicity and the branding of the movement as ultra-leftist would have on its effectiveness as a political force. As a result, Bertrand Russell resigned as president of CND, and the Campaign and the Committee henceforward pursued their separate, though sometimes overlapping ways.

The opponents of direct action within CND, whether pacifist or nonpacifist, centered their case on the inappropriateness, indeed the harmfulness, of such methods in a democratic society. They supported the idea of individual civil disobedience if a law were obnoxious to a man's moral sense, as for example in the case of a conscientious objector to military service, or its collective practice as an act of protest in a country where either the majority or a minority were deprived of their civil rights as occurred, for instance, in British India or with the Negro population in the southern United States. But in a genuine democracy, the critics of direct action claimed, there was—apart from the conscientious refusal of individual citizens to obey a thoroughly immoral law—rarely, if ever, room for such action. If engaged in on a wide scale, it would undermine parliamentary institutions and in all probability usher in eventually a dictatorial regime as a consequence of bypassing the ordinary democratic processes. Canon Collins complained of the Committee of 100's "deliberate breaking of laws, which in themselves cause no offence to conscience, in order to gain publicity and to bring pressure to bear upon governments." [61] He accused its members, while obviously still a small minority, of attempting to enforce their policy on the government by a species of nonviolent blackmail instead of waiting until they had convinced a majority in the country of its correctness. Since tactics of this kind were anyhow unlikely to be successful, the final result would be to discredit the entire antinuclear cause and retard its further development.

In reply, spokesmen for civil disobedience pleaded the urgency of the situation in extenuation of their action. We cannot afford to wait, they said in effect. The nuclear threat and the extinction of the human race, which could result from prolonged competition in nuclear armaments, justified a shortcut in the democratic procedure. In their view civil disobedience, with the readiness of its practitioners to suffer arrest and imprisonment for their witness, would alone serve to arouse a still too apathetic public and to break through the wall of silence with which the British establishment attempted to surround the subject of nuclear disarmament. No amount of marchings and meetings, the direct actionists asserted, would avail. As one might employ radical measures to disarm a lunatic, so shock treatment in the form of direct action was needed to deal with the insane policies of the nuclear deterrent. To the charge that their tactics were essentially anti-democratic, the direct actionists countered both with the traditional appeal to a higher law and by the argument that nonviolent direct action provided a peaceable means for expressing radical dissent, which would prevent its deterioration otherwise into violent channels.[62]

During the first two years of its existence the Committee of 100 organized several dramatic sit-downs and other acts of civil disobedience, which led to the jailing of Russell and other participants. By 1962, however, a change had taken place in the Committee's objectives. From an organization which, like the CND out of which it had sprung, aimed primarily at Britain's unilateral abandonment of the nuclear deterrent as a first step towards international nuclear disarmament, the Committee now became a body devoted to a somewhat vaguely conceived nonviolent political revolution, a total restructuring of society, which would eliminate the Bomb along with the social order generating it. The Committee's social revolutionary aims, however, further limited its appeal, since even among the comparatively small numbers who proved ready to participate in direct action not all were prepared to follow the Committee to this ultimate conclusion. A note of desperation now crept into its demonstrations, a purposelessness began to show itself in some of its acts of civil disobedience: direct action, as it were, for direct action's sake. A strange amalgam of old-school Trotskyites and militant anarchists imparted a flavor of scarcely suppressed violence to a movement that had at first found its inspiration in the Gandhian philosophy of *ahimsa*.

The Committee of 100 had originally hoped to set going a mass movement of protest and, by its cultivation of civil disobedience and its nonviolent suffering of the legal consequences of such disobedience, to awaken tens of thousands to the nuclear danger. One of the Committee organizers felt that

demonstrations must not end with the sit-in. Otherwise after two days of headlines and a certain amount of inconvenience for the courts the authorities are in the clear. We must begin to pledge people in their thousands to carry the challenge further. If ten thousand have to be carried into court where they refuse to say a mumbling word: if ten thousand have to be jailed—then we shall realise the meaning of civil disobedience and I dare say so will the makers of [nuclear] bombs.[63]

Yet this vision proved an illusion. The Committee remained small, if at first select. The masses failed to rally behind its slogans. After a little, its acts of civil disobedience ceased to make much

248 TWENTIETH-CENTURY PACIFISM

impact on the public, though the Committee itself did not finally cease to function until September 1968. Long before this, however, enthusiasm had begun to ebb; rifts and secessions appeared.

The Committee's decline seems attributable to two basic shortcomings. In the first place, there was the ambiguity (already noted), which developed concerning the Committee's ultimate objectives. Did it aim by means of mass civil disobedience to bear witness in the most dramatic way possible to the evil of nuclear war? Or was its purpose to generate something like a general strike against war, which (as syndicalists and anarchists had long been urging) could then be used as a lever to carry out a far-going political and social revolution? It soon became clear that the revolutionary situation, which the second alternative presumed, did not exist in Great Britain at that date. A second source of weakness lay in the Committee's inability (perhaps in part on account of this rapidly developing ambiguity as to its aims) to make its protest an effective symbol in the public mind of the truth it sought to convey. Success in this regard Gandhi had always emphasized as essential in a *satyagraha* campaign. The Committee's failure here may also have derived from the difficulty of arranging a clear confrontation with the evil it opposed. Breaking the law by sitting down in Trafalgar Square, or even by obstructing the entrance to an atomic missile site, did not provide the same immediately obvious connection with nuclear war as Gandhi's illegal manufacture of salt had done with the evil of alien rule or a southern Negro's sit-in at a segregated lunch-counter with the shame of racial discrimination.

The United States

A movement for nonviolent direct action to further world peace developed in the United States at the same time as it was emerging, on a rather wider scale, in Great Britain. Apart from a short-lived revival immediately after World War II when the explosion of the first atomic bombs aroused some alarm concerning the future, the American pacifist movement remained in the doldrums until its gradual reactivation towards the end of the fifties. The relaxation of East-West tensions which resulted from the fall of Stalinism in the Soviet Union, combined with a growing awareness throughout the States of the threat presented by thermonuclear war, created a more receptive atmosphere for pacifist ideas than had existed during the years of the Cold War. In addition, a new generation, more susceptible to pacifist arguments than its fathers had become, had by now arrived on the scene.

As in Great Britain, active interest in Gandhian techniques was confined at first to a small section only of the pacifist movement.[64] The American Fellowship of Reconciliation, like the British PPU, decided early on that it could not sponsor civil disobedience as an instrument of pacifist policy, although members remained free to engage in such action as individuals. Official support, it was felt, would destroy the all-embracing character of the Fellowship. The secular War Resisters' League showed itself more sympathetic to the idea of nonviolent direct action. In 1948 a group of WRL members calling themselves the "Peacemakers" had enunciated a program which included nonregistration for the draft, refusal to pay taxes destined for military purposes and the development of nonviolent techniques for achieving social change. The program represented a fusion of Gandhian and anarchist ideas and showed the influence, too, of the Marxist critique of capitalist society. But the Peacemakers did not flourish for long.

A fresh beginning came in 1956 when in March of that year a new journal of ideas appeared. *Liberation,* as it was named, was intended by its founders to serve as organ for a direct actionist variety of pacifism, which would be neither liberal-democratic, for it advocated a social revolution, nor Marxist, since it stood for nonviolent means to achieve the revolution. This new pacifist left was inclined towards a decentralized society. Some of its supporters had been interested in the communitarian movement, which survived the war here in a more flourishing state than its counterpart in Great Britain. (Staughton Lynd, for example, one of the pacifist left's leading figures in the sixties, lived for a time in a Brüderhof settlement.) In any case the direct actionists were all profoundly disillusioned with the established political parties and utterly without hope of achieving social change or a peaceable revolution through orthodox political channels.

For American pacifist radicals, Gandhi remained both teacher and guide for action (and A. J. Muste with his call for "holy disobedience" was his prophet). "To understand the significance of Gandhi for American pacifists," one of the radicals has written, "it is necessary to look at the conflict between two fundamental ideas and orientations in the peace movement: the idea of *non-resistance* and the idea of *non-violent resistance*. . . . The shift from one to the other represents a change from a conservative, individually-oriented pacifism to a radical, social action pacifism." [65] Moreover, whereas before the last war Gandhi's influence in America was purely intellectual, in the decades after 1945 activists began to put Gandhian techniques into practice.

The application of Gandhi's ideas in the struggle for civil rights has been discussed in an earlier section of the present chapter. This aspect represents in many ways the most dramatic and successful part of the story. But nonviolent direct action was also used in the United States, as in Great Britain, against war preparation, and in particular in protest against nuclear armaments. Of course, American pacifists and peace-minded nonpacifists were no more united in regard to the value or justifiability of direct action than the contemporary British peace movement was. No exact equivalent to CND emerged in the United States. The organization known as SANE (National Committee for a Sane Nuclear Policy), which had been set up in 1957 by a number of pacifists and nonpacifists concerned at the increasing threat posed by nuclear weapons and anxious to achieve nuclear disarmament, was officially less uncompromising in its unilateralism and organizationally much less widely based than the British CND was. It lacked the latter's mass appeal. SANE, too, proceeded from the beginning along entirely separate lines from the direct actionists, who in June 1957 had established a Committee for Non-Violent Action (CNVA) to coordinate their hitherto dispersed efforts.

In some respects CNVA's activities paralleled those of the direct actionists in Britain. Its supporters sat down outside atomic plants and missile sites; they "invaded" Polaris submarine bases and conducted vigils before germ-warfare research stations. In New York City they disobeyed the order to take shelter in the annual civil defense drills. They distributed antiwar leaflets among workers engaged on projects connected with nuclear armament. Sometimes the demonstrators were arrested and fined or jailed. Sometimes they were received with hostility by the local people, who might often be dependent for their livelihood on the arms industry. But they were also successful on occasion in enlisting local sympathy, especially when the demonstration was carried over a long enough period to allow for calm consideration of their case. A hopeful sign was increasing participation of college students in the movement: one manifestation indeed of the growing campus revolution.

Three special forms of nonviolent protest were developed by the American direct actionists: refusal to pay taxes for war; "trespassing" within the area set aside for atomic testing; and the organization of international peace walks. The first two necessarily involved civil disobedience, while the third might do so in certain circumstances.

Tax refusal was an old pacifist technique, though only seldom used. Radical Quakers like the saintly John Woolman in the eighteenth century had practiced it. Henry David Thoreau in 1845 in his classic act of civil disobedience, which led first to his spending a night in the Concord jail and then to his writing an essay whose reverberations have continued to echo up till now, was refusing to pay a tax which in his view supported slavery and war. Where the whole tax, or the greater part of it, was clearly for military purposes, it was easier for the war resister to refuse payment, and his witness gained in consistency and potential impact. The issue at stake was less clear, however, where the government allocated only an undefined—but by the twentieth century often a very large—portion for war preparation.

Most pacifists in mid-twentieth-century America have paid their taxes, feeling that it would be wrong to refuse support for the beneficial activities of their government and impossible to subtract with any degree of accuracy the fraction devoted to war. A few war resisters so reduced their income as to fall below the taxable level. And there were those, too, who refused cooperation with the federal tax authorities and were ready to go to jail rather than pay. Civil disobedience in this case was conceived both as witness to the truth as the resister saw it and a challenge to the warmaking power. One of the most consistent among recent tax objectors, the Presbyterian minister Maurice McCrackin, declared: "By giving my money I was helping the government do what I so vigorously declared was wrong." [66] Since war was a worse evil than bawdy houses or gambling dens, was one really more justified, he asked, in paying taxes, of which some three quarters went for war, than one would be if they went instead for the upkeep of institutions of the latter sort?

An equally arresting and even more novel type of nonviolent direct action was inaugurated by CNVA in 1958 with the attempted sailing of the *Golden Rule* into the Americans' atomic test area around Entiwetok Atoll in the Marshall Islands. The boat had a four-man crew commanded by an ex-naval captain and convert to Quakerism, Albert S. Bigelow. Like the British Quaker couple, the Steeles, in the previous year, the *Golden Rule* was unsuccessful in reaching its destination; the crew being stopped and brought to Honolulu where they were tried and imprisoned. As convinced Gandhians, Bigelow and his colleagues had conducted their whole enterprise in the open, feeling that secrecy would have undermined the message they wished to convey.[67]

The sequel to the story is not uninstructive. An American anthropologist, Earle Reynolds, returing home across the Pacific with his family in their yacht, the *Phoenix,* after a long absence overseas, heard of the *Golden Rule* and thereupon determined to take over its uncompleted mission. Reynolds hitherto had been unconnected with either CNVA or the pacifist movement in general. His boat managed to enter the restricted zone but was subsequently halted, and its owner found his way into jail along with the crew of the *Golden Rule.*[68]

The forbidden voyages did not bring about a cessation of the nuclear testing. Indeed it is unlikely that the participants regarded immediate success in this regard as a likely outcome of their action. Their purpose was to dramatize the evil of nuclear warfare by a direct confrontation, in which the crews incurred the risk not merely of a short prison term (which resulted) but of death in the nuclear explosion. Their action was an exemplification of a basic principle in the Gandhian philosophy of nonviolence: *tapasya,* or self-sacrifice voluntarily undertaken in the name of a declared truth.

The two enterprises did in fact gain greater publicity and more sympathetic coverage for the antinuclear cause than any previous pacifist demonstrations. They marked a decisive stage in its development; the clouds of apathy hitherto covering public discussion of the nuclear deterrent were at last beginning to disperse.

During the first half of the sixties, CNVA, influenced by such ventures in nonviolent direct action as the Freedom Rides into the Deep South (discussed above), began to organize a series of international peace walks. In contrast to the British CND's annual Aldermaston marches, the example of which may also have been influential on CNVA's tactics now, the peace walkers were specially chosen and the number of participants restricted to two or three dozen. These walks, like the voyage of the *Golden Rule,* represent a type of selective *satyagraha* such as Gandhi had sometimes preferred to larger scale enterprises (an example of this is the Vykom Temple Road *Satyagraha* of 1924–25 discussed in Chapter III).

In 1960–61 an international team made the journey from San Francisco to Moscow where their Russian host endeavored (unsuccessfully) to convince them that the Soviet Union, although armed with nuclear weapons, was entirely peaceable.[69] The marchers did not practice civil disobedience *en route;* their object was to center attention—through the walk itself—on the nuclear threat to mankind and to demonstrate in favor of a nonviolent way to resolve conflict. In a later peace walk (Quebec to Washington to Guantanamo, 1963–64) the marchers, however, did run into trouble in the South on account of the integrated character of the team and their determination to witness against the denial of human brotherhood contained in racial discrimination. In Albany, Georgia, they were arrested and jailed. "The prolonged fast," wrote one of the participants in the walk, "is our chief weapon. We have others. A number of walkers practice kinds of civil disobedience other than fasting. Some refuse to walk into their cells. They oppose the prison system in principle. Others will not walk to court. They cannot recognize an apparatus created in the name of justice for the purpose of denying justice. By these acts they offset, indeed annihilate and make ridiculous, the mantle of power and authority that the Albany court has gathered about itself." [70]

By the second half of the 1960s the practice of nonviolence appeared to many in the West to be an instrument with as yet unmeasured potentialities, but one fraught at the same time with serious dangers and also (as the Indians had discovered after independence when nonviolent resistance was often undertaken irresponsibly) open to abuse. This new source of power was still, as it were, at a similar stage of development as electricity had been at the time of Marconi and Edison.[71] In certain circumstances it could obviously be wielded with effect by a subject people or an oppressed minority to extract concessions from the government, even without a total commitment to its use on the part of all participants in a nonviolent campaign. Past experience, however, could throw only an uncertain light on its possibilities as a substitute for armed defense by the nation-state.

There were some pacifists[72] who thought that in the complex twentieth-century world *ahimsa*, like patriotism, was not enough. Today, they claimed, the truth which a *satyagraha* campaign sought to exemplify could usually be reached only through elaborate quantitative research in the social and statistical sciences. To expand this kind of "peace research" directed toward the nonviolent resolution of conflict had now become, in their view, the most important task of the neo-Gandhian movement.

At any rate, whether resulting from scholarly research or from the urgings of the spirit, the adoption of nonviolence would seem to entail a fairly radical restructuring of society. A country, which pursued imperialist domination or tolerated far-going political or economic inequality, could scarcely expect to practice nonviolent resistance with success. Nonviolence, therefore, had social revolutionary implications.

Concerning the practice of nonviolent direct action within a framework of genuine political democracy, a wide divergency of view, we have seen, existed within the peace movement where such action entailed civil disobedience. In fact, in no country of the "free world" had either legal political demonstrations, or symbolic civil disobedience of an individual character, or attempts to obstruct the nuclear effort succeeded in persuading a government to abandon its reliance on the nuclear deterrent or to take steps toward implementing a nonviolent strategy of civilian defense. To some extent the peace movement had been able to spread awareness of the nuclear threat, but there was no evidence as yet that either in the United States or in any other country a majority of the population was in favor of relinquishing nuclear arms—not to speak of conventional weapons.

WAR AND CONSCIENTIOUS OBJECTION: THE UNITED STATES TODAY

Whereas in Great Britain conscription was abolished in 1961, in the United States compulsory military service, set at two years since 1951 and organized on a selective basis, had continued almost without a break since the wartime system of conscription came to an end in March 1947. With the country's increasing involvement in the war in Vietnam the problem of conscientious objection began to take on new relevance in the sixties. In addition, the idea of war resistance now spread from pacifist circles outwards to embrace many who did not share quite the same approach to war and peace.

"During World War II and the Korean War," a veteran antimilitarist has written, "there was little feeling among pacifists that *this* war must be stopped and we will do everything within our power to stop it. Not that any of them wanted war to continue, but the dominant psychology was one of personal nonparticipation in a catastrophe which had been sanctioned by the democratic process and, in any event, was beyond their power to shorten or stop." [73] The growing awareness of the dangers of nuclear war described in previous pages contributed of course to the subsequent extension of antiwar feelings in the population. Opposition to the Vietnam War proved an even more effective agent in creating such sentiment. Many Americans, who were far from considering themselves to be war resisters in the traditional meaning or even nuclear pacifists, regarded the conflict as an unjust war (in a sense roughly approximating the Thomist definition).

Thus not only a convinced pacifist such as Martin Luther King but men like Dr. Benjamin Spock, who had indeed supported America's participation in the Korean War, were prepared to risk imprisonment by urging all those who opposed the war to resist the draft if called upon for military service. Mass parades against the war in Vietnam filled the streets of the major American cities with thousands of demonstrators; sit-ins took place in front of army induction centers. Some young men of military age burned their draft cards in public or handed them back to the authorities. Others crossed the border into Canada. Draft "dodging" may perhaps be considered a species of *hijrat,* a voluntary exile. Gandhi had commended *hijrat* as an alternative, neither dishonorable nor cowardly, to submission to wrong for those who did not feel able, if they stayed at home, to face the consequences of resistance (which in the present circumstances might involve a five-year jail term) or for those who considered this kind of resistance was

not meaningful for them. There were even a few cases where opponents of the war—we may cite the Quaker Norman Morrison or
the Roman Catholic Roger LaPorte—following the example of
Buddhist monks and nuns in South Vietnam, protested by setting
fire to themselves and died. Opponents of the war, while prepared
to pay tribute to the self-sacrifice this involved, did not generally
feel that such self-immolation, such altruistic suicide, though perhaps not essentially different from a fast unto death which had
been undertaken by Gandhi and others on occasion, was an appropriate method, at least in Western society.[74]

Conscientious objection, on the other hand, was to some extent
built in, as it were, to the American political structure: a situation
which did not exist, for example, throughout most of the European
continent. In the United States even members of the far left who
supported the Hanoi government's war effort (a small minority,
let me add, within the antiwar movement) also sometimes sought
the 1-O classification, which now gave conscientious objector status.
But most political objectors to the war in Vietnam did so because
they condemned the United States's intervention in that country
rather than from any desire to whitewash all the policies of
America's "enemy" in this undeclared war.

Yet, according to the letter of the law, only religious pacifists,
with belief in "a Supreme Being" (until this phrase was omitted
when the duration of military service was extended once again in
1967), continued to be eligible for exemption as conscientious objectors and subsequent assignment either to noncombatant or
civilian alternative service. Nonreligious objectors to all wars
as well as the various kinds of political objector, including "selective" objectors to the Vietnam War, were still excluded from the
benefit of the act.

An advance occurred in 1965 with the U.S. Supreme Court's
decision in the Daniel Seeger case, though the decision was possibly
not quite as liberal as that of the Second Circuit Court of Appeals
in 1943 in the Kauten case (mentioned in Chapter V). Seeger,
a pacifist who disclaimed belief in a personal God, was appealing a
sentence of imprisonment imposed after his application for exemption had been rejected. The Supreme Court ruled in Seeger's favor,
stating its opinion that "the test of belief 'in relation to a Supreme
Being' is whether a given belief that is sincere and meaningful

occupies a place in the life of its possessor parallel to that filled by the orthodox belief in God of one who clearly qualifies for the exemption. Where such beliefs have parallel positions in the lives of their respective holders, we cannot say that one is 'in relation to a Supreme Being' and the other is not." [75] At the same time, the Supreme Court stated its view that "essentially political, sociological, or philosophical views," however genuine, did not constitute a conscientious objection to war within the meaning of the act. Nonetheless it would seem that henceforward any fully pacifist objector qualified for exemption, unless he absolutely insisted that his objection was not religious even under the Supreme Court's broad definition of this term.

The problem of the selective objector remained. A not unrepresentative exposition of this viewpoint, and one more typical than the old-style socialist objection which predominated earlier in the century, may be found in the statement submitted by Benjamin Sherman explaining why he was resisting the draft. "I am not a pacifist," he wrote. He did not feel able to be "completely and lovingly non-violent." Nevertheless, he did not believe violence or killing "for any reason" could be right. "I am trying to clean myself bit by bit," he went on. "I am seeking this status of conscientious objection to the war in Vietnam although I know objection to a particular war is not permitted in the C.O. statutes, because I believe our conscience is often the truest guide in achieving some sort of understanding, love, and compassion for our fellow human beings. And our conscience *must,* not the written statutes, be our guide if we are ever to achieve world peace, and, in a narrower sense, peace of mind." [76]

Selective objectors, among whom were some whose scruples concerning participation in this particular war were religiously motivated, cited precedents such as the Nuremberg trials for refusing induction into an army engaged in a war they considered a crime against humanity. And had not obedience to the orders of one's superiors, likewise, been dismissed when Eichmann pleaded this in extenuation of his deeds? Serving soldiers who developed an objection to fighting in the war in Vietnam—but not to war in general—frequently had recourse to the concept of a higher code of international law, in addition to the appeal to a superior moral sanction such as we have just seen illustrated in Sherman's statement quoted above. Neither the civil courts nor military tribunals, however, were willing to admit such arguments.

In view of the alternatives facing them of long terms of imprisonment or of voluntary exile (in this case without term), there were selective objectors who were prepared to play "semantic games with the Selective Service forms." They were ready to state an objection to "war in any form" while adding, as an inward reservation, "given the international environment while I am eligible for the draft." [77] That there was often indeed a quite genuine "situational" element in the objections of young draftees taking the C.O. stand was recognized by those in close contact with them. These young men left the question of participation in a future war open, by no means wishing to exclude the possibility of an indefinitely continued war resistance. At any rate, the burden of proving that a war was "just" lay, in their view, with the government. Pacifists, of course, hoped that this stance would form the prelude to full conversion to pacifism. They felt it sufficient, however, for the time being to say, as in the words attributed to the founder of Quakerism, George Fox, in conversation with the young William Penn: "Wear [thy sword] as long as thou canst."

As the war in Vietnam continued, and the involvement of the United States in it increased and the demands of the military for manpower grew larger, concern spread at the continued refusal of the administration to give legal recognition to sincerely held objection to a particular war. This concern reached far beyond the limits of the peace movement *stricto sensu*. Opponents of recognition have maintained that, if claims to political objection of this kind were sustained, they could eventually undermine a country's military security and destroy its effectiveness in prosecuting its war aims. Besides, was there any more justification for admitting a selective objection to military service than for allowing a selective objection, let us say, to paying income tax? To these arguments the answer has been given, first, that in fact experience has shown that the number of men ready to take the objector stand does not normally constitute a security threat—unless, of course, the antiwar movement outside the ranks of the objectors has already reached formidable dimensions! In the second place, respect for the rights of religious conscience *vis-à-vis* participation in war has become a recognized part of the Western tradition, and more particularly of Anglo-American political practice. The extension of this same respect to embrace all conscientious opposition to military service is as valid as the recognition extended today in other areas to nonreligious conscience or to the claims of a situational ethic.

The war in Vietnam has, from one angle, imparted renewed vitality to the American pacifist movement. Antimilitarist sentiments have grown immensely, especially among the young and on college campuses. Widespread interest in conscientious objection, antimilitarism's classic form of expression in the countries embraced by Anglo-American political tradition, has taken the place of previous apathy or disdain. Organizations like the FOR have expanded both in numbers and in range of activities as well as in outreach to new sections of the population. The FOR, for example, reports that a third of the monthly intake of new members are Roman Catholics, "including many priests and nuns": elements that hitherto had been largely unreceptive to the pacifist message.

Yet this situation has its obverse side, too. Above all, of course, there is the deteriorating international situation, for which American intervention in Vietnam has been one of the factors most responsible, as well as the continuing danger of a resulting international crisis exploding into full-scale nuclear war. The peace movement, despite talk of organizing war resistance, has shown itself hitherto incapable of thwarting national policies which, in its view, are driving toward disaster. There are indications of a general swing within the country toward the right, due *inter alia* to such factors as the White "backlash" and the reaction of the older generation toward student revolt, a swing which could bring in its wake a setback to the antiwar forces too.

Again, cleavages have been revealed within the pacifist camp (as in the wider peace movement). Over against those pacifists who have remained profoundly sceptical of Communist aims and sympathetic to the values represented by American democracy, there have been others who have supported a revolutionary stance and felt a certain kinship with "heroic forces like the Cuban Fidelistas and the Viet Cong," despite disagreement with these latter over means.[78] They have felt, as the FOR left had done in the interwar years, that the choice was not simply between violence and nonviolence, but a much more complex one between violence used to promote a desirable social revolution and to ward off external attack, on the one hand, and violence serving to uphold an outmoded social order and to quash the aspirations of those seeking to establish a more just way of life for their people, on the other. As Staughton Lynd, a Quaker and one of the prophets of the New Left, expressed it: "Although I may be a *personal* pacifist, I am by no means of the opinion that both sides [in the Vietnam War] are equally guilty or that it is a matter of indifference how the struggle ends." And he went on to say that, if he were a citizen of a country whose cause he deemed just, he would participate in the struggle, though "as a noncombatant." [79]

In regard to the future prospects of the pacifist movement in the United States (or indeed elsewhere), two points seem certain.[80] First, it is scarcely likely that within the foreseeable future pacifism by itself, or the extension of conscientious objection, could bring about the cessation of wars among men. The pursuit of peace in the modern world is too complex an activity to be comprised within the old pacifist slogan "Wars will cease when men refuse to fight"; though this, of course, is not to say that conscientious objection does not still retain validity as a moral stand or pacifism as an individual ethic. However—and this is the second point to be made in conclusion—mankind in the nuclear age stands in dire need of an alternative to violence if its conflicts, either domestic or international, are not to bring it sooner or later to extinction. Ultimately, therefore, the gospel of reconciliation, the Gandhian approach, may prove sounder politics than a philosophy of violent deterrence.

NOTES

1. James Reston, as quoted in *Speak Truth to Power: A Quaker Search for an Alternative to Violence* (Philadelphia: American Friends Service Committee, 1955), p. viii.

2. George Orwell, *Shooting an Elephant and Other Essays* (London: Secker and Warburg, 1950), p. 111.

3. Lawrence Stephen Wittner, "The American Peace Movement, 1941–1960" (Ph.D. diss., Columbia University, 1967), p. 192.

4. Hugh Tinker, *Re-Orientations* (New York: Frederick A. Praeger, 1965), p. 137. See Chap. 9: "Magnificent Failure? The Gandhian Ideal in India," for the movement after Gandhi's death.

5. See Hallam Tennyson, *Saint on the March: The Story of Vinoba*

(London: Victor Gollancz Ltd., 1955); Lanza del Vasto, *Gandhi to Vinoba: The New Pilgrimage*, translated from the French (London: Rider and Company, 1956); R. P. Masani, *The Five Gifts* (London: Collins, 1957).

6. Vishwanath Tandon, *The Social and Political Philosophy of Sarvodaya after Gandhiji* (Rajghat, Varanasi: Sarva Seva Sangh Prakashan, 1965), p. 123. This volume contains an excellent bibliography of the Gandhian movement in the fifties and sixties.

7. See the semi-official history by Suresh Ram, *Vinoba and His Mission— Being an Account of the Rise and Growth of the Bhoodan Yajna Movement*, 3rd revised ed. (Rajghat, Kashi: Akhil Bharat Sarva Seva Sangh, 1962).

8. Tandon, *op. cit.*, p. 193; Vinoba Bhave, *Bhoodan Yajna [Land-Gifts Mission]* (Ahmedabad: Navajivan Publishing House, 1953), p. 53. See similar statements by Vinoba and Narayan reprinted in D. Mackenzie Brown, ed., *The Nationalist Movement: Indian Political Thought from Ranade to Bhave* (Berkeley and Los Angeles: University of California Press, 1961), pp. 184, 198, 199, 204.

9. Tandon, *op. cit.*, pp. 194, 196–198.

10. I have drawn heavily in the exposition which follows from Vinoba's book *Shanti Sena*, translated from the Hindi (Rajghat, Kashi: A. B. Sarva Seva Sangh Prakashan, 1961). See also the pamphlet by Narayan Desai, *Shanti-Sena in India* (Rajghat, Varanasi: A. B. Sarva Seva Sangh Prakashan, 1962).

11. Appendix I in James E. Bristol, *Non-Violence and India Today* (Philadelphia: Peace Education Division of the American Friends Service Committee, 1963).

12. Jayaprakash Narayan, *Sarvodaya Answer to Chinese Aggression* (Thanjavur: Sarvodaya Prachuralaya, 1963), p. 36.

13. Bristol, *op. cit.*, p. 4.

14. Tandon, *op. cit.*, p. 156.

15. Bristol, *op. cit.*, p. 3.

16. Quoted in *ibid.*, Appendix VI.

17. Quoted in William Robert Miller, *Nonviolence* (New York: Association Press, 1964), p. 291.

18. H. J. N. Horsburgh, *Non-Violence and Aggression: A Study of Gandhi's Moral Equivalent of War* (London: Oxford University Press, 1968), p. 165.

19. J. E. Bristol, "The Freedom Struggle in Southern Africa," in *Nonviolence Today* (New York: "Liberation," March, 1967), p. 5. See also for example Nelson Mandela, *No Easy Walk to Freedom* (London: Heinemann, 1965), Chap. 15.

20. James Farmer, *Freedom—When?* (New York: Random House, 1965), p. 53. See pp. 53–65 for the Gandhian roots of CORE.

21. Quoted in Wittner, *op. cit.*, pp. 99, 109.

22. M. K. Gandhi, *Non-Violence in Peace and War*, 3rd edition, vol. I (Ahmedabad: Navajivan Publishing House, 1948), p. 127. The remark was made in 1937.

23. Earl Charles Chatfield, Jr., "Pacifism and American Life: 1914 to 1941" (Ph.D. diss., Vanderbilt University 1965), p. 590.

24. See James Peck, *Freedom Ride* (New York: Simon and Schuster, 1962), for an account by a participant of the movement which developed out of the 1947 ride.

25. Wittner, *op. cit.*, p. 150.

26. The question has been raised whether believers in nonviolence are morally entitled to appeal for federal protection in furthering civil rights, although obviously they have a legal right to do so. A. J. Muste, for example, felt that they were not; he pointed to the potential danger of a federal intervention turning into a full-scale civil war. See his article "Nonviolence and Mississippi," in G. Ramachandran and T. K. Mahadevan, eds., *Gandhi: His Relevance for Our Times* (New Delhi: Gandhi Peace Foundation, 1967), pp. 213–215, 217, 218.

27. The following account is derived mainly from autobiographical passages in King's *Stride Toward Freedom: The Montgomery Story* (New York: Ballantine Books), first published in 1958.

28. *Ibid.,* p. 81.

29. *Ibid.,* pp. 174, 175.

30. *Ibid.,* p. 71.

31. Quoted in Miller, *op. cit.,* p. 301.

32. King, *Stride Toward Freedom,* p. 67. *Gandhi Marg* (New Delhi) devoted its July 1968 issue (vol. XII, no. 3 [47]) to King's contribution to nonviolence. For "the transformation of black radicals from the singing, integration-directed marchers of Montgomery, Alabama, in 1955 into the avowed guerilla fighters and alienated rebels of the late 1960's" (p. 325), see Vincent Harding, "Black Radicalism: The Road from Montgomery," in Alfred F. Young, ed., *Dissent: Explorations in the History of American Radicalism* (DeKalb: Northern Illinois University Press, 1968), pp. 319–354. A sharp critique of the "nonviolent commitment" expressed by the civil rights movement in its initial stages is given in Chapter 10 of an important sociological study by Inge Powell Bell, *CORE and the Strategy of Nonviolence* (New York: Random House, 1968).

33. Miller, *op. cit.,* p. 305.

34. Farmer, *op. cit.,* p. 77.

35. William Mahoney, "In Pursuit of Freedom," in Staughton Lynd, ed., *Nonviolence in America: A Documentary History* (Indianapolis: Bobbs-Merrill Co., Inc., 1966), pp. 427, 428.

36. Miller, *op. cit.,* p. 306.

37. Howard Zinn, *SNCC: The New Abolitionists* (Boston: Beacon Press, 1964), pp. 220, 221 and 34.

38. Miller, *op. cit.,* p. 311. See Paul Ramsey, *Christian Ethics and the Sit-In* (New York: Association Press, 1961), Chap. 3, for a conservative, yet not unsympathetic discussion of the relationship between nonviolence and the sit-in.

39. Quoted in Miller, *op. cit.,* p. 83.

40. King, *op. cit.,* p. 178.

41. Reprinted in full in Lynd, ed., *op. cit.* The two passages cited here are on pp. 466, 474.

42. Hugo A. Bedau, "On Civil Disobedience," *The Journal of Philosophy,* vol. 58, no. 21 (1961), p. 656.

43. James W. Vander Zanden, "The Non-violent Resistance Movement Against Segregation," *The American Journal of Sociology,* vol. 68, no. 5 (March, 1963), p. 549.

44. L. John Collins, *Faith Under Fire* (London: Leslie Frewin, 1966), p. 268.

45. See Christopher Driver, *The Disarmers* (London: Hodder and Stoughton, 1964), Chap. 1, for an account of CND's origins.

46. Frank Earle Myers, "British Peace Politics: The Campaign for Nu-

clear Disarmament and the Committee of 100, 1957–1962" (Ph.D. diss., Columbia University, 1965: University Microfilms, No. 66–1719), p. 103.
47. *Ibid.*, pp. 328–330.
48. Frank Parkin, *Middle Class Radicalism: The Social Bases of the British Campaign for Nuclear Disarmament* (Manchester: Manchester University Press, 1968), p. 39. See also Myers, *op. cit.*, pp. 345–348.
49. Horsburgh, *op. cit.*, p. 15.
50. Quoted in Myers, *op. cit.*, p. 116.
51. Collins, *op. cit.*, p. 349.
52. Stephen King-Hall, *Defence in the Nuclear Age* (London: Victor Gollancz Ltd., 1958), p. 14.
53. *Ibid.*, p. 173. See the AFSC's book *In Place of War: An Inquiry into Nonviolent National Defense* (New York: Grossman Publishers, 1967), for rather similar American proposals.
54. Adam Roberts, "Unilateralism—Gesture or Policy?" in April Carter, ed., *Unilateral Disarmament: Its Theory and Policy from Different International Perspectives* (London: Housmans, n.d.), p. 8.
55. Bedau, *op. cit.*, p. 657.
56. For the direct actionist movement down to the end of 1957, see Hugh Brock, *The Century of Total War* (London: Peace News Ltd., n.d.), pp. 21–36.
57. Quoted in Driver, *op. cit.*, p. 49.
58. Collins, *op. cit.*, pp. 328, 329.
59. Alan Lovell, "Direct Action?" *New Left Review* (London), March–April, 1961, p. 24.
60. Myers, *op. cit.*, p. 154.
61. Quoted in Miller, *op. cit.*, p. 78.
62. For a development of this argument, see Gene Sharp, *Civil Disobedience in a Democracy* (London: "Peace News," 1963), a fragment of a very much larger work: "The Politics of Nonviolent Action" (D. Phil. diss., University of Oxford, 1968), which I did not consult.
63. Ralph Schoenman, "Mass Resistance in Mass Society," in David Boulton, ed., *Voices from the Crowd: Against the H-Bomb* (London: Peter Owen, 1964), p. 110.
64. See Charles C. Walker, "The Impact of Gandhi on the U.S. Peace Movement," in Ramachandran and Mahadevan, eds., *op. cit.*, pp. 195–208.
65. Roy Finch, "The New Peace Movement," *Dissent* (New York), vol. 10, no. 1 (Winter, 1963), p. 89. This whole article, which appeared in the Winter and Spring 1963 issues, is a useful source of information.
66. From a mimeographed statement by McCrackin, "Pilgrimage of a Conscience" (1961), in Lynd, ed., *op. cit.*, p. 308.
67. See Albert Bigelow, *The Voyage of the Golden Rule: An Experiment with Truth* (Garden City, N.Y.: Doubleday & Company, Inc., 1959).
68. See Earle Reynolds, *The Forbidden Voyage* (New York: David McKay Company, Inc., 1961).
69. See Bradford Lyttle, *You Come with Naked Hands: The Story of the San Francisco to Moscow March for Peace* (Raymond, N.H.: Greenleaf Books, n.d.).
70. From a report by Bradford Lyttle in Lynd, ed., *op. cit.*, p. 367.
71. I have drawn this comparison from an article by David Dellinger, "The Future of Nonviolence," *Studies on the Left* (Winter, 1965), pp. 90–96, reprinted in Lynd, *op. cit.*, p. 521.
72. For example, the Quaker economist Kenneth E. Boulding, "Why

Did Gandhi Fail?" in Ramachandran and Mahadevan, eds., *op. cit.*, p. 133.

73. D. Dellinger, "Growing Pains in the Peace Movement," in Paul Goodman, ed., *Seeds of Liberation* (New York: George Braziller, 1964), pp. 165, 166.

74. See the interesting discussion of the issues involved here in Gordon C. Zahn, *War, Conscience and Dissent* (New York: Hawthorn Books, Inc., 1967), pp. 192–196: "The Martyr—Saint or Suicide?"

75. Quoted in *The Draft?* (New York: Hill and Wang for the Peace Education Division of the AFSC, 1968), p. 27.

76. Document 55 (dated 1966) in Lillian Schlissel, ed., *Conscience in America* (New York: E. P. Dutton & Co., Inc., 1968). Documents 38–43, 51–54 deal with war resistance and conscientious objection during the years 1965–67. See also James Finn, ed., *A Conflict of Loyalties: The Case for Selective Conscientious Objection* (New York: Pegasus, 1968); Alice Lynd, ed., *We Won't Go: Personal Accounts of War Objectors* (Boston: Beacon Press, 1968); Ralph Potter, "Conscientious Objection to Particular Wars," in Donald A. Gianella, ed., *Religion and the Public Order*, No. 4 (Ithaca, N.Y.: Cornell University Press, 1968), pp. 44–99.

77. *The Draft?* (AFSC), p. 33.

78. D. Dellinger, quoted in James Finn, *Protest: Pacifism and Politics* (New York: Random House, 1967), p. 214.

79. Quoted in *ibid.*, p. 225.

80. This volume was completed and the manuscript in the hands of the publisher at the beginning of 1969. Since then the continuing interest in the United States and elsewhere in conscientious objection, nonviolence and civil disobedience has been shown in the appearance of new books and articles on these subjects. However, as every author must necessarily have a concluding date for his bibliographical material, I have taken the end of 1968 for this purpose. What I have written about pacifism "today," when printed, will already appear as an account of the movement yesterday.

Selected Bibliography

Books

Allen, Devere. *The Fight for Peace.* New York: The Macmillan Company, 1930.

Bainton, Roland H. *Christian Attitudes Toward War and Peace.* New York and Nashville: Abingdon Press, 1960.

Bammel, Fritz. *Die Religionen der Welt und der Friede auf Erden: Eine Religionsphänomenoligische Studie.* Munich: I. & S. Federmann Verlag, 1957.

Beales, A. C. F. *The History of Peace: A Short Account of the Organized Movements for International Peace.* London: G. Bell & Sons Ltd., 1931.

Bell, Julian, ed. *We Did Not Fight: 1914–18 Experiences of War Resisters.* London: Cobden-Sanderson, 1935.

Bondurant, Joan V. *Conquest of Violence: The Gandhian Philosophy of Conflict.* Rev. ed. Berkeley and Los Angeles: University of California Press, 1965.

Boulton, David. *Objection Overruled.* London: MacGibbon & Kee Ltd., 1967.

Bowman, Rufus D. *The Church of the Brethren and War 1708–1941.* Elgin, Ill.: Brethren Publishing House, 1944.

Brittain, Vera. *The Rebel Passion.* London: George Allen & Unwin Ltd., 1964.

Brock, Peter. *Pacifism in the United States: From the Colonial Era to the First World War.* Princeton, N.J.: Princeton University Press, 1968.

Byrd, Robert O. *Quaker Ways in Foreign Policy.* Toronto: University of Toronto Press, 1960.

Cadoux, Cecil John. *Christian Pacifism Re-examined.* Oxford: Basil Blackwell, 1940.

Case, Clarence Marsh. *Non-Violent Coercion.* New York and London: The Century Co., 1923.

Chamberlain, W. J. *Fighting for Peace: The Story of the War Resistance Movement.* London: No More War Movement, n.d.

Conlin, Joseph R. *American Anti-War Movements.* Beverly Hills: The Glencoe Press, 1968.

Curti, Merle. *Peace or War: The American Struggle 1636–1936.* New York: W. W. Norton & Company, 1936.

de Ligt, Barthélemy. *La paix créatrice: Histoire des principes et des tactiques de l'action directe contre la guerre.* Paris: Marcel Rivière, 1934, 2 Vols.

Diwakar, R. R. *Satyagraha: The Power of Truth*. 2nd. ed. Hinsdale, Ill.: Henry Regnery Company, 1948.
Donington, Robert and Barbara. *The Citizen Faces War*. 2nd. ed. London: Victor Gollancz Ltd., 1937.
Finn, James. *Protest: Pacifism and Politics*. New York: Random House, 1967.
Gandhi, M. K. *Non-Violence in Peace and War*. Ahmedabad: Navajivan Publishing House, vol. I, 3rd. ed., 1948; vol. II, 1949.
————. *Non-Violent Resistance (Satyagraha)*. New York: Schocken Books, 1951.
Graham, John W. *Conscription and Conscience: A History 1916–1919*. London: George Allen & Unwin, Ltd., 1922.
Gregg, Richard B. *The Power of Nonviolence*. Rev. ed. Nyack, N.Y.: Fellowship Publications, 1959.
Handboek voor de vredesbeweging: De radical-pacifistische stromingen. The Hague: Nijgh & Van Ditmar, 1954.
Hare, A. Paul and Blumberg, Herbert H., eds. *Nonviolent Direct Action. American Cases: Social-Psychological Analyses*. Washington and Cleveland: Corpus Books, 1968.
Hayes, Denis. *Challenge of Conscience: The Story of the Conscientious Objectors of 1939–1949*. London: George Allen and Unwin Limited, 1949.
————. *Conscription Conflict*. London: Sheppard Press, 1949.
Hershberger, Guy Franklin. *War, Peace, and Nonresistance*. Rev. ed. Scottdale, Pa.: Herald Press, 1953.
Hirst, Margaret E. *The Quakers in Peace and War*. London: The Swarthmore Press Ltd., 1923.
Holmes, John Haynes. *New Wars for Old*. New York: Dodd, Mead and Company, 1916.
Horsburgh, H. J. N. *Non-Violence and Aggression: A Study of Gandhi's Moral Equivalent of War*. London: Oxford University Press, 1968.
Kobler, Franz, ed. *Gewalt und Gewaltlosigkeit: Handbuch des aktiven Pazifismus*. Zürich and Leipzig: Rotapfel-Verlag A. G., 1928.
Kumar, Krishna, ed. *Democracy and Nonviolence: A Study of Their Relationship*. New Delhi: Gandhi Peace Foundation, 1968.
Lacombe, Olivier. *Gandhi ou la force de l'âme*. Paris: Librairie Plon, 1964.
Lee, Umphrey. *The Historic Church and Modern Pacifism*. New York and Nashville: Abingdon-Cokesbury Press, 1943.
Lewis, John. *The Case against Pacifism*. London: George Allen and Unwin Ltd., 1940.
Long, Edward LeRoy, Jr. *War and Conscience in America*. Philadelphia: The Westminster Press, 1968.
Lorson, Pierre. *Un chrétien peut-il être objecteur de conscience?* Paris: Aux éditions du seuil, 1950.

Lynd, Staughton, ed. *Nonviolence in America: A Documentary History.* Indianapolis: Bobbs-Merrill Co., Inc., 1966.

Martin, David A. *Pacifism: An Historical and Sociological Study.* London: Routledge & Kegan Paul, 1965.

Mayer, Peter, ed. *The Pacifist Conscience.* London: Penguin Books, 1966.

Miller, William Robert. *Nonviolence: A Christian Interpretation.* New York: Association Press, 1964.

Morrison, Sybil. *I Renounce War: The Story of the Peace Pledge Union.* London: Sheppard Press, 1962.

Murthi, V. V. Ramana. *Non-Violence in Politics: A Study of Gandhian Techniques and Thinking.* Delhi: Frank Bros. & Co., 1958.

Murty, K. Satchidananda and Bouquet, A. C. *Studies in the Problems of Peace.* Bombay: Asia Publishing House, 1960.

Muste, A. J. *Non-Violence in an Aggressive World.* New York: Harper & Brothers, 1940.

Naess, Arne. *Gandhi and the Nuclear Age.* Translated from the Norwegian. Totowa, N.J.: The Bedminster Press, 1965.

Nelson, John K. *The Peace Prophets: American Pacifist Thought, 1919–1941.* Chapel Hill: The University of North Carolina Press, 1967.

Nuttall, Geoffrey F. *Christian Pacifism in History.* Oxford: Basil Blackwell, 1958.

Peterson, H. C. and Fite, Gilbert C. *Opponents of War 1917–1918.* Madison: The University of Wisconsin Press, 1957.

Power, Paul F. *Gandhi on World Affairs.* Washington, D.C.: Public Affairs Press, 1960.

Prasad, Devi and Tony Smythe, eds. *Conscription: A World Survey.* London: War Resisters' International, 1968.

Raven, Charles E. *War and the Christian.* London: Student Christian Movement Press, 1938.

Roberts, Adam, ed. *The Strategy of Civilian Defence: Non-Violent Resistance to Aggression.* London: Faber and Faber Ltd., 1967.

Santhanam, K. *Satyagraha and the State.* Bombay: Asia Publishing House, 1960.

Schlissel, Lillian, ed. *Conscience in America: A Documentary History of Conscientious Objection in America, 1757–1967.* New York: E. P. Dutton & Co., Inc., 1968.

Seifert, Harvey. *Conquest by Suffering: The Process and Prospects of Nonviolent Resistance.* Philadelphia: The Westminster Press, 1965.

Sharp, Gene. *Gandhi Wields the Weapon of Moral Power (Three Case Histories).* Ahmedabad: Navajivan Publishing House, 1960.

Shridharani, Krishnalal. *War without Violence: A Study of Gandhi's Method and Its Accomplishments.* New York: Harcourt, Brace and Company, 1939.

Sibley, Mulford Q. and Jacob, Philip E. *Conscription of Conscience:*

The American State and the Conscientious Objector, 1940–1947.
Ithaca, N.Y.: Cornell University Press, 1952.

Sibley, Mulford Q., ed. *The Quiet Battle: Writings on the Theory and
Practice of Non-violent Resistance.* New York: Doubleday Anchor
Books, 1963.

Stevenson, Lilian. *Towards a Christian International.* Rev. ed. Paris
and London: International Fellowship of Reconciliation, 1936.

Tähtinen, Unto. *Non-Violence as an Ethical Principle.* Turku, Finland:
Turun Yliopisto, 1964.

Thomas, Norman. *Is Conscience a Crime?* New York: Vanguard
Press, 1927.

Van Kirk, Walter W. *Religion Renounces War.* Chicago and New
York: Willett, Clark & Company, 1934.

Weinberg, Arthur and Lila, eds. *Instead of Violence.* Paper ed. Boston:
Beacon Press, 1965.

Wherry, Neal M. *Conscientious Objection.* 2 Vols. Washington, D.C.:
Selective Service System Special Monograph No. 11, 1950.

Pamphlets, articles and dissertations

Berkman, Joyce Avrech. "Pacifism in England: 1914–1939." Ph.D.
dissertation, Yale University, 1967. University Microfilms, No. 67–
6994.

Bowers, Robert Edwin. "The American Peace Movement, 1933–41."
Ph.D. dissertation, University of Wisconsin, 1949.

Braithwaite, Constance. "Legal Problems of Conscientious Objection to
Various Compulsions under British Law," *The Journal of the Friends'
Historical Society* (London), 52, no. 1 (1968), pp. 3–18.

Carter, April, David Hoggett and Adam Roberts, eds. *Non-violent
Action—Theory and Practice: A Selected Bibliography.* London:
Housmans, 1966.

Chatfield, Earl Charles, Jr. "Pacifism and American Life: 1914 to
1941." Ph.D. dissertation, Vanderbilt University, 1965. University
Microfilms, No. 66–19.

Fortas, Abe. *Concerning Dissent and Civil Disobedience.* New York:
The New American Library, 1968.

*Guide to the Swarthmore College Peace Collection: A Memorial to
Jane Addams.* Swarthmore, Pa.: Peace Collection Publication,
1 (1947).

Kennedy, Thomas C. "The Hound of Conscience: A History of the
No-Conscription Fellowship, 1914–1919." Ph.D. dissertation, University of South Carolina, 1968. University Microfilms, No. 68–
5917.

Knowles, G. W., ed. *Quakers and Peace.* London: The Grotius Society Publications. Texts for Students of International Relations, No.
4, Sweet and Maxwell, Limited, 1927.

Krahn, Cornelius, Fretz, J. Winfield and Kreider, Robert. "Altruism
in Mennonite Life," in *Forms and Techniques of Altruistic and*

Spiritual Growth, Pitirim A. Sorokin, ed. Boston: The Beacon Press, 1954.

Lund, Doniver A. "The Peace Movement among the Major American Protestant Churches, 1919–1939." Ph.D. dissertation, University of Nebraska, 1955.

Manthey, Fred R., Jr. "Christians and War: A Survey of Christian Thought in the United Kingdom 1914–1948." Ph.D. dissertation, University of Edinburgh, 1952.

Miller, William Robert. "The Mightier Pen: American Peace Journalism, 1815–1960," *Fellowship* (Nyack, N.Y.), vol. 26, no. 9 (May 1, 1960), 21–26.

———— ed. *Bibliography of Books on War, Pacifism, Nonviolence and Related Studies.* Nyack, N.Y.: The Fellowship of Reconciliation, 1960.

No-Conscription Fellowship. *Troublesome People.* London: Central Board for Conscientious Objectors, 1940.

Paullin, Theodore. *Introduction to Non-Violence.* Philadelphia: The Pacifist Research Bureau, 1944.

Pontara, Giulano. "The Rejection of Violence in Gandhian Ethics of Conflict Resolution," *Journal of Peace Research* (Oslo), 2 (1965), 197–215.

Sibley, Mulford Q. *The Political Theories of Modern Pacifism.* Philadelphia: The Pacifist Research Bureau, 1944.

Sills, David L., ed. *International Encyclopedia of the Social Sciences.* 17 vols. New York: The Macmillan Company & The Free Press, 1968. Articles by Christian Bay ("Civil Disobedience," vol. 2, pp. 472–487); Johan Galtung ("Peace," vol. 11, pp. 487–496); Mulford Q. Sibley ("Pacifism," vol. 11, pp. 353–357).

Thomas, Norman. "Pacifism in America," *Playboy* (Chicago), 15, no. 12 (December, 1968), 155, 278–283.

Witte, William W. S. "American Quaker Pacifism and the Peace Settlement of World War I," *The Bulletin of Friends Historical Association* (Swarthmore, Pa.), 46, no. 2 (Autumn 1957), 84–98.

————. "Quaker Pacifism in the United States, 1919–1942, with special reference to its relation to Isolationism and Internationalism." Ph.D. dissertation, Columbia University, 1954.

Wittner, Lawrence Stephen. "The American Peace Movement, 1941–1960." Ph.D. dissertation, Columbia University, 1967. University Microfilms, No. 67–15, 529. [A revised version of this dissertation was published by Columbia University Press (New York) in 1969: *Rebels Against War: The American Peace Movement, 1941–1960.*]

Woodcock, George. *Civil Disobedience.* Toronto: Canadian Broadcasting Corporation, 1966.

Index